P9-CQZ-111

Tough Plants
for
NORTHERN GARDENS

Low Care, No Care, Tried and True Winners

Copyright 2003 Felder Rushing

All Rights Reserved. No part of this book may be reproduced or transmitted in any form, or by any means, electronic or mechanical, including photocopying, recording, or by any information storage and retrieval system, without permission in writing from the publisher.

Published by Cool Springs Press, a Division of Thomas Nelson, Inc., P. O. Box 141000, Nashville, Tennessee, 37214.

Felder Rushing, 1952-
    Tough plants for northern gardens : low care, no care, tried and true winners /
    Felder Rushing.
        p. cm.
    Includes bibliographical references.
    ISBN 1-59186-063-6 (pbk.)
    1. Landscape plants--Snowbelt States. 2. Low maintenance gardening--Snowbelt States.
    I. Title.
SB407.R878 2004
635.9'52--dc22
                                    2003021652

First Printing 2004
Printed in the United States of America
10 9 8 7 6 5 4 3 2

Managing Editor: Jenny Andrews
Horticulture Editor: Carol Wallace
Copyeditor: Sara J. Henry
Designer: Starletta Polster
Production Design: S.E. Anderson

Cover Photo by Felder Rushing

Visit the Thomas Nelson website at www.ThomasNelson.com

Tough Plants

for

NORTHERN GARDENS

Low Care, No Care, Tried and True Winners

Felder Rushing

COOL
SPRINGS
PRESS

A Division of Thomas Nelson, Inc.
www.ThomasNelson.com

*Pearl Townsend Boyer,
Felder's Great-Grandmother*

Dedication:

This book is to the gardening women in my family: great-grandmother Pearl, who taught me about wildflowers and daffodils; grandmother Louise, whose daylilies were garden club blue-ribbon winners; Wilma, who just grew zinnias by her concrete chicken; Margie, my mother-in-law, who grew hollyhocks and hot peppers outside her Cleveland, Ohio, apartment; Wilma Gene, my mother whose zest has inspired everyone around her; Terryl, my longtime best friend and wife whose dracaena won a state fair ribbon; and daughter Zoe, the gal who grows the sweetest turnips on Earth— in a purple tire planter.

Acknowledgements:

Thanks to all y'all who helped inspire and tweak this book—Master Gardeners, garden club and plant society members, and my gardening friends. Special credit goes to Terry Conner ("he who lives with Yankees"); Scott Kunst of Ann Arbor, Michigan, who was the first to raise an eyebrow over my writing about Northern plants; Michael Petrie, quirky garden guru of the Delaware Valley; and Carol Wallace, the horticulture editor who gave my manuscript the fine-comb treatment before giving my efforts the "thumbs-up."

I'd also like to credit all the horticulturists (especially university types) who have overcome their scientific training enough to relax and be better "garden variety" gardeners. And the many professional but fun-loving members of the Garden Writers Association (who my wife thinks are weirder than horticulturists).

Special acknowledgment also goes to Jenny Andrews and Hank McBride at Cool Springs Press, who had to pull down deep for patience as we turned this lifelong love of tough plants into something I can share with others. There are special crowns in Heaven for them both.

Table of Contents

Foreword

The first time I laid eyes on Felder Rushing he reminded me of a kind of dignified hippie. The date was February 14, 2003, Valentine's Day. The occasion was a talk he was giving on garden art sponsored by our county's Cooperative Extension Master Gardeners. I didn't realize that this first encounter would lead to a great friendship with one of the most "down-home" gardeners I've ever met.

In *Tough Plants for Northern Gardens* Felder provides gardening information pertinent to the Midwest and North. Written with Southern charm, Felder breaks down the barriers of the high tech talk of botanists and horticulturists that can leave the average gardener scratching his/her head in confusion. Using language and words easily understood by even the most uneducated of gardening enthusiasts, Felder proves in this book that a degree in botany isn't necessary in order for a gardener to easily grow and have a beautiful garden.

I experienced firsthand Felder Rushing's charm when he and I struck up a conversation after his lecture. Felder put me at ease by answering my gardening questions without using the sometimes-bewildering jargon I read in a lot of gardening publications. You'd never know from talking with Felder just how intense his gardening background really is. The list of his accomplishments and contributions to horticulture would be too large to include in this short foreword.

What I found to be one of the most fascinating features of this gentleman is the way he went about doing the research for this book. I'll have to admit that I was quite surprised when I received an email from Felder several days after his lecture asking if I'd be interested in tagging along with him as he poked around up here in my neck of the woods. We arranged a meeting place and time, and Felder paid us a two-day visit. During Felder's stay, I witnessed just how spirited and enthusiastic this man goes about his work.

It all begins when Felder straps on his camera and gets behind the steering wheel of his truck. I sat next to him one day as we drove the back roads looking for interesting plants and gardens. Stopping on a dime when he spotted something of interest, Felder would jump out of the truck and off he'd go, with gusto that'd make your head spin! Politely asking folks about their plants and gardens, arranging meetings with my wife's herb club lady friends, noticing what wild "gully flower" was blooming, Felder's abilities to gather useful and just plain simple information for this book amazed me. Northern gardeners will love this book!   —*Terry Conner*

Green
SIDE UP

This book is about unkillable plants in the cold-winter regions of our country. Its aim is to increase the number of people who garden—without a lot of "bells and whistles" science—by highlighting what decades of experience have shown to be the toughest survivors of the Midwest and Northeast.

Some of the plants are common as dirt, but can be used very successfully—indeed, they are often found growing in the finest botanical gardens on Earth. Think of the fable of Rumpelstiltskin, who wove golden garments from common straw.

The late garden author Henry Mitchell wrote that "there are only two kinds of people—those who garden, and those who do not." Americans are constantly told by pollsters that we are a nation of gardeners, yet an observant drive around any neighborhood usually shows that few of us actually garden with gusto. Truth is, we're mostly lawn mowers and shrub pruners, with maybe a potted plant or two by the television to keep us in touch with nature.

Yet most of us remember grandmothers and aunts, even dads and uncles, who grew all sorts of interesting flowering shrubs, trees, bulbs, perennials, and lots of other weird plants. Most of us today have a pot or two of something tropical in our home or office. Truth is, we *need* to grow something—anything—that depends on us at least a little bit. Or as my friend Russell Studebaker, world-famous horticulturist from Tulsa, Oklahoma, says, "We'd just as well be sittin' around polishin' silverware."

I have spent a *lifetime* scratching and sniffing around landscapes and gardens all over the world, coast to coast and top to bottom in our great country, and along many back roads from west of Des Moines, to Long Island, and Bar Harbor, Maine, across southern Canada and into Alaska, always searching for forgotten plants surviving (even thriving) in utter neglect.

My *opinions* on plants and gardening come from being raised by real gardeners, including a horticulturist great-grandmother who showed me her more than 350 different kinds of daffodils and shared her love of wildflowers, a grandmother whose daylilies and African violets won many blue ribbons, a country grandmother who just loved zinnias and her concrete chicken, and parents who struggled with vegetables and a lawn while raising a bunch of rowdy kids and pets.

Throw in years of experience working in garden centers, a couple of university degrees, more than two decades as an urban "consumer horticulturist" with a university Extension Service (and more than twenty years as host of a call-in radio program), and you can imagine how much I have learned from the experiences of hard-working but fun-loving gardeners.

I have also taken copious notes while on many intimate "behind the scenes" plant safaris, from steamy jungles on both sides of South America

Boyertown, Pennsylvania

to the snowy peat bogs of northern Canada, from wind-swept cemeteries on tiny Caribbean islands to the temperate rain forests of Alaska. I have waded in Lake Itasca where the mighty Mississippi begins its flow, discovered scarecrows in hamlets in the Green Mountains of Vermont, and eaten daylilies in Massachusetts. I have evaluated plants and their combinations on several trips to Europe—including one where I took an educational television film crew to show how the English and French use our native wildflowers, including at Louis XIV's ultra-formal Versailles and Monet's overstuffed garden in Giverney. Not to mention the countless flower shows I have "done" in every corner of our country and Europe as well.

Sadly, many people seem to have gotten away from gardening. Blame it on TV or fast food or El Niño, or preening dilettantes who make us feel bad if we don't garden exactly the way they recommend. Better yet, forget the excuses—there are at least eight very simple and understandable reasons why good people, even flower lovers, have miserable gardens:

Vermont

- We are too tied up mentally, physically, and emotionally with other parts of our lives—family, church, meetings, sports, housework, the Internet, and myriad other distractions that preoccupy us. There isn't enough time to dedicate to all the gardening we love and need to do, so that much of it becomes a chore. Might as well just have a big lawn to cut mindlessly every other weekend.

- The weather won't cooperate when the mood for gardening strikes us right; it's either too hot or cold, too wet or dry, too dark after work, or there's just plain too much humidity to overcome. One week the dirt is hard as concrete, the next it's gummy and sticks to the shovel. And the Weather Channel says more is on the way.

- Our bodies ache just thinking about the physical challenges of gardening. After even half a day of digging or planting, our backs, knees, and hands aren't always up to the task, and the easy chair by the TV beckons.

- Spiders, snakes, and bees unnerve us, and we are worried about whatever mosquitoes might be carrying this year. It's less scary to just stay inside and stare through the plate-glass window as birds flock to their feeders stocked with store-bought sunflower seed.

- Too many rules to remember for how to garden, what to do, and when. We feel daunted, as if we will mess up or waste time and money no matter what we try. And the experts just pile up stuff we are supposed to do or know.

- The neighbors will talk about us if we garden publicly, as if our efforts will make their plain landscapes look bad. We don't want to look like fanatics, so we just hide in the backyard and mow the front.
- Bugs and blights ruin our best efforts. They kill our attempts at gardening—or worse, make our gardens look bad and perform poorly. And though there seem to be way too many pests in the North, we are beginning to realize that pesticides are bad for the environment and our health. Even "natural" kinds of bug-and-blight-and-weed controls are expensive and a lot of fuss.
- Plants die, no matter what we do or how hard we try. So we give up.

There is a simple solution to all the above: Find and plant things that grow whether we tend to them or not! And arrange them in combinations that make neighbors at least think we know what we are doing.

This book is filled with the kinds of plants that have proven themselves over many decades, even centuries, to be useful, beautiful, adaptable, and downright easy to grow. In fact, some are all but unkillable, having performed for generations of cold-climate Northern gardeners with little or no care. They just keep on going, even when planted in miserable soils, and survive back-to-back floods, droughts, prolonged freezes, summer heat, and benign neglect.

That's the premise of this book—to highlight perennials, bulbs, annuals, vines, shrubs, trees, and even roses that have been planted by a wide range of gardeners, of all styles and abilities, for many years and have proven themselves to grow well without "artificial life support."

These many dozens of easy-care plants have been gleaned from country homesteads, cottage gardens, less affluent parts of town, abandoned gardens, and even cemeteries. They're popular, rewarding, and tough, plus they can be displayed and enjoyed in any landscape style, even in the front yards of suburban homes. And most are easy to root, seed, divide, or otherwise propagate for sharing with family, friends, and neighbors.

MASTER GARDENERS are men and women who have been given forty, fifty, or more hours of intense training in all aspects of home horticulture by university Extension Service professionals. In return, they have given an equal number of hours (sometimes many, many more) teaching others about gardening. They are the "take it to the streets" part of university horticulture departments. Find out more, or how you can become involved, by calling your county Agricultural Extension Service office, or do a "word search" on the Internet for your state's Master Gardener program. The entries in the book have passed muster with Master Gardeners, who gave excellent insight on which plants are truly hardy—and which ones some folks thought I should omit because they are *too* easy!

Criteria Used for Selecting the Plants for This Book

Of the thousands of plants we can possibly grow, including old favorites and exciting new cultivars, only a few pass muster to survive "garden variety" gardens across the North; many disappear because they simply aren't tough enough. I have personally seen the plants in this book being grown across the entire Midwest and Northeast, in botanical and collectors' gardens, and in rural cottage gardens alike, all enjoyed because they have these benefits:

- Possess strong values, such as beauty, better flavor or fragrance, and multiple-season effects, and are heirlooms.
- Grow in ordinary soil with little or no watering or fertilizer.

- Tolerate local climate and weather extremes, including heat, drought, rain, and prolonged freezes—with or without snow cover.
- Resist insect pests and diseases.
- Don't require the gardener to have a horticulture degree—these plants all but grow themselves.
- Are "no fuss" and easy to groom in the off season.
- Can be found at local garden centers or through mail-order sources.

You won't find a lot of horticultural "how-to" in this book, for two reasons: It is covered thoroughly in nearly every other garden book, which you probably

Fisherville, Wisconsin

already have, and most of these plants simply don't need a lot of fuss. Most require only two acts on your part: Dig a little dirt, and plant them "green side up."

In this book you will find chapters on annuals, which have to be planted anew every year, either from seed or as nursery-grown plants; perennials and bulbs, which generally stay around for many years but "die down" or go dormant part of the year; and shrubs, trees, and vines, which have "woody" trunks and stems and remain a visible part of the

Quad City, Iowa

landscape year-round. There are also short chapters on low-maintenance lawn care, ornamental grasses (which fall sort of between perennials and shrubs in how they are used in gardens), and the toughest tropical plants, which are easily kept for years in pots and other containers in our home or office.

Also throughout the book you will find fast-reference lists of plants for unique growing conditions and uses, based on what many gardeners, especially Master Gardeners, have discovered in average gardens. Also included are quick tips for planting and caring for tough plants, plus landscaping ideas and simple how-to garden shortcuts, all aimed at saving you time, money, effort, and worry.

This book is for both beginners and "old hands" who just want pretty plants, without all the hassle. Have fun, then share with others.

Where in the World Are We As Northern Gardeners?

Why can't we grow bananas, magnolias, or figs? Simply put: This ain't the South. But then we can grow much better raspberries, rhubarb, and peonies, and the weird weather is worth bragging about.

My opinion is that no "American" gardening book trying to cover New England, California, and Texas alike can really suit us all, because even in the northern parts of the country addressed in this book there are huge differences—from widely varied soils to "micro-climates" caused by nearby lakes or mountains—which make some plants suitable or unsuitable in gardens just a few dozen miles apart!

So even this heavily researched book has to be very general, sticking to "tried and true" plants and very simple gardening chores, to suit a largely diverse group of individual gardeners.

The region covered in this book has its western end somewhere in the wetter areas of the prairie states, from Nebraska, Minnesota, Iowa, and Kansas, through the entire Midwest, as far south as Kentucky and the mountainous areas of Tennessee, through the Mid-Atlantic states, and on into upper New England. In other words, where it gets cold in the winter and usually stays that way until spring. Hardiness-zone-wise, it roughly includes Zones 4 to 6, give or take, with a nod to those hardy "Zone 3 souls" who garden where it can reach negative 30 degrees in the winter.

Generally, soils don't begin to warm up enough for planting summer vegetables and flowers until mid-May, and even then the ground may be too wet to plant. Frosts begin to arrive in early September, and it's often very dry in between all that. And there's no such thing as "normal" weather: New England garden author Jacqueline Hériteau sums it best by saying that the weather's "outrageous eccentricities are our favorite small talk."

Other ways you can tell that you might be a Northern gardener:

- Folks wait until after Memorial Day to plant tomatoes.
- You know what "heaving" is—and it ain't about drinking too much.
- Fire hydrants in your town are wrapped for winter.
- Someone in your neighborhood has a large boulder as a lawn ornament.
- It's easier to say "youse" or "youin" than "y'all."
- Your lawn mower has a snowplow attachment.
- You worry about runoff from the driveway or street causing salt damage to plants.
- You have ever actually put snow chains on your personal vehicle.
- You can recognize a groundhog's night work from the kitchen window.
- You know exactly how deep the average frost line is in your soil.
- An unusually warm winter kills plants because there's not enough snow cover.

- You give away your first tomato, as a gift, because it is so special.
- There's a Union soldier statue in the town square.

For a more detailed description of your state's climate, check out the *Month-by-Month* books published by Cool Springs Press, written by well-known garden experts from your state.

Note on Hardiness Maps

The USDA Hardiness Zones are based on "average low temperatures," which are often way off base; the American Horticulture Society's Heat Zone Map is based on average high temperatures and is another good indicator, but not entirely useful by itself. What we need to do is overlay both maps, plus a humidity map, and a wet winter map, a hot humid dry summer map, a clay/sandy/alkaline/acidic soil map, a no-snow-cover map, and a "too tired and hot to garden" map. *Then*

we'll have some useful information! Given the vast array of factors that determine what plants will do well and where, and the vagaries of nature, Hardiness Zone and Heat Zone maps have not been included in this book.

Plant Names

Elvis sang about how his "Mama loved roses" and getting "all shook up" because you're his buttercup. You know what a rose is, so what's a buttercup? You don't have to know a plant's scientific or Latin name to grow and enjoy growing it. But proper names are important when you go looking for more information about any plant, especially its myriad varieties. Just remember that generally similar plants are lumped into *families*, with really close relatives clustered into the same *genus*, and individual kinds sorted into *species*. Plants with minor variations are named as *cultivars* (which are simply "cultivated varieties"). Got that?

Common names are the designations most gardeners relate to, but they can be misleading for serious identification purposes. For example, there are quite a few plants called "buttercups," including nearly anything with pollen that rubs onto your nose when you smell too close. Most common buttercups include yellow daffodils; wild ranunculus; and the "Mexican primrose" with big, floppy, pale pink and white flowers, sometimes called "showy evening primrose" even though it blooms in the day.

The plant names used in this book, both the generally accepted common names and the official Latin names, are important as reference, but not important to the enjoyment of the plants themselves (though some of them are fun to say, and some have very interesting histories). What is important is that you give the plants a try and, if you like them, make an effort to get to know their names in case you want to tell other folks about them.

"Best for Beginners" and "Kinda Tricky" Lists

One man's weed is another's wildflower. No two gardeners will ever agree on a list of "best" and "worst" plants, based on personal experiences as well as social acceptance. Goldenrod, one of our most common roadside beauties, is generally considered "weedy" in America, yet is one of the most popular summer and fall cut-flower perennials in European gardens. One gardener can grow tomatoes with no trouble at all, while neighbors struggle with the challenge. My grandmother grew blue-ribbon African violets, but they quickly melt under my hit-or-miss care.

Yet some plants are so easy to grow that they are considered common, or a weed. Instead of holding our noses in the air, they should be celebrated as great "intro" plants for new or beginner gardeners, especially children who have no expectations, and new home gardeners who are too busy or horticulturally "green" to give them much care. These "Best for Beginners" plant lists scattered throughout the book are good for just-starting gardeners, and have remained popular long since their success has started to wear thin with more advanced gardeners.

On the other hand, after a quarter-century of watching all sorts of gardeners and helping them with problems, I have seen too many popular plants succumb to insect or mite pests, foliage and root diseases, poor adaptation to our climate, or lack of regular maintenance such as pruning or deadheading. These plants—again, very popular, and widely sold in garden centers—tend to cause headaches for beginning gardeners, or gardeners who don't get around to preventive maintenance. They generate a lot of calls to garden experts; I put them in my "Kinda Tricky" lists. Again, they are all great plants, but may take a little extra planning or thought put into their planting, or a little extra care in their growing.

Master Gardeners and "garden variety" gardeners alike helped narrow the lists to a defensible few. You can grow them all, from both lists, but don't say we didn't warn you about some of them!

WARNING: SOME POPULAR PLANTS can quickly escape gardens to cause problems in the natural environment. So-called "invasive exotics" appearing on horticultural hit lists, though often tough and beautiful (and still legal, for the most part), should be planted with caution and kept in bounds. And remember, the most habitat-destructive plantings in our country are called "front lawns"—which many environmentally-correct people have, and mow every week.

Myth of the Five-Dollar Hole

Even though plants have been grown well in "just plain dirt" for centuries, many modern gardeners have been taught to overprepare soil. The saying goes, "It's better to plant a fifty-cent plant in a five-dollar hole than a five-dollar plant in a fifty-cent hole. Yet, while adding a little organic material can help soils drain better and roots penetrate farther and more quickly, too much can cause soils to hold water during wet seasons, dry out quickly in hot summers, and keep roots in a small area. A moderate approach usually works best.

Think "crackers in chili"—a bowl of chili usually doesn't need any crackers at all, but a handful of crumbled crackers can fluff it up and cool it down; more than that turns it into mush. Dig your soil a solid shovel's depth,

turning it upside down and chopping up the clumps. Spread over the area a thin layer of organic material (compost, manure, potting soil, finely ground bark, whatever), and stir it into the native soil.

Use the following as guidelines for how much organic matter to add: trees, tough shrubs, and bulbs, none; roses and perennials, add a one- to two-inch layer of new material over the native soil, and stir it in; annuals, add a two- to three-inch layer. I never add more than three to four inches of organic matter to a shovel depth of soil!

SPECIAL NOTE: Many tough plants die from being pulled out of pots and plugged right into the ground "as is"—and their potting soil keeps roots in a wet-dry cycle that leads to rot. *Always* loosen potting soil from store-bought plant roots—trees, shrubs, perennials, even annuals—and mix it into your soil.

Mulches Make a Difference

Covering the soil with a blanket of porous material has several important benefits. It keeps the soil surface from packing and crusting in heavy rains, cools the soil in the summer (like a hat on a bare head), reduces rapid temperature changes during sunny winter days and cold nights, prevents many weed seeds from getting the sun they need to sprout, and keeps things looking neat. Landscape fabrics do a fair job, but natural mulches of leaves, pine straw, or shredded bark "feed" the soil as they compost or are eaten and relocated deep around roots by earthworms.

It is best to use the mulch evenly in a "doughnut" shape over the root area under shrubs and around flowers—don't pile it up around trunks and stems, or you may be inviting voles and mice to nest there.

A rule of thumb for how much mulch to use: Spread your preferred material over the area just deep enough to barely but completely cover the soil, then add that much more to compensate for settling and natural composting. Refresh once a year or as needed.

Two Rules for Composting

Too much has been written and said about composting. It makes me tired just thinking about all I'm supposed to do: small particle sizes, correct carbon-nitrogen ratio, thermophilic bacteria, bins an exact size, turning and aerating, and all the rest of that stuff!

As anyone with a leaf pile will attest, there are only two rules for composting: Stop throwing that stuff away, and pile it up somewhere. The rest is finesse. If you want to get in a race with someone, call your county Extension Service office for a handout on how to speed things up. Below are a few tips for composting:

- Mix a little green stuff, including grass clippings and vegetable scraps, even weeds, with brown stuff (decaying manure, shredded autumn leaves, and so on), or add a little nitrogen fertilizer.
- Keep the pile moist, but not wet (good bacteria need moisture).
- Turn the pile occasionally to mix and fluff it up (air is also needed for good bacterial action).
- Chop big stuff into smaller particles.

Really, you can forget the rules—just do it!

Water Wisely

There is no good advice for watering tough plants—after all, most have survived the neglect of many, many gardeners with no watering whatsoever! And most can be found around abandoned homes and even cemeteries.

Well-established trees and shrubs rarely need any water at all. But of course, potted plants, summer annuals, and a nicely maintained lawn need help from time to time. Still, a general rule of thumb is that when you have to water, do it deeply, then leave plants alone so their roots can grow deep and strong, and you won't have to water as often. Watering frequently and a little at a time keeps roots shallow, susceptible to damage during dry spells, and needy.

HINT: When you do water, do it twice, an hour or so apart, to give the first watering time to soak in; the second watering really pushes it down deep. Sometimes I even water my plants after a light rain, to maximize the effect.

And remember that for the plants in this book, too much water (like too much fertilizer) is worse than none at all.

Feed Plants for Quality, Not Quantity

Most of these tough plants can go for years without fertilizers—just look around and see for yourself. But giving them an occasional feeding can boost their performance, and invigorate them with healthier leaves, stems, roots, and flowers.

Keep in mind that most of the people telling you to feed, feed, feed your plants either sell fertilizer or are in a race with someone in a plant-nut club or society. All the plants want is a little pick-me-up from time to time, particularly with nitrogen, phosphorus, and potassium (the "big three," N, P, and K, whose numbers are on the fertilizer bag).

In a nutshell, here is what those three ingredients do for plants:

Nitrogen (first number, letter N) makes plants grow, especially green leaves and stems. Foliage plants (the lawn and ferns) like nitrogen, but too much at a time can cause the plants to grow too quickly, making them weak and tender, and even burn them. And too much nitrogen often forces green growth at the expense of flowers or fruit (all vine, no tomatoes). Once or twice a year, lightly, is the most I'd ever use nitrogen.

Phosphorus (second number, letter P) doesn't "make" flowers and fruit, it *helps* them; too much too often can interfere with other nutrients, especially nitrogen. Once every year or two is usually plenty.

Potassium (the third number, letter K, is in potash) helps make strong stems and roots, and lowers a plant's freezing point (it's the so-called "winterizer" ingredient); like phosphorus, it lasts two or three years or more.

BOTTOM LINE: Use an all-purpose, numbers-all-the-same plant food (such as 10:10:10) every year or two, with maybe a little pick-me-up shot of nitrogen in between. For foliage plants, it's okay to use a fertilizer with a higher first number; for flowering or fruiting plants, use one with a higher middle number. Just don't ever overdo it—lean and mean is the best way to keep plants growing but still tough.

Share the Wealth

Multiply and share your own plants by saving seed, digging and dividing in-ground parts of multiple-stemmed perennials and shrubs, or rooting pieces of stems. Dare to share by holding informal plant swaps. Keep it simple by having participants offer only one plant, which should be given a number, and a corresponding number put in a hat to pass around. Pull a number, and that's the plant you get—whether you want it, like it, already have it, or even brought it yourself! The real swapping begins afterward.

THREE HINTS:

- Save seed indoors in a cool, dry place, and it will last much longer.
- Divide perennials in the season opposite from when they are in full bloom or leaf-growth.
- Root mature stems of evergreen shrubs in the summer and deciduous shrubs and trees in the fall.

WHAT YOU CAN'T SEE usually won't hurt you or your plants; if your shrubs or flowers have little bugs or blots or spots or raggedy edges, try looking at them from ten feet away. Take off your glasses, and a lot of garden headaches disappear. If a plant continues to suffer, dump it for another plant—it ain't like you two are married!

Beyond Iceberg Lettuce and Snow Peas

Talk about really cold-hardy plants! After several trips to Alaska, I have come to appreciate those that are dependable even in that Far North country (which, if cut in half, would make Texas only the third largest state). I even spent time visiting "plant hospices"—commercial greenhouses set up for folks to overwinter cherished potted plants, complete with "visiting days." Yet even the toughest of plants can be damaged by excessive spring rain, summer drought, or a lack of snow cover with unrelenting wind. Raised beds, occasional summer watering, and lots of mulch right before the fall's first hard freeze helps protect stuff.

Hardy plants in Alaska include bee balm, fiddlehead fern, hosta, lily of the valley, primrose, windflower, phlox, daisy, mint, sed orange daylily, yarrow, chives, horseradish, and rock arabis. The best bulbs to start w would be daffodils, crocus, and lilies. Rugosa rose, rhododendron, pink-flowered curra daphne, cherries, apples, and raspberries also do well. And, of course, potatoes.

Why Am I Writing About Northern Gardens?

Okay, so I'm from the South—halfway, in fact, between New Orleans and where Elvis is (really) buried in his Memphis side yard. So what do I know about cold climates?

I suppose it depends on how much *anybody* knows—that it's just best to water and mulch one last time in the fall, then hunker down and hope for the best until the ground thaws and the last of the black road sludge melts away. And try not to slip and fall down.

I have had to lean into the breath-taking chilly wind while we buried my mother-in-law in Cleveland, where *snow blows sideways* off Lake Erie. And tried fruitlessly to sleep in the back of an unheated truck camper in Vermont.

I've been intimate with Iowa's summer humidity, so thick you can almost lick it, knowing it can quickly turn into biting cold that sucks out your breath. I've seen the brilliant white fluffy snow (the same stuff that makes even the worst-kept lawn look as nice as a perfectly manicured lawn) turn to nearly-black, road-salted slush. I've tsk-tsked over dead fruit trees whose bark was girdled by bored rabbits. And I've imagined that those undulating mounds of snow hide either dormant clumps of perennials, or a forgotten wheelbarrow.

I have seen your burlap-wrapped shrubs, made snow angels in Alaska, waltzed at the annual "Meen-nee-so-ta/Wis-CON-sin Polkafest" in Minneapolis (which is almost exactly halfway between the North Pole and the Equator—really!), followed the antics of the characters at the Side Track Tap saloon, been an "international peat harvest inspector" north of Calgary, and seen northern lights. I have sat in roadside diners where the guy next to me seemed to radiate cold from his overcoat.

While looking for *real* gardens in the older parts of town, I have spent more time backing up for a second look than going forward.

I know that, unlike the South, where fall segues slowly into winter and blossoms can appear during every break in the weather, Northern gardens come to a complete standstill in mid-winter, when prolonged cold temperatures suppress all growth, and the only things in bloom are in greenhouses and garden catalogs.

None of this, to some of you, is unusual or crazy. But I ask, of those who think only snow-bound gardeners know about cold climates: Does a psychiatrist need his own personal psychosis to know what he's talking about?

"If we had no winter, the spring would not be so pleasant: if we did not sometimes taste of adversity, prosperity would not be so welcome."
—Anne Bradstreet, *Meditations Divine and Moral*, 1655

Boston, Massachusetts

Rumpelstiltskin's Garden

Remember the old fable of the gnome who wove golden garments from common straw? As I wander around my little cottage garden, I realize that it is a "Rumpelstiltskin" tapestry of sorts.

Though it includes scattered collections of rare plant specimens I've coddled from many travels around the horticulture world, my landscape's backbone is of mainstay, nearly zero-maintenance shrubs (hollies, quince, yew, rose of Sharon, euonymus), cherished no-fuss roses rooted from old gardens, many dozens of different hardy bulbs and old-timey perennials (iris, daylilies, sedum, yarrow), clambering vines, and reseeding annuals passed around between generous gardeners of all stripes over many years. All have been "selected out" over generations by real gardeners as being useful, hardy, and easy to propagate; these plants create a strong sense of place.

Because my busy family (wife and long-time best friend Terryl and children Ira and Zoe), relaxes in our garden year-round, we've tried to have plants for every season, punctuated with assorted "yard art" to anchor the ever-changing scenery. We've screened parts of our garden from neighbors using baffles of lattice-like fencing, painted teal and pastels to help give a glow of color without being garish. We have strewn a few comfortable chairs on roomy decks; built a waterfall that soothes the city sounds; and keep a large iron bowl on our deck, crackling with a wood fire on chilly evenings.

And just as we invite colorful birds and other wildlife to delight us with motion and busy chatter, we welcome friends to enrich our lives by sharing stories. The plants in this book come from this perspective, and I welcome you into my view of what a garden could be.

Annuals
THAT ENDURE

It's a given, in the gardening world, that a lot of popular plants live for only a short time and then die no matter what you do. But they are so fun or productive that gardeners continue to replant them, year after year, in spite of the trouble and expenses of time, effort, money, and maintenance.

These annuals—so-called because they have to be replanted every year—are often perennial in some parts of the world, but in the North are killed by either cold winters or hot summers. Some are borderline and may survive for a couple of years or more, but they are so "iffy" that they are considered annuals for most gardeners.

Still, a surprising selection of annuals are tougher than others, tolerant of bad weather and pest resistant to boot, making them worth planting in an "unkillable plants" garden. Some reseed themselves to "come back" many years on their own; others have seeds that are easily saved from year to year or are readily available at garden centers or through mail order. A few are difficult to grow from seed, but cuttings are easily rooted, or they can be purchased as rooted plants.

What makes most annuals high maintenance is the soil preparation often required at planting time, plus fertilization, mulching, weed control, and watering during extremely sunny, windy, or hot spells (even in the winter).

Every seed catalog and garden book has lots of information on growing annuals, but the best knowledge comes from experience. The annuals in this book have been grown for many years with little or no effort throughout the North and are presented here in a "best of the best" list to help you get started with as little effort as possible.

Soil preparation involves digging your soil as close to a shovel's depth as you can, chopping up the larger soil chunks and smoothing the surface. This can usually be done by hand or with a small power cultivator. The expense and storage problems of large power tillers are usually not justifiable, except for large areas where lots of annuals are replanted year after year, such as in a large vegetable garden. Even then, a large, powerful tiller can often be rented for a few dollars.

Organic matter such as compost, soil conditioner, peat moss, composted manure, or potting soil can be added to the soil to encourage annuals to grow roots quickly and deeply, improve drainage in heavy clay soils, and help hold moisture in sandy soils. Generally, a layer of organic matter two or three inches deep (no more than four inches) laid over the previously dug area and then tilled in will work wonders throughout an entire season. It is better to use a little each of two or three different kinds of organic matter, for a total of two to four inches, than a lot of just one kind.

Fertilization means adding a small amount of a balanced or all-purpose fertilizer to your soil during soil preparation or at planting time. Most gardeners overdo this, causing plants to get "leggy" or grow too fast, resulting in poor flowering, or making plants more susceptible to weather, moisture problems, and pest pressures. A general rule of thumb, regardless of what kind of fertilizer you use, is to apply no more than one pound (about a pint jar full) of all-purpose fertilizer for every hundred square feet (ten by ten feet, four by twenty-five, five by twenty, and so on) of planting area. Adding more fertilizer later in the growing season is often helpful, but never overdo it. "Slow release" fertilizers are applied only at the beginning of the season.

Mulching simply means covering the newly worked soil with a layer of pine straw, or shredded or chipped bark, to keep the sun from overheating the soil, to keep the soil from crusting over after hard rains or watering, and to slow the germination of weed seeds. Synthetic fabric mulches do a fair job of weed control, but do not decay and "feed" the soil or its worms. A good

ANNUALS ARE USED FOR FAST COLOR OR SCREENING, as container plants and hanging baskets, and in long-blooming masses or specimen plants. They provide all-season "color bridges" as perennials flush in and out of show, can give solid color in the spring, summer, or fall (even in the shade), and add interest to shrubbery when it is out of season.

guideline to determine how much mulch to use is to see how much it takes of your favorite kind to completely but barely cover the soil, then add that much more to compensate for packing and natural composting over time.

Weed control is usually done by hand pulling, chopping with a sharp tool, mulching after planting, or, in last-case scenarios, using chemical weed killers—which are not always dependable or safe for other plants. For information on weed control, consult your county Agricultural Extension agent or ask a dependable, trained garden center employee to show you products that list your types of weeds and plants on the labels. Landscape fabrics are "high horticulture"— not good gardening. The best experts hand pull weeds!

Watering is necessary for most short-lived annuals, especially when it is hot and dry and the wind is blowing. Some annuals simply do not need it, but most will, at least every few weeks. Container-grown annuals need regular watering, sometimes even in rainy seasons. How often to water and how much to use is so variable that no one can tell you an honest answer; the rule of thumb is to water only when needed, but do it deeply. I almost always water twice when I water, so the first time "sets up" the soil and the second, done a few minutes after the first, really soaks in and lasts longer.

Note on Pest Control

Most of these plants have few pests, practically none that are major. Occasional leaf spots and minor insect infestations can make some plants look bad, and

Legend of the Three Sisters

Can we still learn from our gardening ancestors? The Iroquois and other North American natives "interplanted" corn, beans, and squash together in one hill. Squash covered the ground and helped with weed control, corn supported the beans, and beans provided nitrogen fertilizer for the whole planting. The hill itself stabilized the plants from wind damage, and as a bonus this intercropping made the garden less attractive to pests. Together, these "three sisters" helped one another, and provided a complete diet for the gardeners.

slugs, leaf-eating beetles, and caterpillars are always challenges that defy even the best experts. Still, it is a good idea to avoid pesticides whenever possible to protect bees, butterflies, and other beneficial creatures. When possible, choose a "natural" product such as insecticidal soap, Neem oil, or diatomaceous earth to control minor insect pests. And be prepared to simply pull up annuals that are suffering intolerable problems—something else is always waiting to go in that hole! Also be aware that overwatering or overfeeding can cause tough plants to be more susceptible to problems.

For some plants slugs are a problem. Make a slug trap from a plastic soda bottle. Cut the top end off, and invert it like a funnel back into the bottle. Add a little beer, lay it on its side, and place where slugs can crawl in but can't get back out. Or cut an inch-wide hole in the plastic top of a coffee can or other container, bury the container to its top rim in the soil and mulch, and add a little beer. Slugs drop in through the hole and can't get back out. Good luck!

Note on Seed or Plant Sources

Always shop locally first! While the quality of seeds and annual transplants that arrive at garden centers is usually similar, in many cases—though not always—independent or family-owned garden centers have better-trained staffs who have cared for plants longer than some mass-merchandisers and who have more knowledge about the

plants and their challenges. Shop at a variety of sources for the best buys and the best service. Mail-order firms often have a larger selection of unusual or old-fashioned plants and seeds. And never overlook the value and fun (and heritage) of swapping seeds and plants with friends and neighbors!

Felder's Top Annual Picks

The following annuals, which by no means include all of the toughest, have proven themselves in millions of gardens as beautiful and low maintenance.

Ageratum
Ageratum houstonianum
Sun or light shade

"Flossflower" is one of our most dependable sources of blue in the border. Used for edging or cutting, and as a companion to larger container combinations.

FLOWER: Rounded clusters of tiny powder puffs of blue, lavender-pink, or white, formed constantly all summer.

PLANT: Low-growing, sprawling mass of pointed, fresh green foliage creeps forward and in between other flowers; especially good with snapdragons, begonias, and alyssum; pinch young plants for bushiness.

INTERESTING KINDS: Lavender-blue 'Blue Danube'; extra early, bright blue 'Adriatic'; nine-inch 'Blue Surf'.

Alyssum
Lobularia maritima
Sun or light shade

Perfect spring and summer plant to use as edging, in hanging baskets and containers, or in a rock garden. Produces masses of flowers except in the very hottest weather; tolerates light frost. Often used to hide foliage of spring bulbs.

FLOWER: Many small clusters of tiny pink, white, or lavender flowers create a mass effect, completely covering the plants and blending well with other flowers such as miniature roses or geraniums.

PLANT: Ground-covering or cascading mass of tiny, inconspicuous leaves. Thrives in well-drained soils that are not kept wet (or risk diseases).

INTERESTING KINDS: 'Royal Carpet' and 'Carpet of Snow' flower profusely; 'Snow Crystals' tolerates heat.

Basil
Ocimum basilicum
Sun or light shade

You don't have to have a herb garden—or even be a good cook—to enjoy basil as a summer foliage plant with a crisp bouquet. Outstanding as a flower bed or container companion as well as cooking herb.

FLOWER: Spikes of lavender all summer; flowers are small but edible, and great for butterflies and bees.

PLANT: Upright or rounded mound of pointed green or burgundy leaves; very fragrant when watered, cut, or even brushed; can be pinched to encourage bushiness. Some varieties are much stronger-scented than others.

INTERESTING KINDS: 'Purple Ruffles'; 'Spicy Globe'; and 'African Blue', a large plant with tall flower spikes.

Begonia
Begonia Semperflorens-Cultorum hybrids
Light shade, shade, or sun

Wax begonias, a traditional "six pack" bedding plant, are cheerful bloomers all season, especially in light shade, as border or window box plants; can be brought indoors for a sunny winter windowsill.

FLOWER: Clusters of roundish petals of pink, white, red, coral, and bicolor, with yellow stamens, held atop foliage to make a mass of color, especially in light shade.

PLANT: Crisp, waxy green or bronze leaves in tight mounds up to nine inches tall and a foot wide. Foliage is fine even in dense shade where flowers may be sparse; may burn in hot dry sun.

INTERESTING KINDS: Dwarf Semperflorens-Cultorum forms, or Wing hybrids up to a foot tall. 'Picotee Wings' has soft white petals edged in rose.

Black-Eyed Susan
Rudbeckia hirta
Sun or very light shade

This very familiar native wildflower is one of the best butterfly and cutting flowers ever for growing on a sunny hillside or in a meadow.

FLOWER: Thin, sunflower-like rays of mostly golden yellow on long, stiff stems in the spring and early summer, usually with dark cones or "noses" that become covered with butterflies.

PLANT: Low-growing, linear leaves over the winter; flowering stems sent up in spring and summer. Prefers fall seeding in poor but well-drained soils.

INTERESTING KINDS: Gloriosa daisy and 'Green Eyes' ('Irish Eyes') are outstanding summer cut flowers.

Castor Bean or Mole Bean
Ricinus communis
Full sun to light shade

The word for castor bean is bold—big summer plant, large leaves, perfect for backs of borders or in the center of a bed or large container. Roots are said to repel moles, but no evidence backs that up.

FLOWER: Stalks up to a foot tall with not very showy flowers, but seeds are contained in large marble-sized spiny burrs, the same color as the stems, sometimes bright red (seeds are very poisonous, so remove them where children might garden or play).

PLANT: Tall, branching, woody-stemmed summer annual up to six feet or more tall and half as wide, with large, lobed leaves up to two or more feet across in burgundy or green.

INTERESTING KINDS: 'Sanguineus' has leaves tinged blood red, 'Zanzibarensis' has green leaves with white veins, and 'Carmencita' has nearly-black burgundy leaves.

Celosia

Celosia argentea var. *cristata*

Sun

These plants will grow in sidewalk cracks and reseed themselves for years to come.

FLOWER: Cockscomb (Cristata group) has rounded, fissured heads up to a foot across of blood red and other colors; plume cockscomb (Plumosa group) has smaller plumes of red, pink, golden, or white; another type (Spicata group) has long, slender flower heads in pink or yellow.

PLANT: Summer annual with pointed oval leaves of medium green or purplish, up to two feet or more tall and half as wide. Use as a specimen, in combinations, or in masses.

INTERESTING KINDS: In the Spicata group, 'Flamingo Feather' is four feet tall with long, narrow spikes of pink and white; 'Flamingo Purple' has dark purplish green leaves and pinkish purple spikes; 'Pink Castle' has rose pink spikes.

Cleome or Spider Flower

Cleome hassleriana

Sun or light shade

Tall fluffy plants with marijuana-like, palmate leaves. Good cut flower that wilts when first cut but perks up in water. Excellent butterfly and hummingbird plant, great in masses behind other flowers or combined with bold textured plants in large containers.

FLOWER: Airy heads six inches wide and loosely arranged, with open flowers that have spidery "cat whisker" stamens and long narrow seedpods, in white, pink, or dusty purple.

PLANT: Four- to six-foot branching summer annuals (there are also dwarf forms) with palm-like foliage that is sticky, a not-so-nice aroma when cut, and small prickly thorns.

INTERESTING KINDS: 'Helen Campbell' is snow white, and Queen varieties (cherry, pink, rose, purple, mauve, ruby) indicate color.

Coleus
Solenostemon scutellarioides
Light shade or sun, depending on the type

Old-fashioned foliage plant grown mostly in light shade as a summer annual, either in beds or containers. Large masses are spectacular all summer and fall. Very easy to root cuttings in water or moist potting soil and keep indoors over the winter.

FLOWER: Tall flower spikes are not very showy, but are studded with small, salvia-like blue trumpets. Most gardeners pinch the stalks off to promote new leaf production.

PLANT: Shrubby, many-branched member of the mint family with large leaves, up to six or more inches long and nearly as wide, in many colors, including red, green, yellow, chartreuse, orange, salmon, pink, and purple, most variegated, splotched, or with contrasting edges. Grows best in moist conditions, with light but regular feeding. Leaves can be steeped to make a tea-like tonic.

INTERESTING KINDS: Seed-grown coleus have highly variable leaf shapes and colors. Sun coleus, so-called for their tolerance of hot sun, include 'Plum Parfait', 'Burgundy Sun', 'Freckles', and 'Saturn'.

Copper Plant or Copperleaf
Acalypha wilkesiana
Sun

Bulky mainstay foliage plant for hot summer beds, often overlooked because it is sold as rooted cuttings in larger pots, which are relatively expensive compared with typical cell-pack flowers sold in flats. Lots of bang for the buck, though.

FLOWER: Not very showy tassels of reddish brown hanging from leaf axils.

PLANT: Three-foot or taller mass of mottled bronze, red, copper, orange, and green foliage, held densely around the plant. Grows all right in the shade, but has outstanding heat and sun tolerance; a great "anchor" for companions in a large container, in groups, or as a short summer hedge behind other flowers. Must be pruned and brought in during the winter if you want to hold it over for next year.

INTERESTING KINDS: 'Macafeeana' has large reddish leaves tinged with crimson and bronze; 'Hoffmannia' has narrow, twisted leaves; 'Obovata' has leaves ruffled and serrated, in pink, bronze, and red.

Coreopsis or Tickseed

Coreopsis species

Sun

Common prairie wildflowers that "tame" very well in urban flower borders, containers, and butterfly or cut-flower gardens. Many species are perennial, though some are short-lived.

FLOWER: Cheerful yellow disks two or more inches across from mid-spring through midsummer.

PLANT: Short, stocky clump of linear foliage appears in early winter. Some species have wide, strap-like leaves; others have very delicate, needle-like foliage.

INTERESTING KINDS: *Coreopsis tinctoria* is an airy, openly branched plant, which has a reddish aura around the flower center and finely divided, almost ferny leaves. Calliopsis (*Coreopsis basalis*) is a vigorous, reseeding summer bloomer.

Cosmos

Cosmos sulphureus

Sun

This summer and fall flowering showstopper is one of the most impressive flowers of the season and reseeds itself to the point of being a nuisance. But it's easy to thin out seedlings in the spring and summer.

FLOWER: Showy, single, flat, daisy-like flowers in deep orange-yellow.

PLANT: Large branching plant to eight feet with deep-green, divided, marigold-like leaves.

INTERESTING KINDS: Common cosmos (*Cosmos bipinnatus*) has pink, white, rose, or crimson flowers with yellow centers that bloom in the spring, summer, and fall; very easy from seed sown in spring.

Dusty Miller
Senecio cineraria
Sun or shade

This is the first "white" companion plant I reach for when looking for contrast in container plantings or especially when working on a patriotic planting. Good, solid white.

FLOWER: Fairly showy, loose clusters of bright, creamy yellow held above the foliage in summer.

PLANT: Upright, spreading, many-branched shrub-like mound to two feet or taller of soft, dusty white foliage; sometimes needs shearing to thicken up the foliage near its base.

INTERESTING KINDS: 'Cirrus' is a dwarf form; 'Silverdust' is very compact and finely textured. Other silvery or white garden plants in the aster family include *Artemisia* and several *Centaurea* species, which are also called dusty miller.

Globe Amaranth or Bachelor's Buttons
Gomphrena globosa
Full sun

Historic summer annual, the perfect companion for other flowers because of its tall, airy growth. Super easy to dry for long lasting flower arrangements. Fairly good butterfly plant.

FLOWER: Bristly, round, button-like clover heads of red, purplish red, pink, or white on long stems up to three feet tall.

PLANT: Often-reseeding summer annual with narrow foliage that is not much to look at. Very pest resistant and incredibly drought and heat tolerant.

INTERESTING KINDS: Compact purplish red 'Buddy', tall red 'Strawberry Fields', and pink 'Lavender Lady'.

Impatiens
Impatiens walleriana
Shade or moderate sun

Very showy shade mainstay, great for containers or borders, especially showy when inter-planted with caladium or dusty miller. Requires watering during prolonged dry spells, but usually perks up quickly.

FLOWER: Masses of flat flowers in white, red, rose, lavender, salmon, pink, and bi-colors are produced constantly all summer.

PLANT: Upright, branched, with dark green leaves, stems almost succulent and easily broken.

INTERESTING KINDS: Many good ones on the market in a variety of heights. 'Victorian Rose' is an impressive double; the Super Elfin series makes great container or hanging basket additions. The new Infinity series has darker leaves, which show off the large, bright pink, red, and salmon flowers. New Guinea impatiens are larger plants with larger flowers, and tolerate much more sun.

Johnny Jump-Up
Viola tricolor
Sun

Favorite "old garden" winter annual, planted in the fall and flowering through the worst winter. Perfect for containers, mass planting over taller daffodils, or borders.

FLOWER: Sweetly fragrant, purple and yellow pansies about the size of a quarter. Blooms spring into summer; seedlings pop up in the fall.

PLANT: Floppy many-branched mounds of small roundish leaves, to a foot or more tall and wide, set out in the fall or late winter as transplants. Reseeds.

INTERESTING KINDS: Various cultivars exist, with flowers ranging from soft lavender to nearly black.

Joseph's Coat
Alternanthera ficoidea
Sun or light shade

Grown entirely for its generally compact habit and solid green, golden, or variegated foliage, this is the most popular annual for creating living floral emblems or to spell out words in flower beds. Tolerates close shearing and roots readily (fallen clippings often root in the mulch).

FLOWER: Insignificant white stars throughout the foliage.

PLANT: Solid little "mini-shrub" from six inches to three feet tall with small leaves.

INTERESTING KINDS: There are many varieties in green, gold, burgundy, rosy red, scarlet, and chartreuse forms. 'Rosea Nana' has rose-colored leaves; 'Golden Threads' has narrow leaves in green, yellow, and white.

Larkspur
Consolida ambigua
Sun

Larkspur is a small "delphinium," producing prolific spikes of pastel colors, perfect for a cut-flower garden or as a companion to late spring or early summer perennials; reseeds well. Outstanding for hummingbirds.

FLOWER: Narrow, dense spikes of a half inch or longer, interesting violet-like flowers of deep or pale blue, pink, or white, produced in late winter through midsummer; some are double flowered. Single-flower varieties have a "rabbit head" structure in the center, complete with ears and buck-teeth!

PLANT: Airy, branching, three- to five-foot-tall plant grows best in early spring. The old-timey single form reseeds prolifically.

INTERESTING KINDS: Giant Imperial and Regal strains are many-branched. A similar, smaller larkspur is C. *regalis*.

Lettuce
Lactuca sativa
Full sun

This European native grown for edible foliage is too often overlooked as a pretty container plant, considering its many forms and ease of culture. Mixing several kinds of seed together creates colorful and delicious "mesclun."

FLOWER: Yellow flowers on tall seed spikes occur when weather is very hot. Allow them to mature for collecting seed.

PLANT: Shallow-rooted leafy balls, tight heads, or loose rosettes of green, chartreuse, yellow, burgundy, red, or speckled. Needs regular light feeding and soakings for continued production. Flavor sweetens after frost. Use scissors to snip only the outer leaves you want to eat, and the plants will continue to produce.

INTERESTING KINDS: 'Red Sails', 'Tennis Ball', 'Oakleaf', green 'Buttercrunch', 'Bibb', and many, many more.

Melampodium
Melampodium paludosum
Full sun

Its unfortunate lack of a common name scares new gardeners off, but this is one of the top ten summer flowering annuals for massing in hot, dry, parking-lot type garden spots.

FLOWER: Buttery yellow daisies produced in nearly solid sheets, from spring to frost.

PLANT: Mounding plants from two to three feet, deep green foliage. Requires heat to grow.

INTERESTING KINDS: 'Showstar' is compact, under two feet tall; 'Medallion' can get over three feet tall and half that wide.

Mexican Sunflower
Tithonia rotundifolia
Full sun

Fast-growing tall screen or accent that flowers nonstop in heat, drought, and humidity, all the while covered with butterflies and hummingbirds.

FLOWER: Marigold-like flowers up to four inches across with orange petals and yellow centers. Blooms spring to frost, good as cut flowers and outstanding for butterflies.

PLANT: Large (to six feet or more) multi-branched summer "shrub" with hand-sized leaves. Reseeds well.

INTERESTING KINDS: 'Sundance' and 'Goldfinger' are more compact, to three or four feet.

Moss Rose
Portulaca grandiflora
Full sun

This solid mass of bright flowers opens only for people who are outdoors in the middle of the day. Perfect for rock gardens, edging, and spilling out of containers in hot, dry locations.

FLOWER: Compact, inch-wide, rose-like clusters of brilliant red, magenta, pink, yellow, and white that open only when summer sun shines directly on them, right up until frost.

PLANT: Low mounds, six inches tall by a foot wide, thick with fleshy, cylindrical leaves to an inch long. Reseeds prolifically in hot, dry areas.

INTERESTING KINDS: There are double- and single-flowered strains of cylindrical-leaf moss rose; the popular flowering purslane (*Portulaca umbraticola*) has flat leaves and flat, single flowers.

Nasturtium

Tropaeolum majus

Full sun or light shade

Cheerful masses of vibrant colors contrasted with bold foliage make nasturtiums popular throughout the North. Their edible flowers are almost too pretty to eat.

FLOWER: Flattened trumpets of bright yellow, orange, cream, apricot, mahogany, or red produced abundantly, especially in cool weather. Flowers are zesty and edible, and can be strung on fishing string by kids to make necklaces or crowns.

PLANT: Trailing, semi-trailing, or dwarf mounding forms all have roundish leaves with wavy margins and prominent lighter veins. Requires very little fertilizer. Seeds are tough, but sprout better if soaked overnight.

INTERESTING KINDS: 'Fordhook Favorite' is a vigorous variety, and the Alaska hybrids have beautiful variegated leaves.

Pansy and Viola

Viola × *wittrockiana* and *Viola cornuta*

Full winter sun or part shade

Pansies and violas have become some of the most popular annuals, and probably the only truly reliable ones for providing color and interest in the cool weather months, connecting fall to the following spring.

FLOWER: Flat and up to four inches across, in white, blue, purple, red, yellow, orange, sometimes with large blotches or contrasting "eyes," produced from fall to late spring. Remove spent flowers for optimum continued production.

PLANT: Compact six- to eight-inch-tall mounds of slightly lobed, roundish leaves. Requires cool weather for best growth; generally dies from heat by midsummer in the North. Best grown from transplants.

INTERESTING KINDS: There are many hybrid strains and colors of pansies, from big floppy kinds to compact freer-flowering ones. New hybrids, called bedding pansies or violas, between the smaller *Viola cornuta* and the larger pansies have midsized flowers and more compact growth, and come in many hues of white, yellow, apricot, blue, purple, and others.

Pentas or Egyptian Star-Cluster
Pentas lanceolata
Sun or light shade

This medium-tall shrubby plant was grown for many years as a Victorian "pot plant" and has made a tremendous comeback as one of the best butterfly plants for the summer garden.

FLOWER: Six-inch-wide clusters of small, starry florets of deep red, white, or pink bloom atop the foliage.

PLANT: Upright, branching "shrub" to two or more feet tall. Grows best in hot weather.

INTERESTING KINDS: Several strains on the market, all about the same.

Pepper
Capsicum annuum
Full sun or light shade

Ornamental peppers, with a huge array of sizes and fruit colors, are seriously overlooked additions to flower beds, herb gardens, and containers. Most ornamental peppers are edible, but very hot!

FLOWER: Small, starry, white flowers from late spring to frost; fruits are tiny birds-eye pods to long and thin, from green to yellow, orange, red, purple, and almost black.

PLANT: Shrubby summer annuals from six inches to four feet or taller, many branched with oval leaves of green, purple, or variegated with white or yellow.

INTERESTING KINDS: There are many, many forms of *Capsicum annuum*, including sweet, jalapeno, and chili peppers. *Capsicum frutescens*, the tabasco pepper, is a large shrub with hundreds of narrow fruits in green, yellow, and red held upright; *C. chinense* includes the habanero pepper, which is fiery hot and has beautiful, gnarly, orange fruits.

Periwinkle

Catharanthus roseus

Sun

One of the most drought-tolerant plants on Earth, periwinkle flowers continually with no care at all.

FLOWER: Flat, five-petaled disks of pure white, pink, or red, sometimes with a darker "eye," produced in masses atop foliage from spring to frost, more in hot weather.

PLANT: Compact mound of glossy green foliage up to two feet tall, usually a foot or less. Reseeds prolifically into nearby hot, dry areas. Resents water and heavy wet soils.

INTERESTING KINDS: Many strains on the market, with more or less creeping or compact habits and larger flowers.

Petunia

Petunia × *hybrida*

Sun

Old "grandmother's garden" varieties are not as showy as modern hybrids, but give a wonderful cottage-garden element to mixed borders and containers.

FLOWER: Flat or ruffled trumpets of white, pink, red, purple, blue, or rose, with or without stripes; some strains have flowers four inches or more across. Blooms best in cool weather.

PLANT: Sprawling vine-like summer annual that tolerates a little cool better than extreme heat. May need "pinching" to thicken scraggly growth. Often reseeds.

INTERESTING KINDS: Too many to mention, but cascading 'Purple Wave' takes the most summer heat, needs no pruning to thicken it up, and smells of heavenly spices, all day and night.

Queen Anne's Lace
Daucus carota
Sun or very light shade

Nothing but a wild carrot, this common butterfly plant reseeds all over meadows with poor soil.

FLOWER: Single stemmed with many branches, each topped with a flat, round, white flower head. A single flower in the very center of each disk is burgundy.

PLANT: Ferny foliage tolerates severely cold weather. Skinny roots smell like carrots.

INTERESTING KINDS: Queen Anne's lace is in the same family with several herbs, including coriander, fennel, dill, parsley, and caraway.

WHO HASN'T TRIED TO DIG UP A WILD QUEEN ANNE'S LACE, just to have it wilt and die? It's because the plant flowers right at the end of its natural life—no way to dig and save it. Instead, collect seed to sow in the late summer or early spring, and they will all sprout and thrive!

Salvia
Salvia coccinea and *Salvia splendens*
Sun or light shade

Salvias are summer mainstays with spikes of red, sometimes pink, purple, white, or peach.

FLOWER: Spikes of small exotic trumpets, mostly red, from spring to frost; great for butterflies and hummingbirds.

PLANT: Upright, branching, small shrubby plants to two feet tall or more; solid green leaves give great contrast to the spikes of flowers. Reseeds prolifically everywhere, including into hard clay.

INTERESTING KINDS: *Salvia coccinea* is the most heat- and drought-tolerant plant of all, will be covered with butterflies, and reseeds everywhere. It's the last annual besides periwinkle to die from drought. Common red salvia (*S. splendens*) also comes in several other colors; may need watering in full sun.

Snapdragon
Antirrhinum majus
Sun or very light shade

Among the best "vertical accent" flowers for cutting, flower borders, or containers, these old-fashioned "workhorses" of the garden have inspired generations of children and adults alike.

FLOWER: Spikes of inch-or-longer yellow, pink, white, or reddish pastel colors, each with two upper and three lower petals and a "jaw" that opens like a dragon's mouth when pressed between thumb and index finger. Deadhead for many weeks of repeat flowering.

PLANT: Upright plant, from six inches to three feet tall. May get "rust" if watered too much. Frost tolerant and will overwinter in milder areas if kept mulched.

INTERESTING KINDS: Dwarf, fluffy 'Tahiti', and many more of different heights and colors for borders or cutting.

Sunflower
Helianthus annuus
Sun

Classic tall annual for the back of the border or even the vegetable garden. Easy to grow from seed directly sown in the ground. Newer cultivars make this "country cousin" look at home even in more "sophisticated" gardens. Plant something in front to hide its bare legs.

FLOWER: Wide, usually flattened heads of golden flower disks surrounded by rays of yellow, gold, cream, rust, and red. Edible seeds mature by midsummer or fall.

PLANT: Tall, to eight feet or more, sometimes branching, with large, pointed, oval leaves up to a foot wide. Sometimes needs staking, or grow it with annual vines to help as a support.

INTERESTING KINDS: Too many to single out, varying in plant height, flower size and color, and quality of seeds (for birds or people); pollen-free kinds are best for cut flowers.

Sweet Potato
Ipomoea batatas
Full sun to moderate shade

Ornamental sweet potatoes are fast growing, trailing (not climbing) vines with beautiful foliage color for large containers, hanging baskets, or ground covers. Astounding in masses or entwined with other summer plants.

FLOWER: Not very showy, small "morning glories."

PLANT: Heart-shaped or lobed foliage on long, trailing vines that root as they "run" from spring to frost. Does best in poor soils with low fertility. Forms edible tuberous roots.

INTERESTING KINDS: 'Blackie' has deep burgundy, almost black foliage that is deeply divided; 'Margarita' has shocking chartreuse foliage; 'Pink Frost' ('Tricolor') has variegated white, green, and pink leaves, and is not as vigorous as the other two; 'Black Heart' has black-green leaves with streaks of lighter green. The dark-leaved varieties can fade a bit in full sun.

Zinnia
Zinnia angustifolia and *Zinnia elegans*
Sun or very light shade

One of the very best "starter" flowers for kids and adults alike, outstanding for butterflies and cut flowers, best used in masses or behind other plants to hide its ugly lower foliage.

FLOWER: Flat or double daisy-like flower heads, up to three or more inches across, in all possible colors, even white (no black), usually with yellow stamens; produced freely all summer and fall on long stems. Deadheading can increase the number of flowers produced.

PLANT: Many-branching, compact mounds or tall specimens to four feet or more, with pleasing oval leaves. Sometimes prone to powdery mildew, but plants keep on flowering. Usually reseeds.

INTERESTING KINDS: Narrow leaf zinnia (*Zinnia angustifolia* or *Z. linearis*) is a loose mound of smaller, non-stop, orange or white flowers, with outstanding heat and drought tolerance in containers, edging, or rock gardens.

Other Annuals Worth a Try

Bachelor's Buttons (*Centaurea cyanus*) or **cornflower**, is an airy blue, pink, or white spring cut flower. Sow seed in fall or late winter. Reseeds prolifically.

Burgundy Mustard (*Brassica oleracea*, Acephala group) has cool-season foliage of deep red or maroon, sometimes with white midribs, and tall airy spikes of clear yellow spring flowers. Edible, but hot.

Calendula (*Calendula officinalis*), or **pot marigold**, has clear yellow, edible flowers; tolerates frost.

California Poppy (*Eschscholzia californica*) has bright orange flowers in spring and reseeds readily. Often used in wildflower seed blends.

Candlestick Plant (*Senna alata* or *Cassia alata*) has dramatic, big fall blooms with a tropical touch.

Chard (*Beta vulgaris* var. *flavescens*) is a beet relative grown for colorful edible leaves.

Cushion Mum (*Dendranthema* × *grandiflorum*) is best used as one-shot masses of autumn glory, expensive but showy. Compost them when they freeze, and replant with bulbs and pansies.

Forget-Me-Not (*Myosotis arvensis*) blooms profusely with tiny blue flowers. An excellent companion with ground covers in sun or shade.

Four-o'-Clock (*Mirabilis jalapa*), has very fragrant evening trumpets of red, yellow, pink, or white; very fast small bush from seed, and great for hummingbirds.

French Hollyhock (*Alcea rosea* 'Zebrina' or *Malva sylvestris* 'Zebrina'), a prolifically reseeding, overwintering plant with lavender flowers streaked in purple.

Jewelweed (*Impatiens capensis* and *I. pallida*) is a tall (to five feet) vigorously reseeding native impatiens with yellow and orange flowers; its sticky sap can be used to cleanse the oil of recently encountered poison ivy from your skin.

Kales (*Brassica oleracea*) include curly and other interesting varieties (including bold-textured collards) for winter and spring color in containers, raised beds, and gardens.

Love-in-a-Mist (*Nigella damascena*) is a reseeding annual with finely cut leaves and blue, white, or rose flowers. 'Miss Jekyll' has blue, semi-double blooms.

Marigold (*Tagetes* species) has showy yellow or gold flowers and fragrant foliage. Often peters out in midsummer from spider mites and heat, but can be replanted for a fall show.

Mexican Heather (*Cuphea hyssopifolia*) is a small, clump-forming, pink-flowered heather look-alike for hot weather.

Million Bells (*Calibrachoa* hybrids) is a mounding or trailing plant covered with petunia-like blossoms of hot pink, purple, white, peach, red, or yellow. Great for hanging baskets or containers.

Nicotiana (*Nicotiana alata* or *N.* × *sanderae*) or **flowering tobacco** blooms with panicles of white, red, pink, yellow, or mauve in cool weather; the tall, white flowering tobacco (*N. sylvestris*) is a knockout in the summer shade garden.

Poppy (*Papaver rhoeas*), or **corn** or **Shirley poppy**, is the cheerful spring-flowering type seen in roadside wildflower mixes. Can be sown over bare soil in fall or spring, and reseeds prolifically except where mulched.

Touch-Me-Not (*Impatiens balsamina*) or **garden balsam** is a shrubby plant with large, toothed leaves and two-inch, sometimes double, flowers along the stems. Seedpods snap open violently to throw seeds everywhere. Sun tolerant.

Wishbone Plant (*Torenia fournieri*) looks like a miniature gloxinia, blue with a purple throat, or pink. Can flower indoors.

Attractive Edibles

Just because you can eat it, doesn't mean you have to, but anyone who's ever had a pansy stick to the roof of his or her mouth has learned the subtle delights of edible flowers. From the sweet, raw-peanut taste of redbud flowers, to battered and fried daylily buds, there's some mighty good eatin' in the garden. Best commonly grown edible flowers to try (when no one is looking): basil, broccoli, chives, daylily, Johnny jump-ups, nasturtium, pansy, redbud, rose, squash, and violets. There are many more, of course, but you get the flavor.

BEST VEGETABLES FOR BEGINNERS: (Vegetables are considered annuals, too. Newer varieties of some are even attractive enough to include in flower garden spaces.) cabbage, Irish potato, lettuce, peas, pepper, Swiss chard, tomatoes.

VEGETABLES WORTHY OF EXPERTS: beets, broccoli, Brussels sprouts, cauliflower, corn, onions, pumpkins.

👍 Best for Beginners:

- Begonia
- Celosia
- Coleus
- Dusty Miller
- Gomphrena

- Moss Rose
- Pansy
- Periwinkle
- Sweet Potato
- Zinnia

Kinda Tricky: 👎

- Annual Verbena (mites)
- Impatiens (root rot)
- Marigolds (spider mites)
- Sweet Peas (wet weather)
- Tomatoes (pests, training)

Fast-Reference Lists for Annuals

In Shade or Semi-Shade
- Ageratum
- Alyssum
- Begonia
- Caladium
- Coleus
- Impatiens
- Pansy
- Pentas
- Salvia
- Snapdragon

For Hot, Dry Spots
- Castor Bean
- Celosia
- Copper Plant
- Cornflower
- Cosmos
- Dusty Miller
- Four-o'-Clock
- Globe Amaranth
- Joseph's Coat
- Melampodium
- Mexican Sunflower
- Moss Rose
- Okra
- Perilla
- Periwinkle
- Queen Anne's Lace
- Sunflower
- Sweet Potato
- Zinnia

Tolerate Frosts
- Alyssum
- Black-Eyed Susan
- Calendula
- Cornflower
- Cosmos
- French Hollyhock
- Johnny Jump-Up
- Larkspur
- Lettuce
- Mustard
- Nasturtium
- Pansy
- Poppy
- Queen Anne's Lace
- Snapdragon

For Poor, Unimproved Soils
- Castor Bean
- Celosia
- Cleome
- Coreopsis
- Cosmos
- Globe Amaranth
- Moss Rose
- Nasturtium
- Periwinkle
- Queen Anne's Lace
- Sweet Potato

Usually Reseed Themselves for Years
- Alyssum
- Castor Bean
- Cleome
- Coreopsis
- Cornflower
- Cosmos
- Forget-Me-Not
- Globe Amaranth
- Impatiens
- Johnny Jump-Up
- Larkspur
- Love-in-a-Mist
- Moss Rose
- Nicotiana
- Periwinkle
- Petunia
- Poppy
- Queen Anne's Lace
- Zinnia

Good Cut Flowers
- Ageratum
- Celosia
- Cleome
- Cornflower
- Cosmos
- Globe Amaranth
- Larkspur
- Pentas
- Poppy
- Queen Anne's Lace
- Salvia
- Snapdragon
- Sunflower (pollen-free varieties)
- Zinnia

Colorful Foliage
- Basil
- Caladium (in Bulbs)
- Castor Bean
- Coleus
- Copper Plant
- Dusty Miller
- Joseph's Coat
- Kale
- Lettuce
- Mustard
- Sweet Potato
- Swiss Chard

Easy Edging
- Ageratum
- Alyssum
- Begonia
- Dusty Miller
- Joseph's Coat
- Lettuce
- Marigold (dwarf)
- Nasturtium (dwarf)
- Pansy
- Petunia
- Sweet Potato
- Swiss Chard
- Zinnia (dwarf or narrow-leaf)

Fast Backgrounds or Screens
- Candlestick Plant
- Castor Bean
- Cleome
- Copper Plant
- Cosmos
- Hollyhock
- Mexican Sunflower
- Sunflower
- Zinnia

Butterfly Plants
- Coreopsis
- Cosmos
- Globe Amaranth
- Mexican Sunflower
- Pentas
- Periwinkle
- Queen Anne's Lace
- Zinnia

Wedding of the Flowers

My great-great-aunt Bernice, a retired New Orleans school principal who visited her old home place in north central Mississippi quite often, was a heck of a gal. It was she who first told me that flying saucers were coming out of the center of the earth, through a hole in Antarctica (and had a magazine with pictures to prove it). She studied teaching in New York City, and took flying lessons from Charles Lindbergh himself (for that, we have REAL photos).

After she passed away, I found some of her old notes and stuff, including a crumbly, printed Victorian parlor word game in which a story was told with blanks left in the narrative, to be filled in with plant names. This particular one was called "The Wedding of the Flowers" and its faded penciled-in answers were hard to read. With help from friends and family, I took on the project of filling in the blanks. Here is the complete story, with the answers underlined:

Black-Eyed Susan married Sweet William after he Aster. His rival had been Ragged Robin, but the groom's Tulips sealed the engagement under towering Sunflowers. Their Four O'Clock wedding in Virgin Bowers was announced by Bells of Ireland and Bluebells. The bride was given away by Poppy, as the groom's mother whispered to him "Forget-Me-Not." Jack-in-the-Pulpit officiated.

Though the groom was giving up Bachelor Buttons, he brought to his bride Peppermint and Candytuft. The rings were made of Goldenrod and the bride's Paper-white gown was trimmed with Queen Anne's Lace (with Cowslips underneath). Bridesmaids were Quaker Ladies, including Lily, Iris, Daisy, and Rose. Their dresses were Lilac and Pinks, and they received Foxgloves and Cockscombs. The groomsmen were Jon-quil, Dan-delion, and Chrys-anthemum.

There was a crowd at the wedding—Phlox—but Seven Sisters and Old Maids were left behind. Singers included Larkspur and the great Bird of Paradise. A brief scene was created when Johnny Jump-Up objected to the wedding, but Bleeding Heart, Bittersweet, and Weeping Willow, all rejected lovers of the American Beauty, kept their Peace.

They ate their wedding cake from Buttercups, and had Lady Slippers tied behind their carriage. Their new home will be on Cape Jasmine, where they will spend the rest of their Everlasting lives in Sweet Peas (peace), hopefully with Baby's Breath.

Here's hoping their Passionflower love affair, made under the Star of Bethlehem, doesn't turn into Touch-Me-Not!

UNBEATABLE
Bulbs

My great-grandmother Pearl, who lived right across the street from my childhood home, grew many kinds of bulbs, including more than 350 varieties of daffodils. I was raised thinking bulbs are the toughest garden plants there are, and I can't imagine my garden without a single one of its dozens of nearly zero-maintenance beauties.

Beginner gardeners overlook flowering bulbs and bulb-like perennials. These have traditionally been planted as afterthoughts or all by themselves, partly because so many of them have temporary shows and we forget about them the rest of the year. But they can easily be worked into overall landscapes to add or prolong color and provide foliage even in "off" seasons.

Not all the plants in this section are true bulbs, which as a general rule are "onion-like." Many grow from rhizomes, corms, tubers, and other forms of underground structures. In addition to traditional, true bulbs such as long-lived daffodils and beautiful but fickle tulips, there are hardy native liatris; delicate, super-early snowdrops; fragrant lily-of-the-valley; and shrub-like, large flowered peonies. Tropical cannas, caladiums, and gladiolas are examples of bulb-like plants that must be replanted every spring.

Flowering bulbs need plenty of sunlight, at least when their foliage is out, which means many spring bulbs get all the sun they need even when planted under summer-shady oaks and tall deciduous shrubs, because the trees still haven't leafed out by late winter and early spring. Be careful, however, to avoid planting them in the shadow of the north side of a building or evergreen shrubs, because the winter and early spring sun is so low in the southern sky, combined with the low-light setting, that the bulbs won't get enough light.

Most bulbs also require well-drained soil and certainly shouldn't be planted where water stands for hours after a rain. Avoid water-related bulb rot by thoroughly blending a little organic matter into heavy soils, or plant in raised beds or containers—or better yet, just don't plant those susceptible kinds of bulbs!

Garden centers, mail-order (including Internet) catalogues, and specialty nurseries have many dozens of different kinds of bulbs, each with several distinct species and sometimes hundreds of unique cultivars. It's always a great idea to try new kinds—you never know when one will turn out to be an all-time favorite in your garden. But for long-term success, see if there aren't enough different kinds of bulbs described here to keep you entertained for many years with little care. The planting rule of thumb for true bulbs, unless otherwise indicated, is "twice as deep as they are tall." Big bulbs go deeper than smaller ones. You can even plant smaller ones above larger ones!

Interplanting with Bulbs

Why waste precious garden space for "one shot" flowers when you can set great plants between one another to prolong the season? Large shrubs, bare winter lawns, and overstuffed patio pots can all be gussied up with bulbs as well. Bonus: The emerging foliage of one can hide the fading leaves of the other.

The biggest considerations for interplanting flowers include making sure that all of them get the amount of sun or shade they need and that watering or fertilizing one type doesn't harm the others.

Bill Lee, with the American Daffodil Society, says his organization uses all of the following in their gardens, which complement one another without causing harm to any: daffodils, daylilies, liatris, purple coneflower, salvia, iris, black-eyed Susan, yarrow, phlox, and coreopsis. I would add chrysanthemums, dwarf golden-rods, and artemisia. Lee also recommended the following annuals, several of which can reseed year after year: larkspur, poppy, cleome (which, in general, may also help deter deer in the garden), ageratum, gomphrena, and mealy-cup sage.

Bulbs for the Shade

Ever see bulbs growing in old home sites that are all grown up with trees? These "naturalized" beauties have spread by seed, because their fruiting pods were left intact instead of being mowed or clipped before their seed ripened.

The trick to getting them to grow and multiply in the shade is planting them under trees that lose their leaves in the winter, giving them late winter sunshine, and leaving them alone after flowering so they have time to form flower buds underground inside the bulbs for the next season. This is especially important for daffodils, which form their next year's flower buds in the six weeks or so after they flower.

THE BOTTOM LINE: Plant bulbs, especially early flowering kinds, where they get winter sunshine, and then leave them alone after they flower—and don't cut or braid their foliage!

BULB FOODS ARE BEST FOR BULBS. Like all plants, bulbs need a balanced fertilizer containing nitrogen, phosphorus, and potash, all in small amounts. Bone meal alone has only phosphorus, just one of the main ingredients needed for overall plant health and growth. Researchers in U.S. universities worked with Dutch bulb growers to develop Holland Bulb Booster and other perfectly formulated brands of bulb food. They're expensive, but they go a long way.

Protect Bulbs from Critters

Voles are small, mouse-like rodents that burrow and eat roots and especially tender bulbs (with the amazing exception of daffodils). I have actually seen them in action, watching plants start to wobble and then disappear into tunnels! Not much will control these destructive pests—they are even difficult for cats to catch! Here are some "tricks of the trade" used by hard-core gardeners, and in botanical gardens:

- When planting bulbs, surround them with gravel or other coarse material, which voles hate to dig through. Folks near the Great Lakes: Try working in zebra mussel shells!
- Place "live" traps near burrows, baited with something smeared with peanut butter.
- When digging beds, place hardware cloth (mesh wire with half-inch openings) in the bottom and up the sides, like an upside-down fence. Cut a trench around the beds and line it with the strip of hardware cloth at least six or eight inches tall, partly sticking out of the ground (mulch will cover the exposed part). Make sure the bottom edge is

curved outward, away from the bed, to guide voles and moles away, not under.

- Plant individual bulbs or plants in wire baskets buried partially in the ground.
- Surround bulbs with plants such as daffodils, which are toxic to voles.
- Protect from digging squirrels, chipmunks, and cats by laying plastic netting or "chicken wire" over the planted area.
- Spray the bitter but non-toxic Ro-Pel or Liquid Fence around bulb planting—very effective for weeks!

How to "Rescue" Bulbs

Not that I'd ever recommend stealing, but if there's an old abandoned home site nearby where you have permission and are sure no one will miss a few daffodils, iris, daylilies, or hyacinths, I say, go for it! But take your time—don't rush out when plants are in full bloom, for two reasons: Digging when in flower often causes them to skip a year blooming (which means it will be two years until the next flowering cycle), and someone you know will invariably come down the road just as you get back to your car with an armload.

Assuming you have permission to dig on private property, here's the way to do it: Cut the flowers from the ones you want, both to enjoy them in a vase, and to keep someone else from seeing them and "liberating" them first. Then, go back a couple of months later to dig, when the plants have formed next year's flower buds and are nearly dormant. Be sure to put a plastic spoon or other discreet label by the ones you want, or you might not find them later.

For more information on bulbs, their planting and care, look for the *Month-by-Month* gardening book for your state, published by Cool Springs Press.

 **Best for Beginners:**

- *Chives*
- *Crocus*
- *Daffodils*
- *Gladiola*
- *Grape Hyacinth*
- *Hosta*
- *Iris*

Kinda Tricky:

- *Allium*
- *Caladium*
- *Dahlia*
- *Garden Lilies* (some)
- *Tuberous Begonias*
- *Tulips* (some)

Caladium

Caladium bicolor

Shade or part sun

Shade lovers, take note: This is one of your best friends! There's no better way to bring pizzazz to a shaded border, brighten a dark patio, or skirt a row of gloomy shrubs with color. Though caladiums will tolerate a lot of sun (with extra soil prep and watering, which is against the principles of this book), these summer annuals perform best by far in the shade.

Caladiums are so striking individually, they really don't need to be planted in large groups in long rows or circles around trees. Better to use them in clusters of three or more, repeated here and there for effect. They are also superb in pots on a shady porch or patio, especially when combined with impatiens.

FLOWER: Not striking at all, a calla-like whorl of white surrounding a pencil-like pollen stem, mostly hidden in the more desirable foliage. Admire the first one or two, then clip the rest off to stimulate more foliage production.

PLANT: Leaves are variable, but mostly pointed heart- or shield-shaped, up to a foot long, of red, white, pink, and green, in countless combinations. Produced in two-foot-tall masses.

INTERESTING KINDS: 'Freida Hemple' has dark red leaves bordered with green; the short, compact 'Miss Muffet' is light green with white ribs and red speckles; 'June Bride' is white.

SOIL: Plant tubers knobby side up, very shallowly in rich soil amended with organic matter, and occasionally water when rainfall is scarce. If plants go dormant, they usually pick back up after rains return. Light, regular feedings promote continuous foliage production.

PROPAGATION: Plant new tubers every year, well after danger of frost is past, or get them started earlier in pots in a bright spot indoors to set out later. Or dig, divide, and save old tubers before frost in the fall; let them dry thoroughly; and keep them very dry indoors over the winter.

TIP: WHAT'S THE DIFFERENCE between bulbs, tubers, rhizomes, and corms anyway? We tend to refer to most of them as "bulbs" and the distinctions can be subtle. All of them are underground structures developed for storing energy, water, and food for new growth and to sustain the plant during dry spells and dormancy. Many plants with such structures are native to regions with regular seasonal dry periods. A tuber is a swollen stem, branch, or root (caladium). A corm is a bulbous stem and is annual, forming new corms from buds on the old ones (crocus). A rhizome is a stem also, but can vary in thickness and branching, and can be near the soil surface (iris). A true bulb is an modified bud, with a thickened stem section and modified leaves (daffodil). Clear as mud, right?

Canna

Canna × generalis

Sun or very light shade

Almost nothing says "tropical" more than cannas, second only to gladiolas as a widely planted summer annual bulb (though neither are true bulbs). Because they are so common around "poor folks" gardens and homes, some upscale gardeners refuse to grow them. Yet the exotic Victorian foliage favorites are showcased in every botanical garden on earth. The biggest problem is what to do with the huge gap they leave after gardeners clean up their wilted, frozen remains once they are dug at first frost. One solution is to interplant with evergreen shrubs or ornamental grasses, or place a "hard feature" such as a gazing globe or statue nearby.

FLOWER: Sometimes very showy, gnarly masses of irregularly shaped flowers in orange, red, yellow, apricot, salmon, and mixed. Hard, round, bristly seedpods can be interesting as well, especially on old Indian shot canna (*Canna indica*). Cut faded flowers to promote more leaves.

PLANT: Large, almost banana-like, slick tropical leaves are long and wide, sometimes pointed, in green, bronze, dark burgundy, and striped. Plants grow in masses of leafy stems that can get up to six feet tall, although compact and dwarf forms are common. Very good for container culture, near pools or water gardens, around patios, and in Victorian mixed plantings.

INTERESTING KINDS: Cultivars include Pfitzer's dwarf varieties, which get two to three feet tall; 'Bengal Tiger' has bright yellow stripes with maroon margins and orange flowers; 'Tropical Rose' grows well from seed; 'Red King Humbert' has bronze leaves and reddish orange flowers; 'Tropicana' has shocking stripes of red, pink, and orange. There are many others available in nurseries or by mail order.

SOIL: Rich and moist soil preferred. Loves water, but tolerates extreme neglect and drought once established. Some fertilizer beneficial, but too much causes tall foliage to flop.

PROPAGATION: Divide thick rhizomes in fall soon after the first frost turns their foliage slimy. Cut (don't pull) off the leaves, let the rhizomes dry completely, then store indoors until warm weather returns. If moving or dividing while actively growing, cut the foliage back—it will recover quickly.

TIP: WHAT ABOUT THOSE WORMS? Canna leaf rollers are the larvae of night-flying moths, for which little can be done. Chemical controls often burn the plants by concentrating in the leaf whorls, and even natural materials such as biological worm sprays or diatomaceous earth kill the caterpillars, but still leave plants looking ratty. What I do is simply cut the plants down low, throw away the debris (and the worms), and let new growth quickly return.

Chives or Onion Chives

Allium schoenoprasum
Full sun or part shade

Chives are a must in any herb garden. Their thin, grasslike leaves have a mild but distinct onion flavor and bouquet, and are excellent when cut fresh and used as a garnish for soups, salads, cream cheeses, and herb butters, and especially over egg dishes. The plants are outstanding year-round, in all weather, even as container plants, and can be used in groups with other perennials, in a rock garden, or as a border—the spring flowers are an exceptional bonus. Interplant chives with daffodils for winter companionship or as a complement to cascading oregano or thyme. Great foil to iris as well, and both prefer dry soils.

FLOWER: Round clusters of lavender-pink florets, up to two inches across, on stems up to a foot or more tall. Edible as garnishes, even in soups. Cutting flowers results in more foliage.

PLANT: Small clumps of grasslike foliage. Leaves are hollow, like quills, and may reach more than a foot long. May die back in severe winter weather, but never fails to return by mid-spring.

INTERESTING KINDS: 'Forescate' is a robust grower with rosy pink flowers; 'Shepherd's Crook' has interesting contorted leaves. Garlic chives (*A. tuberosum*) has flat, garlicy leaves and showy masses of white flowers.

SOIL: Well drained, high in organic matter. Can live in an old container of potting soil for years.

PROPAGATION: Seedlings grow slowly; so it's best to get more plants by dividing clumps in fall or spring. Readily available at garden centers. Small plants can be kept indoors over winter on a sunny windowsill.

TIP: PLEASE DON'T EAT THE DAISIES! But go ahead and munch on the flowers of chives, nasturtiums, pansies, and daylily buds. Edible flowers can bring more than flavor to the table—they can add beauty and a little surprise to dishes, especially if you're having friends over for dinner. There are more things to eat in the garden than vegetables!

WHAT MAKES ONIONS SMELL? The distinctive scent of members of the genus *Allium* is because of sulfur compounds, and is released when plant parts are slightly bruised. For the most part ornamental onions do not spontaneously waft their aromas through the garden as do such intensely sweet-smelling plants as hyacinths. Not that onions smell bad to everyone, though chopping vegetable onions can bring us to tears. But the onion fragrance can also remind us of new-mown lawns in summer and favorite foods being prepared, and some alliums even have a faint violet-like scent. So dry your tears and embrace this sensory aspect of alliums in the garden.

Crocus

Crocus species
Full sun or light shade

One of the first flowers to greet us in the spring, holding its flowers above the slender, grass-like foliage for weeks on end. Its early bloom season and variety of colors make it one of the most commonly grown spring flowering bulbs. And it's cheap, too!

FLOWER: Small, upward-facing, open chalices of overlapping petals in white, purple, striped, and yellow, in early spring or mid-fall.

PLANT: Small corm with grass-like foliage that matures and begins to die down soon after the lawn needs mowing at the first of the season.

INTERESTING KINDS: "Dutch" crocus (*Crocus vernus*) has large showy flowers; *C. flavus* is golden yellow; *C. tommasinianus* is early, soft lavender, and rated "most rodent resistant" by the Brooklyn Botanic Garden. Showy crocus (*C. speciosus*) is a fall-flowering crocus, blooming before foliage appears. Autumn crocus (*Colchicum*) is another fall-flowering plant that looks like crocus. The saffron spice is made from the dried golden stigmas of *Crocus sativus*—an ounce of the spice requires more than two thousand flowers!

SOIL: Plant in well-drained soil, including under shade trees, spread naturalistically in the lawn, or among low-growing ground covers. Amend heavy or clay soils with organic matter at planting time.

PROPAGATION: Order new varieties from bulb catalogs in the spring or summer, or buy from garden centers in the fall. Plant after the weather starts to cool down in September or October. If you want to dig and divide existing clumps after flowering, allow their foliage to mature to form the next spring's flower buds.

TIP: CROCUS BULBS WILL SPROUT through "hardware cloth" with half-inch openings that prevents squirrels from digging and eating them; where voles are a problem, plant in a wire mesh basket or line the planting holes with gravel.

Daffodil
Narcissus species
Full sun, mostly in winter and early spring

A garden expert shouldn't have a favorite flower, so I won't admit to my passion for daffodils. But my earliest childhood memories are of row upon row of many different kinds, including the very fragrant paper-white narcissus (with multiple flowers on each stem) and the skinny yellow jonquils with their heady bouquet. Though not the earliest bulbs, they herald spring for me.

Besides, it isn't just me—old home sites can be located deep in the woods by the naturalized daffodils left behind to spread on their own. Deer and chipmunks, even voles, leave them alone; many varieties (though not all) multiply rapidly year after year, and they come in a wide array of flower forms and fragrances. When I smell them, I'm transformed into a little boy in the garden of my ancestors.

FLOWER: Varies with the species. Stalks from six inches to more than two feet tall produce single blooms or clusters of six-"petaled" flowers, usually with an elongated cup in the center. Double forms, large-cup, short-cup, split corona (cup looks like it has extra petals), in white, yellow, gold, pink, orange, and many combinations. The biggest flush of flowers is in March and April, but early, fragrant paper-white narcissus may appear around Thanksgiving (indoors), with 'Twin Sisters' blooming into early May.

PLANT: Leaves are mostly strap-shaped, butter-knife-like in clumps, from a few inches to a foot or more long, depending on species. *Narcissus jonquilla* has distinct, reedy foliage similar to a porcupine quill. Leaves first appear in mid-fall, and begin to die down by early spring. *Very important:* Do not cut or braid old foliage, which reduces food transported to the bulbs and cuts down on next year's flowers; let leaves yellow and flop naturally. To help hide fading foliage, interplant daffodils with white or pink yarrow or daylilies, all of which are dormant in the winter but whose emerging foliage hides the flopping leaves of daffodils in the spring.

INTERESTING KINDS: Though there are many dozens, even hundreds, of great daffodils to try, these have proven themselves to be long-lived and prolific bloomers: 'Tête-à-Tête', 'February Gold', 'Ice Follies', 'Geranium', 'Cheerfulness', 'Tahiti', 'Carlton', 'Thalia', pheasant's eye daffodil (*N. poeticus*), true jonquils (*N. jonquilla*), and of course the very fragrant paper-white narcissus (*N. papyraceus*) for forcing indoors.

SOIL: Any well-drained or fairly dry soil, even in the lawn or under trees with a sunny southern exposure in the winter. Will not tolerate standing water in winter or irrigation in summer (best to not plant daffodils with roses, hostas, or other flowers that may get a lot of summer water, or they'll rot).

PROPAGATION: Bulb division. Dig as soon as foliage is beginning to disappear in the spring by lifting entire clumps and pulling off bulbs that come apart easily. Best to replant immediately or store in a cool, dry place until early fall planting. Because daffodils make their next year's flower buds after they finish blooming, avoid digging when in flower or risk losing a couple of years of blooms. Mark the ones you want, cut their flowers for an arrangement, and come back to dig when the foliage has died down or at least six weeks after flowering.

Why Daffodils Don't Bloom:

- Too much shade on foliage.
- Poor drainage, and bulbs rot.
- Too much nitrogen fertilizer or no fertilizer at all.
- Crowded bulbs may need lifting and dividing.
- Leaves were cut off too early in the spring.
- Plants were moved when in flower.
- Not a great variety for your part of the country.

For more information, varieties, and sources for this popular old bulb, contact the American Daffodil Society at 4126 Winfield Road, Columbus, Ohio 43220-4606 (www.daffodilusa.org). The site has many tips and lists the e-mails and phone numbers of daffodil clubs in every part of the country.

TIP: WHAT'S IN A NAME? Daffodils are narcissus, and vice versa. Common name, Latin name. Some folks call yellow ones by the common name (or even "buttercups") and fragrant white ones by the Latin, but no matter. Different species sometimes have distinct common names—paper-whites and jonquils, for example. But they're all daffodils. And narcissus. If anyone wants to argue about it, just smile and say "Yes 'm" and let it go.

Garden Lilies
Lilium species
Light shade to full sun (if well mulched)

Garden lilies are among the proudest of garden plants. Generally tall spring and summer bloomers, they have three main requirements for long life: deep well-drained soil high in organic matter, moisture year-round (their roots never really stop growing), and lots of mulch or leaf litter to keep roots cool. In other words, edge-of-the-woods conditions or well-prepared garden soils (bulb guru Scott Kunst of Michigan says "heads in the sun, feet in the shade"). They are outstanding cut flowers and perfect for the backs of flower beds where their lower stems and any support stakes are hidden.

FLOWER: Mostly large trumpets produced from late spring into the summer atop straight, tall (three to six feet or more) stems. White, orange, red, yellow, pink, and often spotted. Many are quite fragrant!

PLANT: Dark green rosettes of leaves come up in mid-winter and begin throwing out flowering stems covered with narrow finger-like leaves in the spring. Some flowering stems turn yellow soon after blooming, but always wait before cutting back until all the leaves are totally yellow; never pull on faded stems or you risk pulling up the plant, bulb and all, or creating a situation conducive to bulb rot.

INTERESTING KINDS: Regal (*Lilium regale*, early summer, white and fragrant), tiger (*L. lancifolium* or *L. tigrinum*, pendulous orange flowers spotted with dark brown), turk's cap (*L. martagon*, pink, curved-back petals on downward-facing blossoms), 'Stargazer' (hybrid Oriental lily, raspberry red with creamy white edge).

SOIL: Must have deep soil (at least a foot), high in organic matter, that does not stay wet all winter or completely dry out in summer. Mulches and leaf litter help keep roots and bulbs cool and moist. Moderate fertility is good for steady growth.

PROPAGATION: Seeds sprout slowly but surely; better to dig and split apart bulbs, which have many smaller "bulb scales" encased in papery sheaths around a central stem (like garlic). Plant each bulb scale about three times as deep as it is tall, cover with mulch, and leave alone—don't go poking around to see what's coming up or you'll break the new stem.

TIP: SUPPORT YOUR LILIES, particularly the really tall varieties, by planting them behind shorter shrubs (spirea, azalea, quince, barberry, shrub roses) or dense clumps of perennials (black-eyed Susan, bluestar, purple coneflower, goldenrod). By "stair-stepping" plants you can help them stand up on their own, rather than trying to strap them to tall stakes after they're already reached their mature height and are heavy with blooms.

Gladiola
Gladiolus species and hybrids
Sun

Gladiola, the ultimate summer cut flower, is as easy as any plant can be. Just stick a handful of corms into reasonably good dirt, and add a stake to keep the tall rocket from falling over under its heavy flower load. Sure, "glads" are annuals in the North, but they are cheap, and you can plant a few every couple or three weeks for a continuous glorious show and cut-flower harvest.

FLOWER: Narrow, tall, three- to four-foot spike of showy flaring flowers that open a few at a time all on the same side of the stem, from the bottom up, as the flower stem grows. Usually requires staking to keep from falling over under its own weight. Outstanding cut flower in red, yellow, orange, apricot, white, purple, and many combinations.

PLANT: Each corm produces one upright fan of tall, sword-like leaves, from which the flower stem also grows. Most effective in groups, especially when planted behind another kind of plant to help hide the bareness down low.

INTERESTING KINDS: Hardy gladiola (*Gladiolus communis* ssp. *byzantinus*) is an old-garden variety that usually has bright magenta flowers, sometimes white. Abyssinian sword lily (*G. callianthus* or *Acidanthera bicolor*) grows up to three feet or so tall and has large white flowers with a purplish brown blotch.

SOIL: Any well-drained soil. Tolerates moisture, but tough enough without needing extra watering. Corms should be planted two or three times as deep as they are big around.

PROPAGATION: Buy new corms every year, planting a few at a time beginning when the soil has warmed in late spring (May or early June) up until early July for a continuous show. Dig old corms, separate the new ones that form, and save them in a cool, dry place over winter to plant next year.

TIP: FLOPPY PLANTS should be staked discreetly. Gladiola often flops under its own weight, as do dahlias, garden lilies, and other tall boys and girls of the summer. When planting, or when plants are beginning to emerge, and the soil is still moist, push curly rods, teepees made of bamboo or other slender but sturdy sticks, or even specialty plant support stakes, deep beside each plant, up to about half as high as you expect the plants to get. As the plants grow, tie them loosely to the stakes with soft twine. You may also use sections of low, prefabricated, picket-fence type border materials as part of your bulb garden, which will work well to prevent the worst flopping.

Grape Hyacinth
Muscari species
Sun, especially in the winter

Old cemeteries are covered in a mid-winter haze of blue from this prolific little bulb; rock gardens burst into color with short stalks of juicy-looking flowers; lawns become "infested" with fragrant patches of this self-seeding native of the Mediterranean region. Great winter companions for the little bulb include the short violas or Johnny jump-ups, ferny-leafed anemones, and inexpensive Dutch iris. Or just plant it as a naturalistic "river of blue" across the lawn.

FLOWER: Many small, light- to dark-blue urn-shaped bells packed like grapes on short, six- to ten-inch stems formed in clusters, with a delightful faint scent of grapes. Many cultivars are available with various blues, all white, or combinations.

PLANT: Short clumps of thin, grass-like leaves from fall to spring. One of the earliest bulbs to send up foliage, it can get so thick it nearly chokes itself out.

INTERESTING KINDS: *Muscari botryoides* 'Album' has white flowers. *M. latifolium* has much larger flowers than the old-timey grape hyacinth and is better suited for mixed-flower borders where it's less likely to get lost under the shade of other plants. *Muscari armeniacum* 'Blue Spike' has double flowers of pale blue.

SOIL: Any well-drained soil, even in cemeteries, meadows, and under winter-deciduous trees.

PROPAGATION: Division of small bulbs, dug and replanted any time you can find them. Very inexpensive to buy lots and lots to naturalize in small groups, which multiply quickly if left alone after flowering so seed will form and self-sow into surrounding areas.

TIP: PLANT SMALL GROUPS or rows of grape hyacinths in front of other bulbs, both as a "skirt" for tall specimens, and to use their early fall-appearing foliage to mark where other bulbs are planted (so you don't accidentally dig them when setting out pansies and other plants in the fall).

Hosta or Plantain Lily

Hosta species
Shade

Anyone who doesn't grow hostas, or has to buy one, must not have any gardening friends! Though hostas (formerly called "funkia") are queens of the shade, making great little border plants and specimens alike, they are also quite common "cemetery" plants for full sun (though they often look ratty toward the end of a hot, dry summer). Good companions for hostas include ferns, Solomon's seal, astilbe, daffodils, moneywort, and pachysandra. Also play hostas off a big rock or statue or other garden accessory.

FLOWER: A "plus" on some varieties which have blooms more showy and fragrant than on other types. Long spikes with generally white or bluish, narrow trumpets up to three inches long, mostly on one side of the stem; blooms in the summer. Fairly good cut flowers. To prevent crown rot, don't pull—cut the old stalks from the plant.

PLANT: The reason for growing hostas is their leaves! Round, oval, heart-shaped, large, small, green, bluish, golden, variegated, with curly or smooth edges—so many kinds exist that you really need to consult a catalog to choose your favorites. Some plants are miniature, growing less than five inches high, while others can easily get three or more feet tall and wide, or larger. All die completely to the ground at first frost, but come back readily in the late spring (don't get overeager and go poking around in April, or you'll pop off some of the buds). Gold hostas are great for sun, and blue or other thick-leaf types can be slug-resistant.

INTERESTING KINDS: There are more than two thousand registered varieties of hostas. A handful of common ones include *Hosta sieboldiana* or 'Elegans' (green), 'August Moon' (chartreuse), 'Francis Williams' (green with gold edge), and 'Sum and Substance' (huge golden variety). Consult any garden catalog for more, or contact the American Hosta Society at www.hosta.org.

SOIL: Rich, woodsy, high organic matter content. Plant level with the soil around them, mulch to keep soil cool and moist, and water only when very dry. Moderate fertility will encourage steady leaf production.

PROPAGATION: Seedlings take years. Simply order new plants when you can, and divide what you have in the fall when the foliage begins to look as if it's starting to "go down," or in late winter.

TIP: CONTROL SLUGS by avoiding overwatering and using slug baits, traps, and repellents. If voles eat your hostas, plant the hostas in metal or heavy plastic baskets buried with a little of their rim above ground. As far as I know, other than a tall fence, there is no effective way to keep deer from browsing hostas.

Iris

Iris species

Sun or light shade

Iris, named after the rainbow goddess because of her range of colors, is one of the all-time great perennials of the world. I have seen the same, stubby-foliaged "sweet flags" iris (*Iris germanica florentina*, the one introduced to America as "orris root," an herbal fixative) growing both around hot metal storm sewer grates in blazing sun and nestled between the gnarly roots of an ancient oak. It is common in cemeteries, in both sun and shade, and was the original pattern for the French *fleur de lis*. Yet it is hardly available commercially. You have to get it from someone who got it from someone who got it . . . Luckily, it is easy to divide any day of the year, and about all you need to know to grow it is "green side up."

The range of different kinds of iris available for the gardener's palette (there are between two hundred and three hundred species alone, not counting thousands of cultivars) includes cut-flower bulbs, evergreen woodland ground covers, roaming masses of rhizomes, and erect swords for the water's edge. Because of several flower types and how the foliage texture (even when not in flower) is a fantastic complement to shrubs and other perennials, the choices are more than sufficient for several to suit every garden style.

The iris borer worm and rots are major problems. The best way to deal with either case is by digging and cutting away infested parts, reworking the soil, and replanting. Avoid mulching or overwatering iris!

FLOWER: Variable in size, atop sturdy stems in the spring, in an astounding array of colors and combinations, including nearly black; some have a strong cinnamon scent as well. The two main parts of the flower are the "standards" (three inner petals that

generally stand upward or are nearly horizontal) and the "falls" (three outer petal-like sepals that are held at various angles, mostly horizontal or drooping). "Bearded" iris have fuzzy caterpillar-like fur on the falls; "beardless" iris have smooth falls; and "crested" iris have comb-like crests on the falls. There are a few "remontant" (repeat bloomers) around, available mostly through specialty nurseries, but most iris flower in May or early June.

PLANT: Narrow, pointed leaves ranging from only a few inches long on creeping rhizomes to thick stubby points to tall thin swords up to four feet tall. Mostly evergreen, perfect as a "skirt" for other flowers or to accent a water garden or focal point.

SOIL: Most iris require dry, well-drained average soils, especially the thick-rhizome bearded kinds, which should be planted near the top of shallow trenches in the soil with the tops of the rhizomes baking in the sun. Iris is also one of the few perennials that do not tolerate mulches, which can lead to rot, slugs, or other problems. Most types cannot tolerate wet roots; however, Siberian, Louisiana, and Japanese iris perform very well in bog gardens and at the edges of ponds.

PROPAGATION: Dig and divide thick, root-like rhizomes in the summer, so they can get established before winter. If the weight of abundant foliage causes new plants to flop over and uproot, cut it back and new growth will resume shortly.

TIP: TO GIVE IRIS DIRECTION, new rhizome growth of iris goes where the tips are pointing. When setting out iris for the first time, situate rhizomes so the new or leaf end is pointing in the direction you want the plant to grow. Planting three or more in a group, eight or ten inches apart and facing outward from the center, like spokes in a wheel, will produce a nice clump quickly that will continue to grow into a mass of foliage.

Some Common Iris Types:

- **BEARDED:** sword-like leaves grow from stubby rhizomes planted nearly on top of the soil, various species and hybrids

- **DUTCH:** small, inexpensive bulbs to plant in the fall for spring cut flowers

- **DWARF CRESTED:** *Iris cristata*, a low, spreading native woodland ground cover, small leaves and flowers

- **JAPANESE:** *Iris ensata*, has the largest flowers of the genus

- **JAPANESE ROOF:** *Iris tectorum*, foot-tall crested iris with glossy foliage and flattened-out flowers

- **LOUISIANA:** various species and hybrids, varying in flower color and height

- **SIBERIAN:** *Iris sibirica*, narrow upright foliage and interesting seedpods

There are many others, some with many hundreds of cultivars. For more information, contact the Iris Society (www.irises.org).

Liatris, Blazing Star, Gayfeather
Liatris species
Sun or light shade

Why do flower arrangers pay more than two dollars per stem for a flower imported from South American farms that grows as a hardy wildflower from Nebraska to Maine? One of the most stunning native flowers of North American woodlands and prairies, liatris is an outstanding cut flower and butterfly plant, and a tall "spiky" element in the flower border. It withstands drought, heat, cold, and poor clay soils. Instead of buying it from florists, we should grow it in the front yard! Combine liatris with coneflowers, ornamental grasses, goldenrod, and other naturalistic flowers in a meadow garden.

FLOWER: Narrow stems from three to five feet tall, studded with small curly plumes of lavender or sometimes white, in the summer and early fall. Flowers open from the top of the stem downward, so cutting faded ends can keep it fresh in an arrangement. Highly attractive to butterflies.

PLANT: Hard tuber whose tufts of leaves elongate into multiple flower stems packed with narrow leaves.

INTERESTING KINDS: Spike blazing star (*Liatris spicata*) is taller than most, except for the 'Kobold' cultivar, which is only about three feet tall; *L. squarrosa* has rounded tufts of purple flowers arranged loosely on the stems instead of in solid bottlebrushes of flowers.

SOIL: Thrives nearly everywhere, including hard clay soils, mostly in open woodlands and fields. Prefers dry, poor soils, but is often found along ditch banks that are briefly flooded in winter. Fertilizer increases size, but at a floppy cost.

PROPAGATION: Seed collected in the fall, stored dry indoors until spring, sown heavily, and covered lightly with moist potting soil either directly outdoors or in flats to be transplanted a couple of months later. Or simply lay pieces of the stems, with seeds down, outside in the late fall and cover lightly with good soil; they'll sprout in the spring. Divide in late winter by digging older plants, carefully cutting away chunks with pointy buds from the hard tuber and planting immediately. Also widely available in nurseries and through mail order.

TIP: LIATRIS AND OTHER WILDFLOWERS don't have to look "wild"—to get away with naturalistic plantings in urban settings, fool the neighbors into thinking you know what you are doing. Start by massing lots of each plant in repeated groups. Combine with complementary plants such as ornamental grasses and other city-accepted favorites. For a "human scale" focal point, add a bench, a section of split rail or picket fence, and a bird house or two, and your garden will look as planned as anything!

Lily-of-the-Valley
Convallaria majalis
Shade to dappled sun

In spite of it being toxic to eat, lily-of-the-valley, one of the toughest perennials for the North, is beloved for its fragrance. The ground cover can be a real thug, though, taking over woodland gardens with thick, difficult-to-eradicate rhizomes. It is an excellent, if invasive, ground cover for places where grass won't grow, such as along a north-facing rock wall, difficult-to-mow shaded hillsides, under evergreen shrubs, or between closely spaced houses. It has become an invasive exotic plant in some Northern forests.

FLOWER: One-sided, arching stems of small, nodding, delightfully sweet-scented, waxy, white bells in spring. Often forced indoors or by florists, and used in weddings. Taller flowering stems can be forced by planting lily-of-the-valley with tall ground covers such as pachysandra or periwinkle. Double- and pink-flowering forms are available. Bright red berries, also poisonous, may appear in the late summer or fall.

PLANT: Rapidly spreading ground cover that carpets everything. Each plant has two broad, six-inch-long leaves that turn yellowish before dying down in the fall. Can get ratty looking in the sun.

INTERESTING KINDS: 'Fortin's Giant' has larger flowers than the species, 'Flore Pleno' is double and white, and the variety *rosea* has pink flowers. Variegated cultivars include 'Albistriata' and 'Aureovariegata' ('Striata').

SOIL: Prefers "woodsy soils" but grows well in well-drained soil, including poor types beneath trees and shrubs.

PROPAGATION: Set out container-grown plants any time, or dig and plant single rhizomes (called "pips"), with good roots and at least one bud, in the spring or summer. Think twice about planting in small areas where it can take over.

TIP: KEEP INVASIVE PLANTS within bounds by planting where they can run without crowding out smaller, less sturdy plants, and with permanent edging materials set at least six inches into the ground, or by hemming in with paving.

Peony
Paeonia hybrids
Full sun to light shade

Peonies are famous for, among other attributes, outliving the gardeners who plant them. These ancient Oriental beauties have come to symbolize the flower border so well that even gardeners in the Deep South make weak attempts at growing them, though they perform better further north.

FLOWER: Sturdy stems up to three feet high are topped with huge, crinkled flower heads, sometimes half a foot across. Flowers of white, red, pink, or salmon can be single, double, or semi-double, many very fragrant, and all make excellent cut flowers. Burn or sear the ends of freshly cut stems to help peonies hold up longer in a vase. For flowers left to bloom on the plant, cutting off small side shoots will increase the size, and increase the sturdiness of the stems. Deadhead or remove faded flowers, though this won't cause peonies to rebloom.

PLANT: Bushel-basket-sized clumps of coarse, deeply divided leaves that remain attractive throughout the summer and fall before dying down at first frost.

INTERESTING KINDS: There are many great peonies, both old and new; the best varieties may be whichever ones you can get a friend to divide with you. Fernleaf peony (*P. tenuifolia*) is early flowering, and tree peonies (*P. suffruticosa*) are magnificent woody shrubs up to four feet tall. Always buy named varieties.

SOIL: Peonies grow in any well-drained soil, but do best in a well-prepared, large planting hole (two feet across, and a foot or more deep, with organic matter added). Plant shallowly for best flowering. Do not add manure to or over peonies, or expect some rotting. After the first summer in the ground, water peonies only during extreme dry spells.

PROPAGATION: Set out container-grown peonies any time, at the same depth they were grown in their pots. Divide old clumps in the late summer or fall; spring-divided clumps may look ratty before fall, but will usually recover the next year. Plant clumps with at least three or four "eyes" (better to have five or more, but don't get greedy), between one and two inches below the soil surface. Do not use manure of any kind in the planting hole, and mulch only when leaf diseases become a problem.

TIP: PEONIES FAIL TO FLOWER the first year or two after transplanting because they were planted too deep, are in too much shade, or have been over-fertilized. Plant them right, and then leave them alone! Unusually cool spring weather, inadequate fertilization, or extreme drought can cause established peonies to fail during some years.

Snowdrop
Galanthus nivalis
Sun or shade

Often popping up in February or March when there is still snow on the ground, few sights bring more joy to winter-weary gardeners than snowdrops—a miniature arrangement on an indoor windowsill is a real heart-warmer!

FLOWER: Small, nodding, white bells, each with three prominent flaring petals and a central notched tube marked with green, on stems above the foliage; double forms are available. Flowers appear in late winter and early spring, and the blooming season can be extended by planting snowdrops in a protected location beside the house.

PLANT: Clump-forming with typical narcissus-like foliage of sleek green blades six or more inches long.

INTERESTING KINDS: British gardeners seek out fantastic new varieties, but the most common include 'Flore Pleno' with double flowers, 'Viridiapicis' with more prominent green markings, and G. *elwesii*, the giant snowdrop. A remarkably similar bulb, summer snowflake (*Leucojum* spp.), not as winter hardy as *Galanthus*, is taller and has flowers more bell-like, with a single green dot on each petal; hardy only in the warmer areas of the region.

SOIL: Well-drained "woodsy" soil high in organic matter. Amend sandy soils with bark, compost, manure, and so on before planting bulbs three or four inches deep.

PROPAGATION: Plant firm new bulbs in the late summer or fall when soils begin to cool, in naturalistic groups. Dig and divide current plantings after the foliage has begun to turn yellow and flop—after the next year's flower buds have had time to form (cutting foliage while it is still green causes a loss of "flower power").

TIP: "MINOR" BULBS, such as snowdrop, squill, and glory of the snow, have traditionally not been used as widely, and are not as large and showy, as the more common tulips, daffodils, and hyacinths. But they are anything but minor in their garden performance!

Tulip

Tulipa species and hybrids
Full sun to light shade

No gardener has ever failed to grow at least one crop of the crayon-colored spring splashes known as tulips. Tulips "shout" spring! Though there are quite a few old garden varieties and "species" (not hybrid) tulips around that bloom for years, the vast majority of those sold in garden centers are florist quality and best treated as one-shot annuals, with those left in the ground flowering less and less over three or four years until they just peter out. Warning: Deer and rodents eat tulips as if they were banana pudding. Protect with wire mesh! When planting tulips in pots, always place the flat side of the bulb outward, toward the pot rim; this makes the first leaf that comes out curl over the edge of the pot. Weird, huh?

FLOWER: Tulips have a typical cup-shaped flower atop a single sturdy stem, and come in every color except true blue—some are so dark burgundy you would swear they are pure black. Whether the flowers are large or small, clean-edged or frilly, fragrant or not, they are always very showy—a good buy for the money even when treated as annuals to be dug and composted at the end of their flowering season.

PLANT: Firm bulbs with one flat side produce sturdy, upright, strap-shaped or narrow leaves from late winter until a few weeks after flowering ends, at which time the leaves turn yellow and the bulbs go summer-dormant. Leaving the foliage uncut helps them form next year's flower buds, if you want to dig and save them.

INTERESTING KINDS: Old-garden and species tulips were bred for gardens, not showy florist pots, so they are hardier. Darwin hybrids are more reliably perennial than most.

SOIL: This is the key to tulip longevity! Plant tulip bulbs six or eight inches deep in regular soil that is well drained and almost completely dry in the summer—think *mountainsides in Turkey*, where tulips originated. Too wet, and they'll rot. Fertilize lightly after flowering to encourage repeat blooming next year.

PROPAGATION: Tulips are very slow to multiply, so it is best to purchase new bulbs every few years to replenish what have gradually petered out. Some species such as *T. clusiana* (early, small flowering kinds) actually set seedpods and can spread into nearby dry garden spots.

TIP: SCOTT KUNST, founder of Old House Gardens in Michigan, shares these tips for getting tulips to bloom forever:

- Choose good varieties—single earlies, species, single lates, and lily-flowered. Keep them dry in the summer—plant where you will never water.
- Plant in a well-drained soil—improve heavy soil, or plant in raised beds. Provide good sun and fertilizer.
- Allow foliage to turn yellow before cutting.

Then there's his age-old method: Dig them up every summer, store in a cool dry spot, and replant in the fall. To make this easier, plant in a basket with good drainage.

72

Other Great Garden Bulbs

There are many other kinds of bulbs to try—some are all-time favorites of mine, but may not be as reliable or readily available for one reason or another. Here are a few worth looking for; you can find much more information on growing them in nearly any all-purpose garden book or mail-order catalog.

Amaryllis (*Hippeastrum* species) is perhaps the easiest of the "big" bulbs to flower—even just in pots on a television set. Their strap-shaped leaves and clusters of huge bell-shaped flowers in red, white, pink, and stripes make them popular old-garden and houseplants. Outdoors, grow in containers or dig up and store before frost.

Camassia (*Camassia* species) is a native meadowland bulb that wows gardeners in Europe. It has sword-like leaves and flower spikes up to three feet tall, topped with a loose arrangement of small, starry, blue flowers. It grows and flowers well in boggy gardens or clay soils, even in shade.

Crocosmia (*Crocosmia* species and cultivars) is a rampant, spreading mass of floppy, sword-shaped leaves with arching stems of vivid orange-red or yellow flowers that seem to sizzle in the summer. It is hardy in warmer parts of the North. Popular cultivars include red 'Lucifer' and yellow 'Jupiter'. Montbretia is an old name for a common orange kind.

Dahlias (*Dahlia* species and cultivars) have been popular summer bloomers for many years with experienced gardeners. Some are short with lots of flowers; others with incredible foot-wide flowers are tall and have to be staked. These Mexico natives require well-drained soil; plant them in raised beds or containers. Dahlias freeze, so dig and store indoors, or just start over with new ones every spring— they're worth it.

Elephant's Ear (*Alocasia* or *Colocasia*) are spreading or upright tropical plants with huge leaves pointing either upward (*Alocasia*) or downward (*Colocasia*). Keep potted to bring indoors in the winter.

Flowering Onion (*Allium* species) are fall-planted, often large-bulb plants with long stems topped by round flower heads that range from the size of a golf ball to the size of a softball in the late spring, summer, or fall. Most are hardy.

Garlic (*Allium sativum*) is a winter-hardy bulb best planted in the fall, harvested in early summer, and replanted every year. Many cultivars, with varying flavor and "heat." Summer flowers are baseball sized.

Glory of the Snow (*Chionodoxa luciliae*) is a dependable, early flower, blue with a white center, above ribbon-like leaves.

Hyacinth (*Hyacinthus orientalis*) is an inexpensive big bang, with foot-tall spikes studded with intensely sweet fragrant flowers in blue, pink, white, pale yellow, or red. They fare poorly in wet or very cold winters and torrid summers, but may return for a few years before petering out. Worth planting a few every year for the fragrance alone! Very good for formal plantings and containers.

Naked Ladies (*Lycoris squamigera*), often called surprise lily, has large straps of leaves in the spring, then bare-naked stems topped by clusters of trumpet-shaped, pink flowers in the summer. The similar *L. sprengeri* is hardy to Zone 5.

Painted Arum (*Arum italicum*) is one of the most overlooked foliage plants around! This surprising heirloom, most often found in old established gardens, has caladium-like flower spathes atop masses of upright arrowheads of green, often variegated leaves in the summer. Orange-red berries can appear later in the summer. A perfect companion for hostas, ferns, and daffodils.

Squill (*Scilla siberica*) has small grass-like leaves and early spring spikes of white or pure blue. Naturalizes in the lawn.

Trillium (*Trillium grandiflorum*), often called "wake robin" by old timers, is a spring-flowering native woodland species with three leaflets and prominent, three-petaled flowers, usually white or pinkish. Protected by wildflower collection laws, it is best to buy from reputable nurseries (who nursery-propagate their plants and don't dig them from the wild), or divide carefully from your own property (be sure to get the entire rhizome).

Tuberous Begonia (*Begonia* Tuberhybrida hybrids) is a very showy, tender, tropical plant with huge flowers (up to six inches across) for shady gardens. Plant after all danger of frost is past, and store indoors during winter.

Tuberose (*Polianthes tuberosa*) is perhaps the most intensely fragrant bulb around—every Victorian parlor had pots of it (for good reason, before air conditioning and deodorants). Most gardeners treat them like gladiolas, by digging and storing, but they do well as easy-to-share potted plants.

Windflower (*Anemone blanda*) has daisy-like flowers and fern-like foliage that are perfect for planting at the base of larger winter bulbs or along edges of winter container gardens. Soak the weird little flattened bulbs overnight before planting shallowly and on their edges.

Winter Aconite (*Eranthis hyemalis*) are excellent, very early flowering small yellow flowers, perfect for naturalizing in woods with high light, or lawns, or working into rock gardens.

Wood Hyacinth or **Spanish Bluebell** (*Hyacinthoides hispanica*) is one of the most enduring old-garden bulbs. Spring flower spikes more than a foot tall are loosely covered top to bottom with open bells of blue, white, or pink, atop tight, foot-tall clumps of dagger-like leaves. Very good in shady old gardens, appearing even under gloomy oak trees.

PLANT LARGE-LEAF TROPICALS
such as elephant's ear, canna, and banana
in tubs large enough to stay moist for more
than a few days, and set them as a backdrop
behind other summer plants where a gust
of wind won't tip them over. By hauling
the container into the garage or basement
at the end of the season you can also keep
such tender plants for use again next year.

Fast-Reference Lists for Bulbs and Bulb-Like Plants

For the Shade
- Caladium
- Camassia
- Dwarf
  Crested Iris
- Hosta
- Liatris
- Lily of the Valley
- Painted Arum
- Trillium
- Tuberous Begonia
- Turk's Cap Lily
- Wood Hyacinth

For Foliage
- Caladium
- Canna
- Chives
- Elephant's Ear
- Hosta
- Iris
- Lily of the Valley
- Painted Arum
- Tuberous Begonia

For Fragrance
- Daffodils
- Garden Lilies
- Garlic
- Hyacinth
- Lily of the Valley
- Tuberose

**For Summer
Flowers**
- Calla
- Canna
- Crocosmia
- Dahlia
- Garlic Chives
- Gladiolus
- Hosta
- Liatris
- Tuberose
- Turk's Cap Lily

**WHY ARE GOOD BULBS SOMETIMES SO HARD TO FIND
COMMERCIALLY?** It's a "supply and demand" thing, in which garden
centers carry mostly what people normally buy; compared with tulips and
hyacinths, some of the great old-garden bulbs are not much in demand—
partly because they seem "old fashioned" and partly because they are so
tough you only have to buy them once! Yet they are available to retailers
from wholesale suppliers, so shop around, ask your local garden center to try
to get them for you, or go on-line, doing word searches for terms like
"old garden bulbs" or the like. When you finally get some, be sure to share
with neighbors!

Quintessence in the Garden

Ever find something that is so "just right" it can't be improved upon? There's a word for something so perfectly apt: quintessence.

Such an item usually does only one thing, but does it so well it would be difficult to replace. Pencils are replaceable; the hand-held pencil sharpener is quintessential. A spatula can be used for scraping windshield ice, but it's mostly for hot skillet stuff—difficult to cook without one. Others would be safety pin, paper clip, smoke alarm, vacuum cleaner, hair brush, coffee filter, toilet plunger, TV remote control, and phone answering machine. And the mouse on my computer. Whether simple or complicated, you could get by without them, but they'd be missed.

There is also quintessence in the garden: wheelbarrows, night lighting, leaf blowers, and other labor-saving tools that we take for granted. Then there are the multipurpose things we use, from five-gallon buckets and red wagons to balls of twine and chicken wire; often these simple tools have no moving parts, other than a gardener.

Then there is the little stuff that falls somewhere between necessary and just plain handy, like crunchy perlite that does nothing but lighten potting soils, and an opposable thumb (difficult to show pride, without hooking a thumb under an armpit). Some we really don't need, but they do a job well while working on the simplest level.

Ideal tools that embody the principles of simplicity and rightness include garden hose, watering can, bulb planter, hose-end water valve, water wand, leaf rake, pincushion sprinkler, flat metal file, self-locking plastic cable ties, and, for flower arrangers, a metal "frog" and a stack of green oasis blocks.

Garden accessories that go to the heart of gardening without adding clutter to our lives are hummingbird feeder, wind chimes, rain gauge, outdoor thermometer, weather vane, hose hanger, tiki torch, and porch swing.

I suppose some living things have carried the essence of the gardening spirit through many centuries, and are the epitome of a garden but don't become the taskmasters. My short list would include gourds, shade trees, seeds of all types, butterflies and bees, rosemary, hot peppers, and a handful of universally grown flowers: orange daylilies, daffodils, iris, violas, and old roses.

These are a mere smattering of "just right, almost can't garden without, everyone needs, and anyone can use" items that do only one thing, but do it so well they'd be difficult to garden without. In other words, they're quintessential!

Grasses
WITH GUMPTION

Ornamental grasses bring the landscape to life! And everyone is getting "on board"—within the past few years, every university horticulture department I have visited has planted extensive ornamental grass display gardens, and now even fast food restaurants include grasses in their landscapes.

The earliest vivid memory I have of grasses is from a shortcut I took home from kindergarten, along a winding hillside path. At one spot, some wild grasses flowed over the path and were swaying in the breeze and making a rustling sound—which to a five-year-old sounded like the rattlesnakes my mom had long warned me to watch for. Though I could see my house from where I was standing, I was paralyzed with fear, unable to move forward or back, until I took a deep breath and, with a yell, plunged on through to the other side. The experience settled me into a life-long fascination with how grasses look, move, sound, feel, and even smell. Add the taste of corn and oats (both grasses), and all the senses are covered! In addition to the other senses, their visual effect is of color, richness, and texture. They come in a wide variety of shapes, colors, variegations, and long-stemmed "flowers" that are long lasting in both fresh and dried cut-flower arrangements. Some grasses grow in tight clumps; others "run" or spread. The plants can be used as specimens, in groups, as a ground cover, in naturalistic masses, and even in containers.

Shrub-like and ground cover grasses have been grown in botanical and cottage gardens for many decades. But other than the common use of miscanthus and bamboo, only fairly recently have grasses become more widely accepted as very tough "foils" to other landscape plants.

Uses of Grasses

Clump-forming grasses work well with perennials, especially coarse-textured ones like daylilies, canna, black-eyed Susan, hibiscus, and sedum, and colorful shrubs such as barberry, and as contrasts to "hard features" such as large rocks, benches, or sculpture. Smaller grasses grow well in rock gardens and containers, and larger grasses make good screens and borders.

Though some prefer shade and a few tolerate moist soils (some even grow in water gardens), most grow best in sunny, dry locations. They put out new growth in the spring, flower in the summer and fall, and have no major pests. Most gardeners leave the foliage alone in the winter, but some cut the old growth back in the late winter to help new growth come out clean and fresh. Be sure to do this before new growth begins to come up, or it may look ragged all summer.

Pests and Care

Other than too much water or fertilizer—which causes rampant foliage growth that often "flops" in midsummer—ornamental grasses have few problems. The worst I have encountered are the wasps and thumb-sized leaf-footed stinkbugs that love to nest in the thick, cool clumps.

Even ornamental grasses need mowing, at least if you want to keep them neat. There's no need to do this, other than for cosmetic purposes—if you don't prune the old growth, new foliage will cover it up by late spring. Once a year, in mid- to late winter, give the old foliage a neat shearing so the new spring growth will come out nice and clean. Don't burn them—as tempting as it may be—or risk killing the center of the clump, not to mention losing your eyebrows! Approach grasses from an angle with sharp shears or a fast-running string trimmer, going around and around like eating an ice cream cone, gradually getting down to the main clump. Tying the clump together with twine below the shearing line makes it easier to collect the cut stalks together as a bundle for hauling them off.

"Shattering" is when ornamental grass blades and flower stalks dry out in winter and flake apart—and if winds and snows hit them they bend and break, and generally make a mess of everything in the vicinity. Carol Wallace, garden writer from upstate Pennsylvania, says: "The best non-shattering grasses for me include *Chasmanthium, Miscanthus* 'Morning Light; *Calamagrostis* 'Karl Foerster', most bamboos, and most types of *Pennisetum* (though pennisetum seedheads DO shatter). And switchgrass (*Panicum virgatum* 'Heavy Metal') holds its form well through winter. So does my all-time favorite, *Hakonechloa macra* 'Aureola'."

BAMBOO IS NOT THE THUG that many people think it is. Most gardeners who have problems with bamboo have the "running" kind, generally a species of *Phyllostachys* that includes "fishing pole" bamboo, giant timber bamboo, beautiful black bamboo, and others. These very cold-hardy bamboos have almost woody underground stems that can shoot in any direction and, when cut, can send new plants up at every joint. They can take over entire landscapes—and gardens of neighbors, too! Other spreading bamboos include the dwarf ground cover *Arundinaria*. Running bamboos can be contained—at least for a while—with trenches, foot-deep edging, and a little luck. Otherwise, herbicides will have to be brought in. Bamboos reportedly do not cross water, so you could plant them next to a stream or build a deep moat around them.

On the other hand, some very beautiful types of bamboos stay in slow-to-spread clumps, such as fountain bamboo, *Sinarundinaria nitida*, hardy to Zone 5. But most clumping bamboos are not hardy in portions of the North. These are in the *Bambusa* genus, with some that get up to ten or more feet high but take many years to spread even a little. Most *Bambusa* species get killed to the ground by temperatures below the mid-teens. The U.S. Department of Agriculture's "bamboo introduction station" for the Southeast United States, located near Savannah, Georgia, has nearly every imaginable variety of bamboo and other grasses. And the American Bamboo Society has members in every state who know and grow the very best kinds for landscapes (including a fantastic garden I photographed near Boston).

👍 Best for Beginners:

- *Blue Fescue*
- *Clump-Forming Bamboos*
- *Fountain Grass*
- *Miscanthus*
- *River Oats*

Kinda Tricky: 👎

- *Horsetail*
- *Japanese Blood Grass*
- *Running Bamboos*

Best Ornamental Grasses:

These super-hardy grasses have been commonly grown for many decades by Northern gardeners:

→ **Blue Lyme Grass** (*Leymus racemosus* 'Glaucus' or *Elymus arenarius* 'Glaucus') is a showy ground cover of stiff leaves up to two feet tall, the bluest grass of all. Aggressive spreader in moist soils, but more manageable in dry soils or clay.

→ **Fountain Grass** (*Pennisetum alopecuroides*) forms knee-high clumps of fine-textured foliage with long, narrow, cylindrical "fox tail" flower heads. Note that though fountain grasses are hardy in much of the North, purple fountain grass (*P. setaceum* 'Rubrum') is strictly a very showy annual.

← **Blue Fescue** (*Festuca glauca*) is a small, compact clump of stiff, evergreen (or "ever-blue"), needle-like, nearly blue leaves, which thrives in cool weather but sulks when it gets hot and humid. Must have good drainage. Best used in groups as an exciting complement to other "blue" perennials such as lavender, salvia, and Russian sage.

← **Feather Reed Grass** (*Calamagrostis* × *acutiflora* 'Karl Foerster'), with its upright clump of stiff but slightly arching foliage, is topped in early summer with sturdy flowering stems to five or six feet tall, persisting through winter.

✦ **Japanese Blood Grass** (*Imperata cylindrica* 'Red Baron') features upright clumps to two feet tall with rich, almost blood-red upper portions of foliage. Spreads slowly but surely, and rarely flowers. Must have good drainage or it will rot.

➔ **Maiden Grass** (*Miscanthus sinensis*) is a versatile clump-forming grass with many cultivars, most of which get only four to six feet tall, with dozens of taller flowers opening as tassels and gradually expanding into soft feathery plumes in late summer and fall. Great cultivars include 'Autumn Light' (reddish fall color), 'Cosmopolitan' (erect habit and broad leaves striped with white), 'Gracillimus' (slender weeping foliage with reddish flowers), 'Morning Light' (five-foot clump with white narrow stripes along leaf edges, overall silvery effect and bronzy flowers), 'Strictus' (porcupine grass, with narrow, erect leaves with creamy stripes that run across the leaves), 'Yaku Jima' (compact to four feet, slender green leaves and tan flowers), and 'Zebrinus' (old-garden favorite, broadly arching clumps to six feet, leaves banded crosswise with yellow). All turn an attractive, completely uniform tan at first frost. Variegated miscanthus cultivars are often used in water gardens because they tolerate wet feet.

✦ **Northern Sea Oats** or **River Oats** (*Chasmanthium latifolium*) is a native grass for full sun or moderate shade, with stiff, knee-high, wiry, bamboo-like stems. Topped with numerous arching flower stalks with two dozen or more dangling florets that have been compared to little fish or even "flattened armadillos," and hold up very well in dried arrangements. River oats can self-seed to the point of being invasive.

➔ **Ribbon Grass** (*Phalaris arundinacea*) is a very aggressive creeping ground cover to two or more feet high, good border plant or "skirt" for shrubbery, or bog plant. Turns brown at frost. 'Picta' has white-striped leaves.

✦ **Switch Grass** (*Panicum virgatum*) is a garden-quality, prairie native with a mist-like cloud of pale blooms on four- to five-foot stalks. 'Heavy Metal' has beautiful metallic-blue foliage and pink-tinged flowers.

Other Good Grasses and Grass Look-Alikes:

➔ **Bluestem** (*Schizachyrium scoparium*), a native roadside or abandoned field grass, has upright, feathery flower stalks with striking orange-red fall color and silvery seedheads, great for dried arrangements.

➔ **Dwarf Bamboo** (*Pleioblastus pygmaeus* or *Arundinaria pygmaea*) is a ground cover bamboo to three feet tall, very thick and aggressive, even in dense shade. Contain with deep metal or plastic edging.

➔ **Feather Grass** (*Stipa* species) is a knee-high clump of fine-textured foliage, topped in summer and fall with a billowy cloud of yellowish flowers on stems up to six feet tall.

← Hakonechloa or **Hakone Grass** (*Hakonechloa macra* 'Aureola') is an outstandingly beautiful, variegated ground cover grass for shaded gardens in warmer areas of the North, but can be killed in a freeze-thaw-freeze type of winter.

→ Horsetail (*Equisetum* species) is a dinosaur-era holdover, evergreen and invasive—difficult to kill, but very easy to hand pull.

← Purple Muhly Grass (*Muhlenbergia* species), a knee-high clump of slender foliage, is not much to look at until late summer and fall when it's covered with airy, billowy masses of striking pinkish red flowers.

→ Tufted Hair Grass (*Deschampsia caespitosa*) is a knee-high clump topped with a billowy mass of golden yellow flowers.

WHAT GOES AROUND, COMES AROUND—or, as an old Chinese proverb puts it, "All the flowers, of all the tomorrows, are in the seeds of today and yesterday." I have an 1890s garden catalog whose tattered cover has an illustration of "zebra grass"—though modern-day horticulturists act as if they practically invented it.

What is an heirloom plant? Does it have to be old, or can it just be memorable from another time, another gardener's garden? Some of my favorite "pass-along" plants are fairly modern crosses and hybrids, some of which I now expect to be grown and shared as heirlooms. Many snazzy hybrids may not survive the whims of fashion, disappearing in the long run under a crush of even more new hybrids. While most popular, hardy plants fall in and out of horticultural and designer favor, many survive in cottage and country gardens in their rightful place in the sun. What is old fashioned today was high fashion yesterday, and will be trendy at some other time down the road.

In a letter written in 1736, John Custis, a wealthy Williamsburg planter whose son was Martha Washington's first husband, expressed his admiration for a striped boxwood and other variegated plants: "I am told those things are out of fashion; but I do not mind that I always make my fancy my fashion."

Your garden—your decision as to what is heirloom or what is mere passing fancy.

Help! I'm a Garden Nerd!

Ever find a sprig of rosemary soaking in a water glass beside the sink, left over from a nice meal out on the town the evening before? Anyone who brings food home to root has a problem, possibly an addiction. I can just hear it now, at a twelve-step meeting:

"Hi, my name is Felder, and I am a gardener . . . " ("Welcome, Felder, we're glad you are here. Come back often.")

"I gardened just this morning." ("Amen.") "Pulled a few weeds on the way down to pick up the morning paper, and before I knew it, started dividing daylilies and repainting a fencepost. During carpool, I found a mail-order catalog under my car seat, and people behind me at the stoplight had to honk to get my attention back on the road.

"I need help, I just can't stop gardening on my own. Even though I don't play golf or own a bass boat, I am sorry for my family because I spent my last paycheck on a new greenhouse door, a big bucket of Miracle Grow, and some shrubs I don't even need, 'cause they were on sale..."

Sound close to home? Here's a simple test to see if you, too, need help:

Do you grow ten or more different kinds of the same plant (rose, daylily, daffodil, iris, African violet, camellia, tomato, whatever), and know their names? Extra points if they're labeled. Do you subscribe to three or more garden magazines? Do you think Roger Swain is funny?

Do you keep a small shovel in your car trunk? Turn your compost weekly? Blow leaves on Sunday morning? Buy birdseed by the fifty-pound sack? Own a $40 pair of pruning shears (bonus points for a leather scabbard)? Are entire flats of flowers still sitting in the driveway because there's simply no more space to plant?

Have you ever willingly taken a tour of a garden by flashlight? Do we need to search your purse or camera case for purloined seeds after a visit to a botanical garden?

Extra points if your cuticles are dirty right now. And last, but not least, triple points if you would appreciate a special someone sending you a load of manure for an anniversary.

I'm not suggesting we gardeners should quit—though we all claim we can, any time. Maybe our motto should be *One Flower at a Time*. And remember, denial is a symptom!

LOW-MAINTENANCE
Lawns

The low-growing, generally flat mat of green plants we call our lawn holds most gardeners in a powerful grip. Though its appeal to American gardeners of all stripes and walks of life, sometimes reaching the level of obsession, is astonishing to many people around the world, the lawn has become a deeply ingrained national cultural icon. Advantages and disadvantages to having a lawn aside, you don't have to be a slave to the whims and fashions of your neighbors. And you can reduce the amount of time, labor, equipment, water, and pesticides your lawn needs.

A Quick History

Early in our country's settlement by Europeans, open swaths of turf were adopted by a relatively small group of landscape gardeners as a sign of Old World culture and prestige. They were based on elements taken from old European manor "garden park" landscape designs. Most were mowed every month or two with long-handled scythes, or grazed by sheep and cattle (kept in bounds by a low ditch called a "ha-ha"). In the 1800s the development of clumsy mechanical cutting machines (often pulled by people), then gas mowers, made the lawn appealing to more gardeners, to whom the wall-to-wall green represented a democratic ideal by which everyone could be proven an equal.

In the early 1900s, newly organized chapters of The Garden Club of America pushed the U.S. Department of Agriculture to develop more uniform lawn grasses, which helped standardize lawn care. Soon equipment, seed, and fertilizer companies began promoting the benefits of their products in ways that today would be considered bordering on brainwashing, with ads suggesting that if you didn't have a nice lawn, you weren't as good or smart or patriotic as your neighbors.

To this day, advice on lawn care—from the size of your mower and edger and leaf blower to the amount of fertilizer, weedkiller, and even the color of the grass—is driven by the marketplace philosophy of "more is better." Anyone who argues with this is seen as wacky.

Benefits

Without question, having a neat lawn is beneficial in several ways. Beyond the physical exercise provided by caring for the grass (assuming you don't ride your mower) and the obvious leisure activities made possible by a uniform lawn, a thick turf has environmental benefits:

1. A thick turf holds the soil against erosion.
2. Lawns keep dust and pollen down in the summer.
3. Turf reduces mud tracked indoors in the winter.
4. Grass shades soil from direct sunshine, which has a dramatic cooling effect.
5. Billions of individual grass plants generate an incredible amount of fresh oxygen while "scrubbing" pollutants from the air.

Plus a neat lawn provides an important design element to the landscape or garden. Its strong shape contrasts with other plants. It can serve as a walkway between flower borders, create a vista to lead the eye to a focal point, and become a crucial "unifying" effect overall.

Labor-Saving Ideas

The lawn's advantages come at a huge cost, requiring gardeners to invest heavily in special equipment, as well as a considerable amount of valuable time and sweaty effort. Some gardeners love their lawns as a hobby; others have them maintained by professionals as a means of proving their social intentions or standing. Most of us, however, simply mow whatever comes up, grass and weeds alike—and then only grudgingly.

There are two things you must understand: (1) There is no such thing as a low-maintenance lawn—even the most slovenly lawn is the single most labor-intensive feature of any landscape; and (2) no two grasses are alike when it comes to maintenance needs—each has distinct requirements for mowing, watering, feeding, and weed control. Find out what kind of grass you have or what kind you want, based on your desires and its needs.

Here are a few tips on how a reasonably neat lawn can be maintained without becoming a taskmaster, ranked in order of importance to the lawn and your neighbors:

- Mow on the high side, which helps turf have a thicker root system and shade out many weeds.
- Create a distinct edge—dig a small ditch around the lawn or line the lawn with a material such as bricks, rocks, broken pottery, or store-bought edging material—and keep the edge crisp and neat with regular cutting. This creates a dramatic appearance for even a ragged turf.
- Water only when the lawn is about to die from drought.
- Fertilize lightly at least once a year, but not as much or as often as fertilizer salesmen tell you to do!
- Weed control is nearly impossible without the use of strong chemicals; if you follow the tips above, your lawn will compete better with weeds and be more likely to survive bad weather.
- Don't look at the lawn too closely, or you will find imperfections that are really not as glaring as you think.
- Look at the big picture, in which even a poor-quality lawn that is mowed regularly and edged occasionally still has a strong visual (and social) impact.

If you think some of these recommendations are a little extreme, consider how little maintenance—especially irrigation, fertilizer, and weedkillers—are used around cemeteries, school yards, country churches, and even your grandmother's old home site: None. Zero. Zilch. Nada. The only people saying you have to do all that "stuff" for a nice lawn are salesmen or suckers! Look around—it's true that you really can just "mow what grows."

But if you want to slightly improve your lawn's appearance and reduce mowing frequency (weeds need mowing more often than turf), you need more detailed tips on lawn care. For this, contact your county Agricultural Extension Service office.

Grass in the Shade

If you have more than 50 percent shade, you are out of the lawn business. Period. In a quarter-century of working closely with home gardeners and landscapers, I have worked with many hundreds of frustrated gardeners who

have tried everything to re-establish grass where it has died out in the shade, even using solid sodding, careful watering, and fertilizing. I cannot show you a single success story. Not one.

The solution, even in front yards where grass has too long been the accepted norm, is either a natural layer of leaf mulch, store-bought mulch, or low-growing ground covers such as pachysandra, lamium, ivy, vinca, wintercreeper, or even moss. There are others, of course, but those are the most commonly used and lowest maintenance.

You can create a landscaped effect by keeping a neat edge between where grass is and is not. Edging materials and low-growing border plants can highlight combinations of taller shade plants such as ferns, hostas, and iris, making a nice scene. Top off the effect with stepping stones or a bench, urn, sculpture, birdbath, or other "hard" feature—which creates a focal point that takes people's attention away from your lack of grass.

Did You Know?

It was Edwin Budding, an engineer in Gloucestershire, England, who in 1830 patented a machine "for the purpose of cropping or shearing the vegetable surface of lawns, grass plots, and pleasure grounds"—the first mechanical lawn mower. Ironically, it was about that time that Justus von Liebig, a German chemist, invented chemical fertilizers for making plants grow faster . . . and the two inventions have battled each other's effects ever since.

Create a "Flowery Meade"

Wildflowers are much more natural than a lawn! And they can easily be used as a foil to the rest of the lawn, with a couple of easy tricks. Think of how golf courses are set up, with a tightly mowed "putting green," a lesser quality but still neat "fairway," and the wilder "rough"—which is where wildflowers fit into the picture. If you can create this effect by just mowing one area more often than another, it can look purposeful, even if you never plant a wildflower. Just the mowing pattern can look interesting—while cutting your mowing chores dramatically! Check local weed ordinances before creating a meadow since residents in some areas are nervous about a "too-wild" look, especially in the front yard.

Avoid the "wildflowers in a can" approach, in which a dozen or more kinds of wildflower seed are mixed for a general effect; it rarely works well. Instead, choose several easy, dependable wildflowers, including purple coneflower, phlox, Queen Anne's lace, coreopsis, liatris, and naturally spreading orange daylilies and daffodils, planted in groups, and then let native grasses and other "weeds" grow up around them for a prairie or meadow effect.

You can set a wildflower meadow off from the rest of the lawn area even more dramatically with a section of split-rail fence, some bird houses, maybe a sign that says "butterfly crossing." All this together creates a sense of purpose that is as easy to look at as it is easy to manage. Mow on the high side once a year, after frost, to keep taller plants under control while letting reseeding winter annuals and low-growing spring wildflowers and bulbs get the sun they need to flower best.

In the long run, the route toward a low-maintenance lawn is easier than most folks realize, at least physically. But mentally it is difficult to let go of that desire for perfection. Plus there are social pitfalls to either avoid or learn to live with. It's your landscape, your spare time. But only you should decide how it affects your reputation!

Sun-Loving Ground Covers

Where a slope is too steep to mow, or you just want to have less grass to mow, choose low-growing, spreading, evergreen plants such as ground cover junipers, creeping euonymus, orange daylilies, Japanese honeysuckle, and similar plants, massed and mulched to reduce weeds.

Mower Care

Get the most out of your power equipment by keeping blades sharp and oil and air filters clean and by changing the spark plug as needed. Every winter, drain the gas tank and run the engine dry to keep fuel from turning into a gummy mess—the leading cause of starting problems in the spring. And believe it or not, string trimmers are designed to be run "flat out"—the engines are more efficient at high speeds.

By the way, keeping mower blades sharp is the easiest trick to a neat, crisp lawn cut, rather than the dingy look created by a dull blade leaving ragged brown grass tips. Get a second blade, so you can keep one on the mower while the other is being sharpened.

Note on Wildflowers

The idea of a wildflower meadow is a romantic one and can be practical in some garden settings where large lawns or borders can be left unmowed. You will need to seed or transplant some plants, whether native or non-native wildflowers, and control some weeds by hand pulling or mowing. Most spring wildflowers are best sown or planted in the fall, and selecting individual plant species is much better than a hodgepodge mixture of wildflower seeds.

Prairies are the last things we think about as lawn substitutes. Truth is, *lawns are artificial prairies*, but without the prairie plants—instead of bison browsing wild grasses and fires keeping shrubs and trees under control, we use mowers. You could say that a flower border is simply a "prairie remnant"—especially if native wildflowers and grasses are included.

Spring Transition Your Lawn

A lot of the stuff I get over the Internet is such passing frivolity, I've rubbed the lettering off my "delete" button. But this insightful, author-unknown bit keeps coming my way, year after year, and deserves a wider audience:

"Spring Transition Your Lawn," the sign outside the garden store commanded. I feed it, mow, rake, and water it, and watch a lot of it die anyway. Now I'm supposed to *transition* it? Imagine the conversation The Creator might have about this:

"St. Francis, what happened to the dandelions, violets, clover, and other stuff I started? I had a perfect, no-maintenance garden plan, with plants that grow in any type of soil, withstand drought, and multiply with abandon. Their flowers and seed fed butterflies, bees, and songbirds. Instead of waves of color, now all I see are green rectangles."

"It's the tribes that settled down there, Lord, the Suburbanites. They started calling your flowers 'weeds' and went to great extent to kill them and replace them with grass."

"Grass? But it's very temperamental, and attracts only grubs. Do these Suburbanites really want all that grass growing there?"

"Apparently so, Lord. They go to great pains each spring to poison any other plant that crops up. They feed the grass, and as soon as it grows, they cut it, sometimes twice a week."

"They *cut* it? Do they bale it like hay?" "No sir. They pay to throw it away. And in the summer when the grass stops growing so fast, they drag out hoses and pay more money for water so they can continue to mow it and pay to get rid of it."

"What nonsense! At least they kept some of my trees, which grow leaves in the spring to provide beauty and summer shade. In the autumn they fall to the ground and form a natural blanket to keep moisture in the soil and protect roots. As they rot, they compost to enhance the soil. It's a natural circle of life."

"Better sit down, Lord, the Suburbanites have drawn a new circle. As soon as the leaves fall, they rake them into great piles and have them hauled away. Then they go out and buy something they call mulch, haul it home and spread it around in place of the leaves."

"And where do they get this mulch?"

"They cut down trees and grind them up."

"Enough! I don't want to think about this any more. St. Catherine, you're in charge of the arts. What movie have you scheduled for tonight?"

"Dumb and Dumber, Lord. It's a real stupid movie about..."

"Never mind. I think I just heard the whole story."

Perennials
THAT PREVAIL

Perennials are "hot" in the gardening world, making a trendy comeback in popularity because so many of them simply grow without any care to speak of. From my very first "starts" of heirloom iris and daylilies to my latest "find" of a new wildflower cultivar, I have come to depend on those plants that "come back" year after year to create a never-ending series of surprises—with little or no work on my part.

Unlike trees and woody shrubs, which are also perennial, herbaceous perennials appear to die down part of the year, only to emerge again the following season from roots, stems, bulbs, or rhizomes. The simple term "perennial" is commonly used when referring to herbaceous perennials. And unlike annuals, which grow and flower rapidly from seed, most perennials require two or more years from seed to flower. Most gardeners start with mature plants, either bought or divided from other plants. Perennials generally require less maintenance and water than annuals.

Once prominent in many landscapes, these enduring plants are being rediscovered for their dependable seasonal effects, treasured and shared by gardeners for their abilities to withstand our climate and soils, often with no care at all. Only the toughest of them all are featured in this chapter.

Lima, Ohio

Designing Perennial Plantings

Because perennials live for many years, their planting requires some planning. Perennial flower beds are usually highly visible and look best when they complement an overall garden design; otherwise, large areas of the landscape may be bare part of the year. Many perennials, like annuals, are effective *en masse* when they are in bloom, but because of limitations on their blooming period, they are often better used in smaller clumps,

96

Lifetime Companions

All plants look and probably feel better when surrounded with friends, as long as the growing conditions are similar. The trick is to find those that are complementary in texture, color, and season. Example: Spring-flowering azaleas look like green meatballs most of the year, so grow them in the light shade of summer-flowering trees, skirted with iris, hosta, daylily, ferns, cushion spurge, or other companion perennials.

Great perennials that live for decades and are compatible with others include yarrow, soapwort, iris, daylily, daffodils, amsonia, artemisia, phlox, violets, hosta, and liatris. For the shade, include ferns, hellebore, violets, and lily-of-the-valley.

where their color and texture can accent other plants. Use small evergreen shrubs, flowering trees, or such hard features as a fence, stone, bench, birdbath, or garden art to enhance a flower garden and "carry" it through all the seasons. One of the easiest design tricks is to interplant groups of flowers that have contrasting shapes. For example, daylilies can have their large flowers set off well by the slender spikes of blue salvia and the round flower heads of yarrow. The large leaves of hosta and sword-like form of iris plants have a dramatic effect when used in groups among other less bold plants.

A natural way to begin planting perennials is to create islands of flowers in an open lawn. But because such beds are easily viewed from many sides, they often require high maintenance to keep them attractive. Border plantings along a wall, fence, or hedge can soften the transition between structures and the rest of the landscape or can create allées of color. Where space is restricted, a simple rectangular bed in front of shrubs or a wall can be easily dug and planted. When planting a perennial border against a hedge, fence, or wall, leave a little space between it and its backdrop. This allows for better air circulation, more light penetration, and easy maintenance from the rear of the bed. Perennial borders often are six to eight feet wide, allowing adequate space for at least a combination of six or more species, front to back, yielding a continual bloom.

To prevent turfgrass from growing into the perennial bed and becoming unsightly, use some form of broad edging or a separating strip. Bricks laid flat, flagstone, bare ground, or a heavy layer of mulch such as wood chips or bark will help keep out grass. Or simply dig a small ditch a few inches deep and wide that can be trimmed when the lawn is mowed, or edged with a shovel when the ground has been softened by a recent rain.

Perennials may be grouped according to color, mixing plants that bloom at different times for a continual display. Early bulbs may be interplanted with spring yarrow and iris, which usually fade before daylilies and daisies begin their season of color. Fall sunflowers and ornamental grasses complete the season. Select plants that have not only attractive, long-lived blooms, but also attractive foliage.

Plant height is a major consideration. In border plantings, the tallest plants are usually placed toward the rear to serve as a backdrop, with a few moved forward to prevent monotony in the design. In island plantings, place tall plants toward the center. Fall-blooming perennials are usually the tallest, making them the best backdrop or accent plants. Most of the middle-height perennial plants are summer bloomers and may occupy most of the middle space. Spring-blooming perennials are primarily short plants to be placed toward the front. Emerging foliage and flowers of later blooming plants can also help hide the fading foliage of earlier flowers. Narrow beds with excessively tall plants are usually not effective displays. Whether in borders or island beds, keep the width of a planting about twice the height of the tallest plant.

Site Selection, Soil Preparation, and Fertilization

Let's cut to the chase here—every other garden book has many more details, illustrations, and photos on planning, preparation, and care of plants, so we won't waste space. Here are what I think are the basics:

Though some perennials such as ferns and pachysandra tolerate heavy shade, most flowering perennials need at least six or seven hours of sunshine a day. Very few will live for long where water stands for more than a couple of hours after a heavy rain. Air circulation is important for avoiding diseases; air that is stagnant, warm, and humid creates ideal conditions for diseases.

Soil preparation for perennials is similar to that for annuals, but you have only one shot at doing it right—or you'll be doing it over again in a couple or three years. I dig my soil a solid shovel's depth, then spread a layer of organic matter (bark, peat, compost, and so on) two or three inches deep, and stir it all together. That's that—I never add more than three or four inches of soil amendments, or I run into watering issues! Adding organic matter improves soil structure, but too much can create soggy conditions. Because different types of organic matter work and decompose at different rates in the soil, it is best to use a little of two or three kinds of organic matter than a lot of just one kind. Lastly,

Chicago, Illinois

I cover the planting area with natural mulches, which slowly break down to replace the organic matter that decomposes in the soil.

Perennials need a balance of several nutrients, including nitrogen, phosphorus, and potassium. Most garden supply stores carry a wide variety of fertilizer mixes, and I choose one with all the numbers about the same, no matter what kind of plant—and I always use fertilizers very sparingly! While most plants will not thrive without regular feeding, many of the plants in this chapter have been known to survive and flower for years with little or none. Too much fertilizer, too often, is worse on some plants than none at all. Really.

Do I worry about soil acidity, and lime, and all that soil testing stuff? Nope. It'd be great to do, but . . . nah! These are tough plants, remember?

Planting Them in the Ground

Set perennial plants in their permanent places so that their roots are completely covered with prepared soil, but avoid burying the stem or crown. Place container-grown plants the same depth that they were growing in their pots; place dormant plants dug from the ground at the depth they were growing during the previous season. To encourage side root growth, make a planting hole twice as wide as deep. With bare-root perennials, spread the roots outward as well as downward. Important: For container-grown plants, loosen encircled roots before planting, and mix any potting soil that falls out into your planting soil.

After planting, water the plants thoroughly to force out any air pockets and to settle the soil. Then mulch the bed surface with straw or bark to keep the soil from drying, crusting, and overheating in the summer and to prevent many weed seeds from germinating.

Care and Maintenance

If you do not mulch your plants, lightly work up the soil surface in the spring and early summer to break and aerate compacted soils. This also helps water and fertilizer penetration. Summer cultivation, by the way, can damage shallow roots. Early in the season, stake tall plants with wire stands or bamboo canes, being careful not to damage roots.

Apply fertilizers sparingly to plants early in their growing season, after new growth begins to show. If plants are growing well, no additional fertilizer may be needed; otherwise, a second light feeding will be helpful several weeks into the season.

Some plants grow so well and spread so rapidly that you simply have to get out once every year or two and pull part of them up. In most cases—obedient plant, goldenrod, phlox, asters, and perennial sunflowers come to mind—they are easy to pull with one hand while you are drinking coffee with the other. All I do is wad them up and drop them right back where they were pulled so they compost and recycle into the soil. Doing this after a good rain or watering is less a chore than it is therapy. Plus, if you pot a few, they provide gifts for unsuspecting new gardeners—who are eager to get new plants before they realize how invasive they are! Think of them as great starter plants for children, too.

In the fall, cut the old plant stalks to the ground after the leaves have fallen, and mulch to protect crowns and roots from the harsh extremes when there's no snow cover—which can cause plants to warm up early and then

Iowa

get damaged by sudden freezes.

A few perennials can be subject to pests (aphids can show up on butterfly weed and sedums, grasshoppers and slugs are fond of hostas, and so on). Problems are worse if plants are stressed. Powdery mildew is more visual than anything, and there isn't much we can do about it. Susceptible plants, including monarda, zinnia, summer phlox, roses, euonymus, and a few others, are not as bothered by it as we think—many plants survive it. Even mildew-resistant varieties can get it, and fungicide sprays are temporary fixes at best. Learn

PRACTICE SAFE GARDENING! When getting new plants from other gardeners, always set them in a trial bed for a few weeks or even an entire season, where you can watch them closely to see if there are insects or diseases—or very difficult-to-control weeds—brought in with the plants. It may be impossible to get rid of a weed or disease introduced into the larger garden. And always remember a rule of thumb regarding new plants: The more someone wants you to "take all you want," the more suspicious you should be of it being invasive!

to prune a little and live with a little, or plant gray-leaf artemisia or dusty miller nearby as a visual complement. When my phlox gets mildew, I put an old concrete chicken nearby—and nobody notices the mildew any more!

Propagation

Again, most garden books go into lots of detail, so here are my basics: Though most perennials may take a couple of years to flower from seed, many are as easily started as annuals. The quickest way to have blooming plants, however, is by vegetative propagation: dividing old plants or rooting stem cuttings. Plants produced vegetatively have all of the traits of the "mother" plant. Propagation by division may seem difficult at first, but most gardeners find that dividing crowns and roots and separating bulbs takes very little training and can be mastered quickly. Try dividing an old daylily for experience; then move on to iris, then sedum, and before long you will have the hang of it.

Clump-forming perennial plants with shallow roots, or with long, fibrous roots such as daylilies, are easily dug up and pulled apart by hand. Thickly intertwined roots may need more forceful separation or cutting with digging forks. Replant only those segments with strong roots and a few intact leaves or crowns. It is best to divide perennials during their dormant or "off" season—divide spring bloomers in the fall and fall bloomers in spring. The worst time to divide plants is when they are in full bloom, although some perennials can be divided any time you feel like it. Some perennials may need dividing every few years, or they will slowly crowd themselves into clumps of non-flowering leaves and roots.

Many perennial plants may be propagated from stem cuttings, which does not disturb the plant's roots. Take stem cuttings during the spring or early summer, choosing stems that are mature and firm but not yet hardened and woody. Stick cuttings in a well-drained flower bed or pots of potting soil where they get bright light—but not direct sunshine, or the cuttings will overheat. I often cover mine with a plastic soda bottle, bottom cut off and cap thrown away, to create a miniature greenhouse effect. It works! Water daily or as needed, and rooting can occur within three or four weeks. By the time new leaves begin to appear on cuttings, roots are usually formed and the plastic bottle should be removed. Water new plants as needed.

Layer long-stemmed perennials by throwing soil over stems that have been first bent or slightly wounded and held down to the ground. Roots will form at the bend or wound during the summer, and you can cut and remove the rooted plants in the fall.

Collecting seeds of some species can be easy or difficult, depending on how closely you watch your garden. When blooms with central cones and "ray" flowers (purple coneflower, black-eyed Susan, sunflowers) fade, seeds are already forming but may not be ripe for a few days. Wait until all the ray petals are completely brown and dry, then snip the cones from stems and put them in a paper bag where they can continue to dry without shattering seeds everywhere. (**TIP:** The seeds of purple coneflower are light colored; the black bits are chaff.)

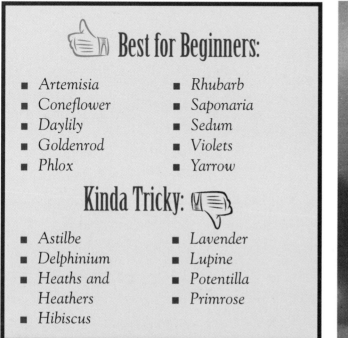

👍 Best for Beginners:

- Artemisia
- Coneflower
- Daylily
- Goldenrod
- Phlox
- Rhubarb
- Saponaria
- Sedum
- Violets
- Yarrow

Kinda Tricky: 👎

- Astilbe
- Delphinium
- Heaths and Heathers
- Hibiscus
- Lavender
- Lupine
- Potentilla
- Primrose

Lamium maculatum 'Pink Pewter'
Pink Pewter spotted deadnettle

Wildflowers That Mind Their Manners

We want nature, but we want it tidy. The following native or naturalized plants are "acceptable" in mixed flower beds in town.

Reseeding Annuals: *Coreopsis, Cosmos, Queen Anne's Lace, Black-Eyed Susan, Zinnia*

Perennials: *Amsonia, Asters, Daisy, Ferns, Goldenrod, Bee Balm, Phlox, Obedient Plant, Purple Coneflower, Black-Eyed Susan, Spiderwort, Sunflower, Violets, Bleeding Heart*

Trees and Shrubs: *Beautyberry, Buckeye, Hollies, Redbud, Sumac, Maples, Clove Currant, Yucca*

Get Started!

Perennial plants have been enjoyed for centuries, both for their flowers and foliage and for their ability to return in our gardens for many years with little trouble. By planting only three or four new types of perennials each year, you can quickly build up a showy perennial garden and then divide the plants for your own use or share them with other gardeners.

Hardy Perennials for Northern Gardens

The following perennials have been proven by "old hand" gardeners to be long-lived, winter- and summer-hardy survivors. And they are generally available from garden centers, mail-order or Internet sources, local plant society and Master Gardener plant sales, and newfound gardening friends—whom you will no doubt meet as you begin growing these treasures. For more information, check out your state's *Gardener's Guide* by Cool Springs Press.

Ajuga
Ajuga reptans
Shade to moderate sun

Bugleweed is a ground-hugging mat of foliage and flowers that spreads relentlessly in moderate shade. This is one "pass-along" plant that just keeps on giving!

FLOWER: Short, springtime spikes of tiny orchid-like flowers in royal blue, purple, pink, white, or rose.

PLANT: Low-spreading rosettes of flat or crinkled leaves, each leaf up to three inches long and almost as wide (some cultivars have leaves up to six inches long). Foliage can be solid green, metallic tinted, or variegated and is evergreen in even the most severe winters (even into Nova Scotia!). Spreads by vigorous runners. Root rot is a problem in heavy clay or poorly drained soils where water stands.

INTERESTING KINDS: 'Alba' has white flowers; 'Variegata' is edged and splotched with cream; 'Burgundy Glow' has green and pink leaves edged with white, with new growth tinged with purple. 'Atropurpurea' and 'Bronze Beauty' are burgundy leaved.

Amsonia
Amsonia tabernaemontana
Full sun to part shade

This "railroad refugee" will grow in damp soils as well as dry, and is one of the most commonly planted North American natives in European cottage gardens and perennial borders.

FLOWER: Tight rounded heads of small, blue, star-shaped flowers atop sturdy, erect, knee-high stems in the late spring. Great for cut flowers; good butterfly perennial in an "in between" season.

PLANT: Many-stemmed dense clump of shoots up to three feet tall, with three- or four-inch willowy leaves the entire length. Works well in naturalistic settings with woodland ferns. Autumn color is bright yellow.

INTERESTING KINDS: *Amsonia montana* is the compact type most often seen in European gardens. *Amsonia hubrectii* has soft, extremely thin, needle-like leaves and is one of the most commonly sold varieties today.

Artemisia
Artemisia ludoviciana
Full sun to light shade

The historic plant, which was originally introduced as a "wound wort" or emergency bandage plant, is one of my "top ten" companion plants for other perennials and shrubs—but may become invasive.

FLOWER: Insignificant, usually not even noticed. Best ignored or cut off.

PLANT: Generally vigorous, bushy or spreading, medium-height ground cover with silver gray or white leaves that are pungent when broken. Excellent source of filler material for flower arrangements and an outstanding contrasting foliage companion to iris, daylilies, and other drought-hardy perennials.

INTERESTING KINDS: 'Silver King' and 'Valerie Finnis' can be invasive. 'Powis Castle' is a fern-leaf hybrid forming a dense, knee-high shrub but may not be as winter hardy in northern areas. 'Silver Mound' (*A. schmidtiana*) makes a tidy little silvery-gray "bun." 'Lambrook Silver' is one of the best varieties for the North, two and a half feet tall and more silvery than other types.

Asparagus
Asparagus officinalis
Full sun

Nothing like fresh, homegrown asparagus in season—then having a beautiful "fern" to enjoy the rest of the summer and fall! As new shoots appear in the early spring, cut and enjoy all you can eat until they start getting thin; then leave the rest to send energy down to the crown for next year's crop.

FLOWER: Small, greenish white, not showy; red berries form on female plants.

PLANT: Clumps of many-branched, medium-green "ferns" from four to five or more feet tall. Crowns are fleshy tuberous roots like daylilies and get larger every year—some clumps can eventually get five or six feet across. Planting the crowns, which requires trenching, can be tricky for new gardeners.

INTERESTING KINDS: Old varieties include 'Martha Washington', but modern heat-tolerant hybrids sold as "all male" (which don't waste energy making seeds) include 'Jersey Giant' and others with "Jersey" in the name. Perhaps the best kind is whatever you can find locally, especially if it's growing in someone's garden where you can vouch for the plant's vigor.

Aster

Aster species

Full sun to very light shade

These autumn flowers pick up gardeners' spirits in the first few cool days of fall like nothing else, especially when combined with other fall-flowering perennials. And they can grow from woodland edge to the concrete chunks packed along an urban drainage creek!

FLOWER: Many loose clusters of flat flower heads made up of numerous ray petals sticking out from a central disk, up to two inches across, from late summer to late fall. Colors range from white to purple, with lots of pinks, reds, lavenders, and blues. Flowering stems tend to be tall and floppy, but can be pinched or lightly cut back before the Fourth of July for a bushier show in the fall.

PLANT: Many-stemmed clumps or tall, floppy plants, most with narrow leaves and an airy look that is best combined with other perennials, tied to a wall, or staked.

INTERESTING KINDS: New England aster (*Aster novae-angliae*) and its close relative New York aster (*A. novae-belgii*) include many cultivars: 'Harrington's Pink', 'Alma Potschke' (dark rose pink), 'Hella Lacy' (lavender with yellow center), and 'Purple Dome' (a shorter, more compact form) are easy to find commercially. Tatarian aster (*A. tataricus*) is a tall, upright fall bloomer with airy, football-sized clusters of purple flowers and large leaves. One of the toughest of all is the aromatic aster (*A. oblongifolius*), which spreads by underground runners into a three-foot mass of solid purple and yellow every fall.

BEST BUTTERFLY PERENNIALS include, in order of bloom: yarrow, phlox, purple coneflower, rudbeckia, salvia, liatris, sedum, aster, and goldenrod.

Astilbe
Astilbe species and hybrids
Light shade

"False spirea" is a standard shade perennial for the North, though it will take some sun if it gets plenty of water. Its flower spikes are among the showiest flowers for the shade, brightening up fern and hosta glades.

FLOWER: Tall, pointy plumes of pink, red, rose, or white billow up to three or more feet high every spring, with early, mid-, and late season varieties helping extend the show into early summer.

PLANT: Clump-forming plants spread into large mats of deeply cut, fern-like green or bronze foliage, attractive both before and after flowering. Good as accents in the light shade, or even as a perennial summer border.

INTERESTING KINDS: Too many great astilbes to mention, although the early flowering 'Fanal' is very popular, as is 'Sprite,' which was the 1994 Perennial Plant Association Plant of the Year.

Bee Balm
Monarda species
Light shade to sun

Bee balm and bergamot are among the first plants new gardeners start giving away, because they just keep on growing—everywhere! Lucky they're so pretty, or we'd call them weeds.

FLOWER: Spring and summer, round clusters of salvia-like tubes that are irresistible to hummingbirds, bees, and butterflies, and are perfectly edible (spicy-minty, good fresh off the plant, in salads and sandwiches). Colors are white to deep burgundy, with pink, lavender, mauve, and scarlet varieties.

PLANT: Aggressive colony-forming native woodland-edge perennial with upright stems and aromatic leaves.

INTERESTING KINDS: Bee balm (*Monarda didyma*) is a vigorous red species, called Oswego tea after the New York State Oswego Indians who made a medicinal beverage from it; common cultivars include 'Cambridge Scarlet' and 'Croftway Pink'. Many bee balms are prone to powdery mildew; resistant varieties include 'Jacob Cline', 'Scorpion', and 'Stone's Throw Pink'. Bergamot (*M. fistulosa*) has pink flowers surrounded with white bracts.

Bellflower
Campanula species
Sun or light shade

Bellflowers have been collected for centuries, and hybridized into more than 250 types. They are long-lived perennials that often multiply—sometimes too well!

FLOWER: Light cups of blue and white, sometimes lavender or pink, appear on stately stems—sometimes to five or more feet tall—from late spring into summer and even fall. They are outstanding cut flowers.

PLANT: Perennial or reseeding biennial plants create soft mounds of green, which are easy to work into the middle of flower borders, where they blend with or soften other plants. A few have become weedy in some regions.

INTERESTING KINDS: *Campanula persicifolia* 'Grandiflora Alba' and 'Telham Beauty' are spectacular; *C. portenschlagiana* usually grows less than a foot tall with heart-shaped leaves and many star-shaped blue flowers, from late spring to summer. *C. carpatica* is a good edger or rock garden plant growing no more than a foot tall, covered with blue or white flowers.

Bishop's Weed or Goutweed
Aegopodium podagraria 'Variegatum'
Heavy shade to light sun

Be sure—be *very* sure—that you want this ground cover, because there's no way to keep it in bounds or get rid of it once you have it established. It does cover a lot of ground, and its variegation brightens the shadiest areas.

FLOWER: Queen Anne's lace type flowers rise about a foot above the leaves.

PLANT: Incredibly invasive ground cover for sun or the very densest shade. Keep bishop's weed in bounds as best you can with edging sunk at least six inches deep, or plant it where it is surrounded with paving. Glyphosate is one of the few environmentally safe herbicides that will control it. If in sun, the leaves burn a bit toward the end of the summer.

INTERESTING KINDS: The species is solid green, rarely used because it's not as pretty and it is much more invasive.

Black-Eyed Susan
Rudbeckia fulgida 'Goldsturm'
Full sun or very light shade

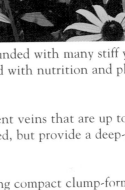

This was the first perennial I set out on my newly bare, hot, dry, pure-clay hillside—a "horticultural hell" where I had just killed all the grass to create a wildflower patch. And it's still growing!

FLOWER: Branched flowering stems in late spring and summer are topped with chocolate-brown "noses" or cones surrounded with many stiff yellow ray petals. Brown cones are packed with small nutty seeds, loaded with nutrition and plant fat for birds migrating into the area for the winter.

PLANT: Flat basal rosettes of pointy-oval leaves with prominent veins that are up to four inches long and half that wide. Flowering stems are sparsely leafed, but provide a deep-green backdrop to the flowers.

INTERESTING KINDS: 'Goldsturm' is a thickly flowering compact clump-former, very heat tolerant. Cut-leaf coneflower (*Rudbeckia laciniata*) is taller and has deeply lobed leaves; 'Goldquelle' is more compact and spreads less aggressively. It is happiest in moist soil at the woodland's edge, but will tolerate full sun if watered well during dry spells.

Bleeding Heart
Dicentra spectabilis
Shade or part sun

Little brightens up a dark corner by the garage or a woodland garden more than the charming—and always fascinating—bleeding heart. It comes with a splash, goes without a whimper, and returns year after year.

FLOWER: Long, arching stems in the spring from which dangle a single row of perfect little exotic pinkish red hearts, each with a white "teardrop" hanging from the bottom.

PLANT: Shrub-like clump of coarse, ferny leaves that usually look ratty or die down in the harsh heat and drought of summer; tuberous roots help keep the plant alive until the following spring.

INTERESTING KINDS: The native "wild" or fringed bleeding heart (*D. eximia*) is smaller and ever-blooming right through the summer, and seeds itself readily.

Coreopsis
Coreopsis species
Full sun

Few native wildflowers are as versatile in bloom as coreopsis, which grows wild across the entire eastern half of North America, from Canada to eastern Mexico. It is extremely drought tolerant and pest free.

FLOWER: Flat, single, or frilly double sunflower-like flowers with golden centers and the edges of each petal jagged or "pinked," nearly always golden yellow but sometimes clear pure yellow or with maroon markings. Stems are long and stiff, making them excellent cut flowers, or meadow flowers held high above other blooming plants.

PLANT: Flattened rosettes or spreading, airy mounds, leaves oblong or threadlike. Plants seriously resent fertilizers and summer irrigation, getting floppy and losing their flower power when grown in too-rich or moist conditions.

INTERESTING KINDS: Threadleaf coreopsis (C. *verticillata* 'Moonbeam') is a mounding summer-flowering perennial; tickseed (C. *grandiflora*) has large flowers, single or double, in late spring.

Cushion Spurge
Euphorbia polychroma
Full sun to very light shade

A member of the same family as poinsettia, with "milky" sap, this ground cover can be breathtaking on a dry hillside in all but the coldest part of the region (it even grows in southern Alaska).

FLOWER: Two-inch clusters of almost fluorescent, greenish yellow, flower-like bracts, about a half inch long, each like little greenish yellow horns, produced in early spring (about the time daffodils bloom); a most unusual color that adds zest to the early spring garden.

PLANT: Spreading mass of upright, pale green stems to about a foot tall, very thin and succulent and easy to trample, with many inch-long leaves that stick straight out. Very good in rock walls, or rock piles for that matter.

INTERESTING KINDS: Donkey-tail spurge (E. *myrsinites*) creeps across the ground with blue-green leaves and brilliant yellow flowers early in the spring. E. *dulcis* 'Chameleon' reseeds prolifically, even in dry shade where little else will grow.

Dandelion

Taraxacum officinale

Full sun or light shade

And *why not?* It has good leaves, pretty flowers, interesting seedheads, is easy to grow, and all parts are useful—plus it's a prolific producer of both nectar and pollen for bees from late winter to late fall.

FLOWER: Stalks are hollow tubes from an inch to a foot tall, each topped with a single bright yellow flower head made up of many dozens of thin, strap-shaped florets that open and close with the daylight and weather. Gossamer seedheads form in a day to release floating parachutes that seemingly all succeed in sprouting somewhere.

PLANT: Flat rosette of toothed leaves that when young are considered a delicacy for salads and sandwiches. A deep taproot is difficult to dig up, but can be used for making acceptable coffee or beer substitutes.

INTERESTING KINDS: A burgundy, variegated, or larger-flower or sterile-seeded cultivar could be worth millions. A few cultivars have been developed for use as a salad green crop.

MASTER GARDENERS ARE TAUGHT that a weed is a "plant out of place"—which logically would include a rose growing in a corn patch, right? And a maple seedling in a flower bed can grow to shade a thousand square feet of lawn.

Ralph Waldo Emerson asked, "What is a weed, but a plant whose virtues have yet to be discovered?" A personal dislike for a plant doesn't make it a weed—except in the offended gardener's domain. The same plant growing in a wildflower patch could be considered a wonderful butterfly plant! The late great plant explorer J.C. Raulston once told me that he thought a weed is "any plant having to deal with an unhappy human."

That's more like it.

Daylily

Hemerocallis species and hybrids

Full sun to light shade

"Wherever the sun shines, there is a daylily," says Canadian-born perennials guru Allan Armitage. These most eagerly grown perennials, second in popularity only to daffodils, are the mainstays of the summer flower garden. They are so easy to grow and even hybridize that there are more than twenty thousand named hybrids—and hundreds of new ones introduced every year.

Daylilies get their scientific name from a combination of Latin words for "beauty" and "day," and come in a rainbow of colors (everything but true white and true blue). They survive an astounding range of climate conditions and soil types, are extremely drought resistant, and have no major insect pests. (Rust, however, has recently become a problem in some areas, especially on plants that are watered and fertilized too much.)

FLOWER: Large, six-petaled, from two to more than six inches across, with the six petals arranged in patterns ranging from circular to triangular, flat or trumpet, thin "spider" to double. Flowers are borne on sturdy scapes (stems) from six inches to six feet tall, mostly in the two- to three-foot range; some varieties have branching scapes with from ten to a hundred flower buds. Colors range from pale yellow to blackish red, and everything in between; flowers can be single colors or have contrasting "eyes" and throats, or be bicolored, banded, tipped, or edged ("picoteed"). Most daylilies flower in the morning and fade by late afternoon, but some remain open for up to sixteen hours, and some even flower in the evening. Some are also fragrant.

PLANT: Many flattened fans of long, slender, grass-like foliage grow from a central crown. Leaves can be six inches to more than three feet long, usually arching somewhat. The dreaded rust disease seems to be worst on daylilies that are planted in soil that is too rich, then overfed and overwatered—it seems to be a "daylily society" disease. Keep plants lean and mean!

INTERESTING KINDS: There are way too many kinds of daylilies to mention here. Some of the most common ones include the old orange species (*Hemerocallis fulva*); 'Hyperion', a tall, clear yellow variety from great-grandmother's day; 'Mary Todd', a free-flowering yellow variety; and 'Stella d'Oro', a foot-high miniature that makes a fine border plant to flower all summer.

NOT TO GET TOO TECHNICAL, but most daylilies have two sets of chromosomes and are called "diploid." Breeders have found ways to double that genetic material into "super" daylilies called "tetraploids" that generally have stronger flower scapes, larger flowers, more intense colors, greater vigor, and sturdier "substance" (thicker foliage and flower petals). Growing a few different kinds of daylilies will quickly convince you that there are great daylilies in both groups—regular and super!

SOIL: Daylilies are tough, but will flower more freely if planted in a soil that has been amended with organic matter to a shovel's depth and then slightly raised to keep the crowns from staying wet in rainy seasons. A light feeding as growth begins in the spring will kick off a good flowering cycle. Note that too much water and fertilizer—which is sometimes recommended by expert growers—often sets plants up for diseases.

PROPAGATION: Very easy to divide nearly any time of year (even when in full bloom, as done by many collectors who want to know exactly what they are getting). Lift entire clumps, then work apart individual or small groups of fans (prying with a digging fork makes this easier). Growing from seed is a bit of a challenge: Sow small, black seeds in potting soil as soon as fat seedpods turn brown and split open, and keep moist; the small, grass-like baby plants can be kept indoors in a sunny window or in a protected area outside and planted in the spring. Most will take another year to reach blooming maturity. To learn more about kinds of daylilies and how to choose the best ones for your garden, find tips on growing and even home-hybridizing them, plus how to find friendly, good growers near you, contact the American Hemerocallis Society, www.daylilies.org. Or do a word search for the American Hemerocallis Society, whose officers and members are scattered throughout all corners of the country.

TIP: THE SINGLE MOST COMMONLY GROWN DAYLILY, the old orange one seen growing along ditches, beside country homes, and in cemeteries—and even found in famous botanical gardens—is despised by "society" daylily growers because of its very commonness. In fact, I've never seen anyone get his shorts in a knot quicker than a daylily breeder when someone mentions that old "outhouse" lily! Yet the "tawny" lily, and the variety *kwanso*, its double-flowering version, continue to be excellent, readily available, easy-to-propagate, "unkillable" summer perennials for starting new gardeners off on the right foot. They do not cause other daylilies to "revert" to the orange species form, but because they are strong spreaders, do not plant them with newer, less vigorous daylilies or the weenie ones will be overwhelmed.

ANOTHER TIP: DAYLILIES ARE PERFECTLY EDIBLE! Their buds have more vitamins than broccoli and can be eaten in the same ways: raw, dipped, steamed, fried, or in soups. Lighter colored yellows and oranges have a less strong flavor. Try chopping daylily flowers into blueberry pancake mix—yum!

Dianthus
Dianthus species
Full sun

"Pinks" are an old cultivated flower, a member of the same family as carnation and sweet William.

FLOWER: Generally flat disks with notched petal tips (where the scissors called "pinking shears" got their name), in white, pink, or red, or combinations on one flower. Prolific bloomers very heavily spice-scented, like sweet cloves. Some make good cut flowers. Deadhead to encourage more flowers the rest of the summer.

PLANT: Compact mounds of grassy foliage are evergreen, often bright green or blue green, and can be important elements of a winter garden.

INTERESTING KINDS: 'Bath's Pink', discovered by Jane Bath of north Georgia, is perfectly hardy in Minnesota or New England, with blue foliage and pink flowers; another low-grower is 'Tiny Rubies'. The 'Zing' group is six-inches tall and bloom all summer. 'Kelsey' also holds up well in both hard freezes and sultry summer humidity.

False Dragonhead or Obedient Plant
Physostegia virginiana
Full sun to part shade

Here's a plant to give to all your neighbors—one so pretty they can't believe you want to pull and pull and pull and then give it all away! This native plant is almost irresistibly beautiful and great for hummingbirds.

FLOWER: Inch-long, tubular flowers, lavender or white, on summer spikes. Outstanding cut flower.

PLANT: Spreading mass of individual stems to three feet or more tall, with long, pointed, deep-green leaves on distinctly square stems. Plants may flop after a rain, requiring staking or interplanting with fall asters. Gardeners gripe about how quickly the plants can spread, but it is easy to pull and share.

INTERESTING KINDS: 'Summer Snow', 'Bouquet Rose', and the rose-pink 'Vivid' are easily found; 'Variegata' has pink flowers, white-edged foliage, and is much less aggressive than green-leaved types.

114

Ferns
All sorts of weird Latin names
Shade to part sun

Ferns add the most drama to shaded gardens, complementing woodland shrubs and trees, marking paths, or accenting benches. There are too many to do justice here. Plant at least two or four kinds!

FLOWER: None, because ferns reproduce by spores rather than seeds.

PLANT: Individual leaves ("fronds") arise from very shallow, often-hairy root-like rhizomes or a compact crown. Ferns can be very small, or to four feet or taller; some ferns die to the ground in the fall, while others are evergreen.

INTERESTING KINDS: Of the many great ferns, here are a handful of the most interesting and hardy:
Christmas Fern (*Polystichum acrostichoides*)—popular evergreen, fronds two feet tall by five inches wide.
Interrupted Fern (*Osmunda claytoniana*)—will take a great deal of sunshine.
Japanese Painted Fern (*Athyrium nipponicum* 'Pictum')—an evergreen clump to eighteen inches, with lower portions of each frond having purplish leaflets, gradually lightening toward the tips in shades of lavender to silvery green. Very attractive and easy for beginners.
Maidenhair Fern (*Adiantum pedatum*)—a delicate-looking small fern to eighteen inches, fan-shaped fronds of leaflets are light green on dark stems. Must have shade. Deciduous.
Ostrich Fern (*Matteuccia struthiopteris*)—the most widely used landscape fern, turns brown at first freeze.

EAT A FERN! New "fiddleheads" of some ferns—particularly ostrich fern—are perfectly edible! Collect when they are two or three inches tall and tightly furled, store in the refrigerator until you have enough to cook, wash then boil them for three or four minutes and serve hot, or cold in a salad. Warning: Not all ferns are edible; some are poisonous. Eat only what you are perfectly sure of (you can be sure ostrich fern is safe, just be sure it's ostrich fern).

Goldenrod
Solidago species
Full sun or very light shade

A garden with goldenrod looks and feels like home! Unfairly blamed for allergies (of which it is innocent—it's the ragweed and grasses that drive our histamines nuts), many great goldenrods are widely appreciated in European gardens, where they aren't considered weeds.

FLOWER: Clusters of small, bright golden-yellow flowers atop long, stiff stems up to five feet tall; some varieties have arching, wand-like flowering stems. Excellent cut flower, and bird, butterfly, and bee plant.

PLANT: Winter rosette of foliage shoots up into tall stems with narrow leaves. Some species spread by underground shoots that are easy to pull up; others are low-growing clump-formers, not invasive at all.

INTERESTING KINDS: Sweet goldenrod (*Solidago odora*) is tall, unbranched, and non-invasive, and has anise-scented leaves; rough-leaf goldenrod (*S. rugosa* 'Fireworks') has arching stems to four feet tall; *S. sphacelata* 'Golden Fleece' is a compact clump to only two feet tall; 'Cloth of Gold' stays under two feet.

Hardy Hibiscus or Rose Mallow
Hibiscus moscheutos
Full sun to very light shade

Dinner-plate-sized hibiscus flowers look so unreal, no one in their right mind would expect them to be winter-hardy. But I've seen old clumps in cottage gardens from Iowa and Chicago to upstate New York.

FLOWER: Huge, up to foot-wide flat flowers, looking like they are straight from the tropics, from July to frost. Dazzling white, pink, wine, and shimmery red, sometimes with contrasting throats or edges.

PLANT: Many-stemmed, deciduous shrub-like clumps with large, heart-shaped leaves. Prefers wetland conditions, but will grow in moderate garden soils and tolerate light shade. Mulch heavily in winter, and allow some insect damage on foliage (not much can be done about it, but it doesn't seriously harm plants).

INTERESTING KINDS: Dozens of hardy new cultivars are being developed in the Midwest, but start with old favorites 'Lord Baltimore' (red) and 'Appleblossom' (pink with red margins). The hybrid 'Kopper King' has copper-colored, maple-shaped leaves; large flowers are light pink with a red eye.

Hellebore

Helleborus species

Shade to light sun

Even the coldest winter wonderland can have flowers. The glossy foliage of hellebores contrasts well with fallen tree leaves, and the clusters of soft-colored flowers, though holding their faces toward the ground, provide a welcome relief from the evergreenness of many shrubs.

FLOWER: Several branching stems up to two feet tall hold clusters of downward-facing flowers, each an inch or so wide, starting in late winter, but the papery bracts can persist for months.

PLANT: Clump of lustrous dark-green leaves up to two feet tall and divided into fans of jagged leaflets. Foliage is evergreen in the worst winters, but will burn in direct sunshine. Slow to establish, but very long-lived, often forming colonies in woodland gardens.

INTERESTING KINDS: Lenten rose (*Helleborus orientalis*); Christmas rose (*H. niger*); bear's-foot hellebore (*H. foetidus*) has interesting, upright, deeply divided leaves and large upright clusters of pale-green flowers.

Hollyhock

Alcea rosea

Sun

This tall, old-fashioned garden favorite is a constant of the cottage garden, and even abandoned gardens. Sow seed this year, and it will bloom the next, and for many years to come.

FLOWER: Large, single, double, or flattened hibiscus flowers up to five inches across, in colors ranging from white to almost black and every pastel shade of pink, rose, salmon, golden, canary-yellow, red, crimson, maroon, and combinations of practically all these colors, with either white centers or white margins. Seedpods follow in late summer.

PLANT: Reseeding biennial or short-lived perennial, an overwintering rosette of large leaves which throws up a tall (five- to eight-foot) spire of flowers by midsummer. Susceptible to foliage diseases and unsightly insect damage, which just means plant the things in the back of the bed, out of sight.

INTERESTING KINDS: 'Nigra' is a chocolate-burgundy variety still around from Thomas Jefferson's gardening days; many others are "out there" and can be grown from seed collected (with permission) and sowed in the late summer.

Japanese Pachysandra
Pachysandra terminalis
Shade to part sun

Pachysandra to the North is what English ivy is to Southern gardens—the most widely used, perhaps most practical, ground cover for shaded gardens.

FLOWER: Loose bottle-brush-like plumes of raggedy tubular white flowers stand up in late winter from the ends of the previous season's growth to lighten shaded gardens where the ground cover is used.

PLANT: Aggressive but not invasive spreading ground cover, with notched, glossy green leaves in whorls, which can be completely knocked off during a rough winter. Root rot and leaf spots are problems of wet growing conditions or overwatering

INTERESTING KINDS: 'Green Carpet' is a low-growing pachysandra favored by landscapers for its more compact growth and deep green foliage. 'Variegata' has mottled white foliage and is less vigorous than the species but can brighten a shaded corner or small area.

Mint
Mentha species
Full sun or light shade

Mint helps the medicine go down, brightens the breath, and makes a stimulating tea and culinary herb. Once started, it can be almost difficult to get rid of. I grow a hardy mint in a crack in my back driveway!

FLOWER: Small pinkish white blossoms on stems above foliage, fragrant and edible but usually not showy enough to enjoy at the expense of foliage, which generally shuts down while plants are in bloom.

PLANT: Invasive underground rhizomes sprout upright stems a foot or more tall. Leaves are aromatic with oils, extremely fragrant when crushed or after a good rain. Most mints need to be trimmed back occasionally to keep them covered with fresh foliage, or they tend to get woody and leggy.

INTERESTING KINDS: With well over five hundred different mints to choose from, the most popular and available is the versatile, heavily scented true spearmint (M. *spicata*).

Mums and Daisies

Dendranthema and *Leucanthemum* species

Full sun

Forget the arguments over the proper Latin names—daisies and mums begin and end the summer gardening season with large, cheerful flowers perfect for butterflies and flower arrangements. The indestructible plants are grown around country cottages with no care other than an occasional pinch for bushiness.

FLOWER: Spring-blooming daisies are flat, many-petaled white flowers up to four inches across with yellow center disks; mums are white, yellow, pink, orange, and red and usually flower in the fall.

PLANT: Many-stemmed shrubby plants to two feet tall with narrow, sometimes toothed, medium- to deep-green leaves up to five inches long, which die completely down at first frost. Crown rot associated with heavy rains and high humidity is the main problem facing these plants. Pinch young flower stem tips to encourage more flower branching.

INTERESTING KINDS: Shasta daisy (*Leucanthemum* × *superbum* or *Chrysanthemum superbum*) is the most famous daisy, with large white flowers on stems up to three feet tall, and includes cultivars such as 'Becky' and 'Alaska', and the double-flowering 'Marconi' and 'Esther Read'. The much sturdier ox-eye daisy (*L. vulgare* or *C. leucanthemum*) is not as showy but has stiffer stems, with the 'May Queen' variety being the longest flowering. My all-time favorite fall-flowering mum is *Chrysanthemum rubellum*, especially 'Duchess of Edinburgh' (reddish); 'Mary Stoker' (yellow with a pink blush); and 'Clara Curtis', sometimes called 'Ryan's Pink' or "country girls," with huge, light pink flowers that spill over flower beds until just before frost.

LITTLE BIRDS LOVE LITTLE SEEDS produced by coneflowers, sunflowers, rudbeckias, goldenrods, and other summer- and fall-flowering perennials. Don't rush to cut dead flower stems down until birds have first had a chance to glean the seeds.

Phlox

Phlox species

Full shade to full sun

Spring wouldn't be right, and neither would summer, without phlox. Among our most eye-catching native perennials, they have been mainstays in European gardens since the mid-1700s. Different species are so distinct they almost seem unrelated, yet all are tough and easy to grow. But then, hey, they're native!

FLOWER: Five-petaled stars up to one inch across of white, blue, pink, lavender, purple, or red (sometimes with contrasting "eyes"), produced in masses on stems above foliage from late winter through late summer (depending on species). Lightly fragrant, incredibly showy, and great for butterflies.

PLANT: Multiple-stemmed plants which, depending on the species, can be creeping woodland ground-huggers or meadow beauties up to five feet tall, with deep-green leaves that are generally oval or oblong. Powdery mildew is a problem on many kinds, and there isn't a lot to be done about it other than thinning out new growth so that what is left has better air circulation, and avoiding excess irrigation.

INTERESTING KINDS:

Creeping Phlox (*Phlox stolonifera*) is smaller and more compact than woodland phlox, well under a foot tall, with more rounded leaves. It spreads well even in dry woodland soils, and it flowers in masses of white, blue, pink, or purple. Cultivars include 'Bruce's White', 'Sherwood Purple', lavender blue 'Blue Ridge', and pink 'Home Fires'.

Downy Phlox (*Phlox pilosa*) is another creeper that stays about a foot or so high, but comes in some sturdy cultivars perfect for container or border edging. Best bets include 'Chattahoochee'

(a hybrid, blue with a wine eye), 'Eco Happy Traveler' (deep pink), and 'Ozarkana' (fragrant, light pink with a red eye).

Moss Pink (*Phlox subulata*), or thrift, is as garish as a plant can be, cascading from hillside gardens and rock walls. Its tiny, needle-like leaves make the plant disappear into the background most of the year—until it covers itself with solid sheets of pink, blue, or white flowers in late winter and early spring. Propagate by sticking small bits of stem right into the ground. This very low-growing phlox absolutely requires low fertility and

drought, and grows best in hot sun in perfectly well-drained soils, making it ideal for tucking into retaining walls, rock gardens, and massed along slopes. Cultivars include 'Scarlet Flame', 'Coral Eye', 'Snowflake', and 'Maiden Blush'.

Summer Phlox (*Phlox paniculata*) is the "tall boy" of summer, sprouting sturdy multiple stems up to four or five feet tall, topped with football-sized panicles of garish pink, white, purple, lavender, or red. Some cultivars are touted as mildew resistant ('David' and 'Robert Poore'); powdery mildew is generally a problem best dealt with by thinning stems in the spring and providing good air circulation or by hiding the bulk of the plant behind a small picket fence or daylilies. Many cultivars, including 'Mt. Fuji' (white) and 'Bright Eyes' (pink with a rosy center).

Woodland Phlox (*Phlox divaricata*), also called wild sweet William or blue phlox, is a low-growing (under fifteen inches), spreading forest plant, usually evergreen except in severe winters, that flowers in early and mid-spring. It creates airy masses of medium true-blue flowers, with enough fragrance on a warm day to fill the entire woods. Perfect complement to naturalized daffodils, ferns, and the unusual native trillium and mayapple that appear at the same time. Its cascading habit also makes it a great winter-hardy potted plant and flower border edge, or accent in a rock garden. Cultivars include 'Fuller's White', 'Louisiana', and pale blue 'Dirigo Ice'.

ROCK GARDEN SOILS must drain well or roots can rot. Blend equal parts topsoil, coarse or sharp sand, and organic matter (peat, compost, potting soil, or finely ground bark). Do not add lime if acid-loving plants will be included in the planting. Mulch to keep the soil in place.

Primrose
Primula species
Light shade

Don't think I'm talking about those pretty little things they sell in grocery stores—overbred, over flowered, and not likely to survive outside, summer or winter. I'm talking *common* primroses—three kinds in particular.

FLOWER: Clusters of flat flowers or balls of small flowers in early spring, in white, red, purple, pink, or yellow.

PLANT: Rosettes of leaves up to nearly a foot long, which require light shade in most areas, certainly in the hotter, more humid parts of our northern region. Too much watering, and they rot; too little, and they just disappear. They need moist, well-drained soil. Excellent rock garden or border plants.

INTERESTING KINDS: Common primrose (*P. vulgaris*) has single, soft yellow flowers atop an eight-inch stem; drumstick primroses (*P. denticulata*) have two-inch round purple or white balls on foot-tall sticks, very unusual in the early spring. 'Wanda' (*Primula × polyantha*) has very early, red-purple flowers with yellow eyes in clusters atop bright green leaves; an old and popular English variety.

Purple Coneflower
Echinacea purpurea
Full sun to light shade

Nearly indestructible in home gardens—unless you try to pamper it with good soil, fertilizer, and lots of water, which simply cause it to grow too tall, flop over, and die. This species is a butterfly magnet.

FLOWER: Dramatic combination of bristly bee hive shaped orange cone and long, thin, pink or white ray petals held above multiple-branching flowering stems. The "noses" are pods of nutty wild bird seed.

PLANT: Basal rosette of dark-green, pointy-oval, sand-papery leaves that shoot leafy flowering stems up to three or more feet in the summer. Plants spread slowly by rhizomes, but also sow viable seed everywhere.

INTERESTING KINDS: Native plant enthusiasts obsess over yellow forms and kinds with scraggly pink ray flowers; gardeners go for the big bold varieties, including 'Magnus', 'Bravado', and the rosy-purple 'Bright Star'; white flowering forms include 'White Swan' and 'White Lustre'.

Rhubarb
Rheum × cultorum
Full sun

Rhubarb—either you like it or hate it, no matter how much sugar you cook it in. It can be used to scrub pots, dye hair, and make insecticide. But it is also a fine ornamental plant for cold-climate gardens, one that Southerners can only wag their okra and sweet potatoes at.

FLOWER: Tall stalks of airy florets, produced in midsummer.

PLANT: Thick, fleshy rhizome produces numerous reddish or green basal leaves, over a foot long on thick, succulent petioles (stems), which are edible when harvested early in the season and cooked a lot. The leaf blades are very high in oxalic acid, which can poison humans. Only the petioles are cooked and eaten. In the sorrel family.

INTERESTING KINDS: 'Valentine' has long red stalks that retain their color after being cooked; 'Victoria' has pinkish red and green stalks; 'Mammoth Red' has four to five foot tall, deep red leaves. *Rheum palmatum* has giant leaves, green backed with burgundy; it prefers a moist location but will grow in ordinary garden soil.

Russian Sage
Perovskia atriplicifolia
Sun

First time I saw this "cloud of blue" perennial was back in the 1980s in central Minnesota, and it almost knocked my socks off—not for its own sake, but for how it set off rudbeckia, daylily, and other "hotter" colored perennials.

FLOWER: Beautiful, powder blue that looks lavender because of its tall, airy, silvery stems. Flowers from early summer to frost, the hotter the better.

PLANT: Airy "sub shrub"—a perennial with a woody base—that needs cutting back in the winter. Silvery-gray foliage has a sage-like aroma when brushed. Best viewed in groups, set off by an evergreen backdrop or as a companion in a naturalistic setting or border.

INTERESTING KINDS: 'Longin' is more upright and narrow than the species, with violet flowers; 'Filagran' is just over three feet tall; 'Blue Spire' has lavender flowers.

Salvia
Salvia species
Full sun to light shade

One of my earliest horticulture jaunts across the country was in search of blue flowers for the summer—and I found them in salvias, several of which are hardy perennials that complement other garden plants, while also attracting butterflies.

FLOWER: Tall, long-flowering spikes of purple or blue, sometimes white, two-lipped trumpets.

PLANT: Spreading masses of upright stems with long narrow leaves, sometimes very fragrant (sage, the widely used culinary herb, is a hardy salvia).

INTERESTING KINDS: Common sage (*Salvia officinalis*) is a somewhat short-lived perennial with highly fragrant leaves and many forms, including variegated; violet sage (*S. × superba*) is a spreading plant with narrow, erect flowering stems to nearly three feet; *S. × sylvestris* 'East Friesland', 'Rose Queen', 'Blauhügel' ('Blue Hill' or 'Blue Mound'), and 'May Night' are all very popular perennial garden favorites.

Saponaria or Soapwort
Saponaria officinalis
Full sun or part shade

Early colonists brought with them this plant for making soapy lather to rinse hair and delicate fabrics. Naturalized along New England riverbanks. Also known as bouncing bet, after English barmaids, called "bets," who used it to rinse bottles. Because of its soapy taste, neither deer nor slugs will mess with soapwort.

FLOWER: Single or double, pink and white, tubes in clusters at tips of branches all summer.

PLANT: Spreading evergreen ground cover with smooth oblong leaves up to three inches long. Leaves are glossy-slick and absolutely evergreen (even in Vermont). Soapiness makes it unpalatable to insects.

INTERESTING KINDS: 'Alba' is a single-flowered white cultivar; 'Rosea Plena' is a pale-pink double; 'Rubra Plena' has nearly crimson double flowers that fade to pink. Rock soapwort (*Saponaria ocymoides*) has cascades of red, pink, or white flowers.

Scabiosa
Scabiosa columbaria
Sun or light shade

Pincushion flowers are long blooming "grandmother's garden" favorites coming back in style for borders or cut flowers.

FLOWER: Domed heads of tiny flowers surrounded with leafy bracts, with stamen protruding beyond the curved surface of the flower head, giving a "pincushion" effect. Excellent for cutting or drying. Deadheading will keep plants in bloom to frost.

PLANT: Basal rosette of large, divided or even finely cut, ferny foliage making a compact mound.

INTERESTING KINDS: 'Butterfly Blue', selected by the Perennial Plant Association as the 2000 Plant of the Year, is a heavy-flowering dwarf perennial with an amazing abundance of two-inch flowers from mid-spring until mid-fall; 'Pink Mist' is a pinkish variation. *Scabiosa caucasica* has very large flowers, grown specifically for cutting; 'Fama' has intense sky blue flowers, 'Alba' is white.

Sedum
Sedum species
Full sun or light shade

With the common name "stonecrop" you know this is one tough group of plants! They survive even in concrete cemetery urns.

FLOWER: Tight, broccoli-like heads or loose panicles of starry flowers in white, yellow, gold, red, or pink.

PLANT: Low-growing and cascading, or upright leafy kinds, all have thick, succulent stems and leaves that break easily but also root readily (even the leaves can sprout into new plants); foliage on some turns red in the winter. Sedums lose hardiness or rot if watered too much. Best in raised beds, containers, rock gardens.

INTERESTING KINDS: Three popular sedums are trailing *S. kamtschaticum*, upright showy stonecrop *S. spectabile* 'Autumn Joy', and mat-forming *S. spurium*.

Solomon's Seal
Polygonatum species
Shade

I once bought a plant just for its name: *Polygonatum odoratum* 'Variegatum'; sounded too good to pass up, and it turned out to be a real winner, spreading along my wooded back garden path.

FLOWER: In the spring, rows of dangling, bell-shaped, green or creamy-white flowers, usually in pairs, hang from sturdy but arching stems, and are followed by blue-black berries. Some types are fragrant.

PLANT: From each plant, individual stalks arise from the underground stems like large, coarse, arching "ferns" with paired leaves the entire length. The mass is very showy when planted with hostas, ferns, and other woodland plants. Leaves are oblong and deeply veined. Fall color is a fair yellow.

INTERESTING KINDS: Variegated Solomon's seal (the long name above) has creamy leaf margins. *Polygonatum biflorum* is a native species; *P. commutatum* is a woodland giant to nearly five feet tall; *P. humile* is dwarf, only six inches high.

Spiderwort
Tradescantia ohiensis
Full sun to deep shade

Native woodland perennial, somewhat difficult to get rid of, but named after England's most accomplished plant explorer, John Tradescant. And it was my horticulturist great-grandmother's favorite childhood plant memory.

FLOWER: Distinct, interesting, three-petaled blue, white, pink, or purple flowers, up to an inch and a half across, produced in small clusters atop knee-high stems. Each flowering stem has several long, dagger-like leaflets that hang down, giving a spidery effect.

PLANT: Slow-spreading, grass-like clump to a foot or more tall, sometimes with arching leaves.

INTERESTING KINDS: 'Innocence' is pure white; 'Red Cloud' nearly red; 'Bilberry Ice' pale lavender with a deeper blush; 'Zwanenberg Blue' deep blue; 'Purple Dome' purple.

Sunflower
Helianthus species
Full sun

Seeing is believing —root-hardy native sunflowers are all over the North, all fall bloomers loaded with rich wild bird seed. Best to put these tall gangly plants to the back of the border or along a fence row.

FLOWER: Daisy flowers with a very dark brown central disk edged with many long golden-yellow ray florets, one to five inches across, arranged in loose clusters atop tall, many-branched flowering stems. Not fragrant.

PLANT: Multistemmed, up to eight or more feet high, covered with narrow or divided leaves, and spreading by underground roots. It's easy to pull what you don't want.

INTERESTING KINDS: Maximilian sunflower (*Helianthus maximilianii*) gets up to eight feet tall with lance-like leaves and bright golden yellow flowers up to four inches; more compact, wider-leafed *H. × multiflorus* gets about five feet tall, with 'Flore Plena' being double-flowered; *H. × laetiflorus* is up to six feet with bright yellow flowers.

Violet
Viola odorata
Shade, sun

Lawn freaks hate violets because they spread so well. But aren't they pretty, even in the shade, and sweet smelling—and edible to boot! Some weed!

FLOWER: "Pansy" flowers up to two inches across, produced in masses on very short stems in late winter and early spring. Very fragrant, and long lasting as cut flowers. Usually deep purple-blue, but sometimes found in pink and white forms.

PLANT: Low-growing dense clump of deep green, heart-shaped or split leaves. Plants spread by somewhat aggressive stolons and seed production.

INTERESTING KINDS: Larger-flowering than the species are 'Royal Robe' (an old purple favorite) and 'Royal Elk' (purple with long stems for cutting). 'Charm' has small white flowers and 'Rosina' pink flowers.

Yarrow
Achillea species
Full sun

Yarrow is another plant I have tried to give away, without enough success. Luckily it's a good cut flower.

FLOWER: Flat, compact clusters up to four or five inches across, atop sturdy stems from two or more feet tall. Common variety is white, but cultivated forms include yellow, golden, pink, cerise, orange, and red.

PLANT: Spreading clump of ferny, fragrant, soft leaves. New growth begins to billow up in the spring, providing a convenient and attractive support for floppy daffodils.

INTERESTING KINDS: Common yarrow (*Achillea millefolium*) is hardy into Alaska; its flowers do not last as long as cut flowers, but beautiful forms to enjoy in the garden include 'Rose Beauty', red 'Colorado', and golden yellow 'Fireland'. Better for cutting are fernleaf yarrows (A. *filipendulina*), with large heads that dry well when hung upside down at full maturity, including 'Coronation Gold'. Hybrids include yellow 'Moonshine' and pink 'Appleblossom'.

Yellow Arum
Lysichiton americanus
Shade or part sun

This most unusual plant deserves greater attention because it is really the first flower of spring—usually well before spring! It is most commonly called "skunk cabbage"—technically a similar plant to which it is very closely related—for its musky odor (intended to attract pollinating insects), or "swamp lantern" for its huge yellow flower spathes. An outstanding, if unusual, addition to wet or boggy garden sites.

FLOWER: Each large golden yellow hooded spathe is nearly two feet tall, appearing with the very first leaves of the season, and containing a single rod- or club-like flower spike.

PLANT: Large, green rhubarb-like leaves persist through late summer. Gives off enough heat to melt snow—up to 70 degrees in the late winter.

INTERESTING KINDS: The true skunk cabbage (*Symplocarpus foetidus*) is much smaller with five-inch Easter-egg-looking "flowers" of mottled reddish-purple with greenish blotches.

Other Good Perennials

Balloon Flower (*Platycodon grandiflorus*) is a very showy perennial border plant, with inch-wide bell-shaped flowers that open from inflated, balloon-like buds. Very drought tolerant, blooms all summer and fall.

Barrenwort (*Epimedium* × *rubrum*) is a long-lived, airy ground cover with heart-shaped leaves on wiry stems, somewhat showy red flowers in June, and reddish fall color that persists through the winter.

Bergenia (*Bergenia cordifolia*) grows in a clump of hand-sized, heart-shaped leaves with saw-toothed or wavy margins, either glossy green with bronze fall colors, or burgundy all season. Small, bell-shaped flowers of pale pink to ruby red or dark purple are produced in compact clusters atop twelve-inch burgundy stems in the early spring.

Blue False Indigo (*Baptisia australis*) is a tall, almost coarse plant with three-leaflet leaves and tall spikes of cool-looking, but heat-tolerant blue pea-like flowers from mid-spring into summer, showy in both meadows or borders.

Boltonia (*Boltonia asteroides*) is a tall, airy native aster with many small white or pinkish flowers in late summer and fall, best as a "filler" with other fall-flowering perennials or in wildflower gardens.

Butterfly Weed (*Asclepias tuberosa*), a knee-high mass of very showy, flat-topped clusters of bright orange-red flowers followed by long pods containing feathery seeds, is an outstanding butterfly plant—especially for migrating monarchs.

Cardinal Flower (*Lobelia cardinalis*) is an outstanding native hummingbird plant with four-foot spikes of cardinal red flowers in late summer. Outstanding perennial for shaded or moist gardens.

Catmint (*Nepeta faassenii*), not to be confused with the "catnip" (*N. cataria*) favored by flower-eating felines, is a hardy, sprawling mint relative with long spikes of purplish blue flowers in late spring, and is hardy to minus 30 degrees. 'Six Hills Giant' grows up to about three feet tall; 'Dropmore' is about half that high.

Coral Bells (*Heuchera* hybrids) are excellent rock garden and edging plants, with small mounds of scalloped maple-like leaves of (depending on the cultivar) purple-bronze ('Palace Purple'), bright garnet ('Garnet'), silvery-blue ('Dale's Selection'), purplish metallic-silver ('Pewter Veil'), or near-black ('Obsidian'). All need dividing every few years.

Cranesbill (*Geranium maculatum*) is a common woodland wildflower with one- or two-inch flowers found growing in the wild with blue phlox and trillium. Very tough and adaptable, surprisingly tolerant of many soils.

Delphinium (*Delphinium elatum*) is a difficult plant, period. Don't be a sucker—stick with prairie larkspur (*D. virescens*) or baptisia.

English Lavender (*Lavandula angustifolia*) is a borderline perennial in all but the warmer areas of our region; but it is irresistible, so plant in a perfectly well-drained, dry site, and hope for snow cover to protect it from deep freezes! Plant in a rock garden, or mulch with white marble to reflect sunlight upward.

Foamflower (*Tiarella cordifolia*) is a charming native ground cover for the shade, a spreading mat of crinkled, overlapping maple-like leaves topped in the spring with ten-inch stems of airy white flowers.

Heaths and **Heathers** (*Erica* and *Calluna* species) are popular, pretty, interesting, and useful—and widely available. But these small rhododendron and blueberry relatives require well-amended, acidic soils and lots of moisture through the summer.

Ironweed (*Vernonia* species) has clumps of five- to seven-foot leafy stems with brilliant purple flowers in late summer and early fall. Outstanding butterfly native; perfect at the back of the border; wet or dry soils.

Jacob's Ladder (*Polemonium* species) is a valuable woodland plant that looks like a coarse fern, a clump of arching leaves with small leaflets arranged like a ladder. Its blue spring flowers are attractive, even showy, but the foliage of some variegated kinds ('Brise d'Anjou', 'Snow and Sapphires') is very showy in the shade.

Joe-Pye Weed (*Eupatorium purpureum*), a many-stemmed native to eight feet tall, features showy whorls of lance-shaped leaves topped with a loose cluster of dusty rose flowers in late summer. Excellent for butterflies and damp soils. 'Gateway' is only six feet tall with purplish stems and flowers.

Lady's Mantle (*Alchemilla mollis*) makes a magical foot-deep mass of scalloped, cupped, silvery foliage that holds shimmering drops of rainwater after a shower. Summer stalks of small, bright yellow star-shaped flowers glow in the shaded garden or border.

Lamb's Ears (*Stachys byzantina*) is a hardy, furry-leaf gray plant with spikes of violet or white flowers. Grows best in raised beds or large containers. Tends to rot in humidity, and has to be cleaned up at least once a year to keep it looking fresh. 'Helen von Stein' is more tolerant of heat and humidity; 'Silver Carpet' spreads rapidly. Don't let it flower unless you want lots of seedlings.

Lamium (*Lamium galeobdolon*) or yellow archangel is a ground cover for difficult dry shade. 'Variegatum' will quickly fill in (almost too quickly). Less aggressive 'Hermann's Pride' has narrower, silver-variegated leaves. Before you plant lamium, be sure you want lots of it!

Leadwort (*Cerastostigma plumbaginoides*) is a beautiful ground cover for small, sunny or lightly shaded areas, a low mat of glossy leaves half a foot deep and covered in the summer and fall with super-blue flowers on reddish bracts. Not hardy in northern areas of the region.

Lungwort (*Pulmonaria saccharata*) is a mounding, low-growing clump of dark green leaves with very interesting silvery patterns and splatters, and even nearly all silvery, with pink-changing-to-blue spring flowers. Very effective foil to woodland plants (even grows under rhododendrons!), ferns, spring bulbs, and the like. Great foliage plant.

Lupine (*Lupinus perennis*) is not a super-hardy perennial for average gardeners, but reseeds well when planted in poor, sandy, dry soil with low fertility. The late spring favorite's unmistakable spires of bright blue flowers signal the coming of summer.

Lythrum (*Lythrum virgatum*) has upright stems of pink to six feet tall. Tolerates many conditions but has become a serious pest in wetlands—even the "sterile" cultivars—and is outlawed in some states. Outstanding for butterflies, however.

Moneywort or **Creeping Jenny** (*Lysimachia nummularia*) is a low-growing, fast-spreading ground cover, invasive in moist shade, with pairs of round leaves from early spring until fall. Golden moneywort ('Aurea') takes more sun.

Oregano (*Origanum vulgare*) is a sprawling, clumpy, almost spreading culinary herb that also makes a fragrant border plant, especially the golden-leaf varieties. Very hardy and deer resistant throughout the region.

Periwinkle (*Vinca minor*) is a shade-loving ground cover with pairs of roundish, glossy evergreen leaves; its bright blue flowers are cheery in May. There are several variegated kinds; 'Illumination' is golden, edged in green.

Potentilla (*Potentilla fruticosa*) is a stemmy little shrub with tiny hand-shaped leaves and bright, clear-yellow flowers that last all summer. It requires good drainage and occasional shearing.

Rose Campion (*Lychnis coronaria*) is a low-growing rosette of dirty gray leaves that sends up a spring and summer spray of the most vivid magenta, sometimes white, starry flowers, which set prolific seed before the short-lived perennial "mother" plant dies. Usually a dependable biennial for hot, dry, well-drained garden spots. *Lychnis viscaria* 'Splendens Plena' has double red flowers.

Veronica (*Veronica spicata*), though sometimes prone to foliar diseases, provides a welcome, thick stand of spiky blue or purplish, white, or pink flowers from mid-spring through fall. Very attractive contrasting companion to clunkier flowers. *Veronica peduncularis* 'Georgia Blue' is a great, green ground cover.

Virginia Bluebells (*Mertensia* species) is either very easy, or impossible—depending on whether you have a naturally moist, woodsy area, like its native habitat throughout the Midwest and the eastern third of the United States. Its tall, nodding blue bells are inspirational on walks through the woods in the spring. Then it's dormant until next year.

Wild Ageratum or **Mist Flower** (*Eupatorium coelestinum*) is a spreading mass of many stems to two feet tall, topped in the fall with fluffy clusters of powdery blue flowers. Vigorous native spreader can be difficult to control; outstanding for butterflies and edges of naturalistic or meadow gardens. Not hardy in northern areas of the region.

Wild Ginger (*Asarum canadense*) is an outstanding native ground cover for dense shade and moist soils—it will even grow under spruce trees! Hand-sized heart- or kidney-shaped leaves are deeply veined and slightly fuzzy. *Asarum europaeum* has smaller, shiny evergreen leaves.

Landscaping for Winter Interest

See those undulating mounds in the snow? There are *supposed* to be plants underneath! During what can seem like an interminably long, wet, or frozen winter season, we often find our landscapes and gardens bare of color and texture. Here are a few ways to spice up this otherwise dreary time of year.

- Clean up the garden, generally neaten stuff up.
- Replace summer annuals as best you can with cold-tolerant kinds.
- Leave frozen winter foliage and flower stems of grasses and perennials.
- Add interesting shrubs, evergreen ground covers, and small trees with good bark or berries for winter form, texture, and color.
- Place a "hard feature"—large rock, birdbath, sculpture, urn, or a trellis, gate, or small section of fence (split rail, picket, whatever suits you).
- Plant bulbs by late October to give them time to settle in before winter.
- Group indoor potted plants near a window for a tropical touch.
- Install low-voltage night lighting to illuminate any outdoor steps for Daylight Savings Time.
- Set up a simple platform-type bird feeding station, stocked with sunflower seed.

Fast-Reference Lists for Perennials

Shaded Gardens
Ajuga
Astilbe
Bee Balm
Bleeding Heart
Cardinal Flower
False Dragonhead
Ferns
Foamflower
Forget-Me-Not
Geranium
Goutweed
Hosta
Iris
Jacob's Ladder
Moneywort
Pachysandra
Phlox
Primrose
Trillium
Violet
Virginia Bluebell
Wild Ginger

Heavy or Wet Soils
Amsonia
Astilbe
Cardinal Flower
Cattails
Ironweed
Joe-Pye Weed

Lythrum
Miscanthus
Rhubarb
Siberian Iris
Skunk Cabbage

Late Summer and Fall Flowers
Aster
Boltonia
Daylily
Four-o'-Clock
Goldenrod
Ironweed
Obedient Plant
Purple Coneflower
Saponaria

Butterfly Plants
Bee Balm
Black-Eyed Susan
Coreopsis
Goldenrod
Ironweed
Joe-Pye Weed
Liatris
Lythrum
Phlox
Purple Coneflower
Sedum
Yarrow

Best Culinary Herbs (Including Annuals)
Basil
Chives
Dill
French Tarragon
Garlic
Mint
Oregano
Parsley
Sage
Thyme

Good Cut Flowers
Aster
Astilbe
Balloon Flower
Bellflower
Bleeding Heart
Daisy
False Dragonhead
Hollyhock
Hosta
Iris
Ornamental Grasses
Phlox
Purple Coneflower
Rudbeckia
Salvia
Violet
Yarrow
most flower bulbs

Interesting (Bold or Cut-Leaf) Foliage
Artemisia
Asparagus
Astilbe
Bergenia
Bleeding Heart
Ferns
Heuchera
Hosta
Iris
Jacob's Ladder
Lamb's Ear
Lamium
Lungwort
Ornamental Grasses
Peony
Russian Sage
Sedum
Solomon's Seal
Wild Ginger
Yarrow

WILDFLOWER MEADOWS ARE MESSY-LOOKING unless you add a few "human scale" features to make them seem less wild. It is perfectly acceptable to use native wildflowers such as phlox, goldenrod, liatris, and purple coneflower in "normal" flower gardens—after all, every flower is wild somewhere! An entire formal English-style flower border, with tall plants to the back and smaller flowers to the front, can be created using only Midwestern or New England natives. Also add a section of fencing, an attractive bench, an arbor, some birdhouses, artwork, and wide mowing paths as points of reference to help visitors think you know what you are doing.

Cut Flowers Don't Have to Be Cut

If it looks good in the vase, it'll look good in the garden—whether you cut it or not. Great no-fuss cut flowers for Northern gardens include:

Annuals: *Celosia, Cleome, Coreopsis, Globe Amaranth, Black-Eyed Susan, Salvia, Sunflower, Zinnia*
Bulbs: *Gladiola, Hosta, Iris, Liatris, Lilies, Daffodils, and Snowdrops*
Perennials: *Daisy, Goldenrod, Purple Coneflower, Black-Eyed Susan, Salvia*
Ornamental Grasses: (flower stalks)
Shrubs and Trees: *Boxwood, Euonymus, Flowering Quince, Forsythia, Hydrangea, Redbud, Roses, Weigela*

Slugs, Japanese Beetles...

Whaddaya gonna do, keep hand-picking the nasty critters (a never-ending job), or continue searching for that elusive "safe" chemical control (another never-ending quest)? Many home remedies are troublesome at best, or work for one gardener, but not for another. Personally, I just ignore the pests as best I can, treating them as a major frustration but not the end of the gardening world. And I try to keep planting new stuff, trying to dilute the pests' appetites, and hope for the best.

The Plant-Society-a-Day Garden

Why does every plant society on Earth think that its favorite plant is the best of all, and treat everything else in Eden as a mere "companion?" My little cottage garden has a "plant society a day"—and you can, too.

There are roses, of course, though most of us have learned to avoid typically fussy hybrid teas. My favorites are the nonstop "gardener friendly" heirlooms like the Buck hybrids that have been growing in the North for half a century, in just plain dirt, from way below zero to being hot and humid and dry for months on end. America's Floral Emblem isn't difficult to grow if you choose easy kinds.

Iris come in every color of the rainbow, but the most commonly grown is the old-timey white "flag," introduced to America early in the 1600s as "orris root" (its rhizomes were used as an herbal fixative). And when my friend Russell Studebaker, horticulturist from Tulsa, Oklahoma, wrote to me after coming across a very old blue iris that blooms a month before the regular bearded kinds, he mentioned that he "asked all the local iris growers about it, but they didn't have a clue. They have their noses too deep in those pumped up hybrids that look like overdeveloped female body-builders—you know, those that have the bulges and curves in all the wrong places . . . " That old iris, by the way, *Iris × germanica*, grown since before the 1750s, is the same one painted by Van Gogh in his *Iris*. It's been a toughie for a long, long time.

And I have many dozens of my great-grandmother's favorite daffodils that are still flowering after thirty years of neglect. By late spring my daylilies are loaded with fat buds atop sturdy scapes. I have a few hybrids from special friends, and really admire the long-blooming 'Stella d'Oro' miniature. Still, in spite of its lack of fashion, my favorite is the old double orange variety *kwanso*, grown for thousands of years now, and still tough enough for me, you, anybody, anywhere, with absolutely no demands. None.

I plant hostas around the daffodils so I won't have summer-bare spots, and my herbs, which, though I do cook with fresh basil, garlic, fennel, rosemary, and mint, are mostly used as "just good plants" with perennials.

Let's see, that's six plant societies represented: rose, iris, daffodil, daylily, hosta, and herbs. Throw in wildflowers (coreopsis, henbit, black-eyed Susan, purple coneflower, phlox, goldenrod, and on and on, providing beauty and food for wildlife through every season), and my garden has enough for a plant society a day.

Then there are societies for hibiscus, dahlia, African violet, sedum, lilac, lily, chrysanthemum, peony, hydrangea, rhododendron, fern, begonia, azalea, clematis, ivy, bamboo, conifer, gladiola, nut growers, and gourds (yes, there's even one for them). And more. All of which I grow.

If we'd start a Compost Club, and a Faded Poinsettia Society—there's gotta be millions of honorary members—and a Friends of Half-Hardy Plants (motto: Good Luck!), I'd be covered. The goal: a plant society a week. Better yet, a Companion Plant Coalition!

Potted
PLANTS

Most of us learned at an early age how to grow simple plants in pots, from the first time a teacher showed us how to put a bean seed in a milk carton. We learned to give it a little sunshine, some water when it got dry, and a little "plant food" to help it grow.

Then it usually died, which set us up for expecting failure with adult plants, from poinsettias and African violets given to us as gifts, to floppy paper-white narcissus, to all those macramé hanger plants that were such a craze in the 1960s and 1970s. And when we or a family member came home from the hospital with one of those mixed pots of baby tropical plants— usually a heart-leaf philodendron, a small palm, a mother-in-law's tongue, and a prayer plant—the prayer plant quickly gave up the ghost.

Then without realizing it, we began learning about tough plants, because that mother-in-law's tongue (known botanically as *Sansevieria*) survived, and the heart-leaf philodendron vine began spreading all around the window. Those simple plants taught us that some potted creatures actually thrive in the low-light, low-humidity, cool-temperature spaceship environments we call home.

This chapter highlights some of the toughest, easiest to grow, longest-lived potted plants found across the North in homes of the rich and the poor, the horticulturally literate and the ungifted non-green-thumbers. They are seen in airports, malls, and offices and on country cottage front porches growing in a huge array of pots, including china vases and old paint buckets.

Environmental Needs

Location, location, location! Most of these potted plants are tropical in origin and can thrive if provided three basic conditions: good light, humidity, and protection from freezing.

Light requirements range from direct sunshine through a clear window to low light that is still easy to read by. No need to get technical—just remember that while some plants will survive for months in very dim areas, most do best either right in or right beside a bright window.

Humidity is not as important for these plants as for, say, ferns or African violets or orchids. At the very least, make sure the plants are not kept in the direct draft from an air conditioner or heater, both of which pull water from the leaves of plants more quickly than they can replace it via roots and stems. Cluster plants close together to create a humid "microclimate." Setting them on trays filled with pebbles and water helps in winter, when the air indoors can get very dry.

Temperature is not as crucial for this selection of plants. Though they prefer the same temperatures we do, they will tolerate down to 30 degrees Fahrenheit for a few hours at a time.

Cultural Needs

Good location aside, how you take care of your plants can determine the difference between their thriving and merely surviving. Water, fertilizer, and occasional repotting are about all these selections need, though an occasional bout of pests may need to be dealt with.

Watering "as needed" is the best approach. Too wet is worse than too dry. To know when plants need watering, stick your finger in the potting soil or lift the pot to check for weight. Never water just on a regular schedule, because variations in environmental conditions, plant type, pot size, potting soil type, and the amount of fertilizer used will cause plants to grow at different rates and need water in varying amounts.

Fertilizer is plant food, and most of these plants need very little at a time. Some can grow for years on just water alone—but that's being abusive. My rule of thumb is to use a good timed-release fertilizer (the long-lasting fertilizer beads) once in the spring, then occasionally hit the plants with a light shot of liquid plant food containing "trace minerals" (iron, zinc, calcium,

Best for Beginners:

- *Airplane Plant*
- *Asparagus Fern*
- *Chinese Evergreen*
- *Devil's Backbone*
- *Heart-Leaf Philodendron*
- *Rubber Tree*
- *Snake Plant*

Kinda Tricky:

- *African Violets*
- *Boston Fern*
- *Bromeliads*
- *Jade*
- *Kalanchoe*
- *Orchids*
- *Palms*
- *Prayer Plant*
- *Weeping Fig*

and so on, which are listed on the side of the container).

Always use plant foods at half the recommended strength—the directions on the containers indicate the absolute highest application amounts the manufacturer can legally get away with, which is simply not necessary for good plant growth. Really. Overfeeding causes many problems.

Repotting should be done when plants have been in the same worn-out potting soil for years or when the plant has gotten too big for its pot.

Pests, including spider mites, mealy bugs, and scale insects, can be annoying, but can usually be controlled by pruning out the infested leaves and spraying with insecticidal soap or misting three or four times with a fifty-fifty alcohol and water spray.

Asparagus Fern

Asparagus densiflorus
Full sun to moderate shade

One of the hardiest, most drought-tolerant potted plants around, this "false fern" is a member of the lily family, closely related to edible asparagus. Though its long cascading "fronds" make it an ideal companion to other tropical plants, it is mostly grown as a hanging basket or pillar plant.

Tiny, needle-like leaflets give the arching stems a light green billowy effect. Occasionally, this plant produces small white flowers and a few scattered red berries. Its roots form hard white tubers, which help the plant get through long periods of drought, but most gardeners cut them off during repotting because they just take up potting soil and root space.

Of the more than three hundred members of the *Asparagus* genus, the most commonly grown potted plant asparagus fern is 'Myersii' or foxtail fern, in the Sprengeri group, which produces many dense, nearly cylindrical spikes of darker green leaves. Asparagus ferns will have greenest foliage in part shade and will tolerate light frosts if left out too long in the fall. They can also make interesting summer ground covers outdoors.

Begonia

Begonia species and cultivars
Bright indirect to moderate light

There are too many kinds of begonias to go into here, but the most common ones seen on windowsills around the North are the cane-type "angel wing" kinds, grown as much for their foliage as their flowers. I have an old friend whose mother roots them in water and shares them with all her children, friends, grandkids, and anyone else who wanders by.

Angel-wing begonias have multiple upright stems, each up to four or five feet tall, with bamboo-like joints sporting pairs of leaves shaped, well, like angel wings, with rounded "shoulders" tapering to points. Leaves are sometimes glossy green, often with light tan or pale pink spots. Flowers are produced in large clusters and range from pure white to medium red, with some pinks and oranges. Long, heavy stems can break, or be pruned, with new flowering stems produced from lower leaf joints; stem cuttings root readily for starting new plants.

Interesting varieties include pink-flowering, large-leaf 'Dragon Wing', which tolerates full sun (with water), and 'Irene Nuss', which has red-and-green leaves and huge clusters of coral pink flowers.

Chinese Evergreen

Aglaonema species

Medium to low light

Expect to find Chinese evergreen thriving in offices and airports where all other plants have slowly wasted away in the low light and low humidity. And expect every single cutting you take to root, even in just water; I have had rooted cuttings live in the same jar of water for years.

Small, canna-like plants usually have several sturdy upright stems; old clumps can easily have dozens of stems, forming a large basketful of foliage that spills over the edges of pots. Each stem is topped with narrow, sword-like leaves up to a foot or more long and four or five inches wide. Each leaf is smooth and glossy (which enables it to tolerate low humidity) and is usually variegated; 'Silver King' and 'Silver Queen' are two popular old variegated varieties of *Aglaonema nitidum*. Flowers look like small greenish white callas, sometimes ornamental but most often hidden in foliage.

Chinese evergreens make superb specimens in ornate pots, or can be used in smaller pots placed on top of the potting soil of larger plants for a ground cover effect. Water only when very dry.

Croton

Codiaeum variegatum

Full sun—the more the better

Go to the tropics, and find this African native beside nearly every doorstep, in the hottest, sunniest part of the yard. In our own temperate-climate homes, put it in a south or west window and leave it there for years, with only an occasional pruning to thicken it up with new leaves and stems.

The wavy, foot-long, leathery leaves, which can be wide like a rubber tree or very narrow and curly, are glossy and splashed in every imaginable combination of green, yellow, orange, pink, purple, red, and bronze—the more sun it gets, the more color it has. It grows best in a sunny greenhouse where humidity is high, but needs to be kept out of air conditioner or heater drafts indoors or placed between larger plants and a window where a humid microclimate is often found. Mealy bugs may be a problem but can be killed with three or four mild alcohol-water mistings a few days apart.

Plants with similar foliage effects include "sun" coleus and copperleaf (*Acalypha wilkesiana*).

Devil's Backbone
Pedilanthus tithymaloides ssp. *smallii*
Full sun to light shade

In the tropics, this densely stemmed tropical shrub is grown even in cemeteries—and can reach waist high or taller, and three feet across. Sometimes called "red bird cactus" because its red flowers resemble birds in silhouette, this milky-sap succulent is most famous for its crooked stems, which zigzag at each leaf joint. Because of its extreme tolerance of neglect, devil's backbone is one of the most difficult potted plants to kill—except with kindness, or freezing.

The most common forms have plain green leaves, pointed ovals produced singly at each leaf joint. But quite a few selections feature green-and-white variegated foliage, which often turns bright pink when the plant is grown in a full-sun window.

A stem piece can root easily even if left on a table top for months until it almost shrivels to nothing; in fact, most succulents actually root better if they are allowed to dry a few days after cutting, to give the cut stem a chance to heal over to prevent rotting in moist potting soils.

Dracaena
Dracaena species
Bright to moderately low light

No office would be complete without a "corn plant" or "dragon tree." From the time they were first hauled out of African jungles, several kinds of dracaena (dra-SEEN-ah) have been among the most popular potted plants, because they can be pruned to thicken back when they thin out from low light and low humidity. All are extremely easy to root from stem cuttings in moist potting soil.

The common corn plant (*Dracaena fragrans*) is often sold as tiered, multiple-stemmed specimens, with each stem up to three inches in diameter and topped with a large whorl of long, curving-downward leaves, each up to three feet long and four inches wide. 'Massangeana' is just one of several cultivars with a broad yellow stripe down the center of each leaf. When a corn plant produces an airy panicle of flowers—rare indoors, but it happens—its intensely sweet fragrance can run people out of the house.

Madagascar dragon tree (*D. marginata, D. cincta,* or *D. concinna*) has much thinner stems, long and twisting or arching, and many thin leaves up to two feet long but only a half-inch or so wide, usually with a narrow margin of purplish red. 'Tricolor' has gold stripes in addition to the red and green. Ribbon dracaena (*D. sanderiana*) is a small white-variegated dracaena with whorls of six- to eight-inch, knife-like leaves, often sold as terrarium or even aquarium plants. The popular "Chinese good luck bamboo" is simply a ribbon dracaena leaned at different angles during production, which produces a twisted or spiral stem.

Dumb Cane
Dieffenbachia species
Bright to medium light, tolerates low light

Know someone who talks too much? *Dieffenbachia* (dee-fen-BACH-e-uh) is the plant for him. Well, not really—swallowing even a small amount of the plant's sap, even accidentally while chewing a fingernail after handling the plant, can paralyze the voice box, leaving a person unable to talk for hours—which is painful and not a nice thing to do.

These striking, upright plants have thick stems topped by wide, pointed, canna-like leaves up to three feet long and a foot wide. Most common varieties have striking white, yellow, chartreuse, or cream variegation, from pale speckles against a dark green background to broad stripes and nearly solid white spots covering most of the leaf. Small pots usually are stuffed with several plants, giving a multiple-stem effect, and can be divided into individual plants, sometimes just one, two, or three to a pot for more "elbow room." Tall plants can easily be cut back severely—to just a few inches tall—to force strong new growth near the base; the cut-off portions are easily rooted.

Moving dumb cane suddenly to bright light can cause leaf scorching, but the new leaves produced will adjust to the growing conditions. Overwatering is worse than prolonged drought.

Dwarf Schefflera
Schefflera arboricola
Bright to moderately low light

This tidy little indoor shrub, much tougher than the large schefflera, has leathery, deep green, hand-sized, many-fingered leaves, and is as durable as indoor plants can be. A law school classmate of my wife's bought one at a parking lot "truckload" sale and did everything in his

power to kill it, before leaving it with us when he moved back to Wisconsin. Since then I have rooted several branches in water and given them away. It tends to get branchy and quite leggy in low light, but pruning thickens it right back up.

Sometimes grown as several plants in one pot with braided trunks, variegated kinds on the market include 'Gold Capella', which has deep green, shiny oval leaves with contrasting intensely yellow variegation.

Schdeffleras are very tolerant of a wide range of growing conditions, even down to near-freezing or over a hundred degrees. However, a well-drained potting soil is a plus, because overwatering may cause roots to rot in low-oxygen conditions, especially in the winter or in dark areas where plants don't dry out as quickly.

Moses in the Boat or Moses in His Cradle
Tradescantia spathacea
Full sun to moderately low light

This purplish burgundy clump-former is so drought tolerant and low care that it's often seen planted on graves or as edging in the tropics. It gets its name from the boat-like flower bracts stuffed with small, three-petaled flowers. This old, old heirloom "pass-along" plant is grown in a huge variety of containers, and must be brought indoors during freezing weather.

Each short stem, up to six or eight inches tall and usually produced in bunches, is covered with a whorl of sword-shaped leaves up to six or eight inches long. Most are solid green on the top, with a maroon or burgundy underside; 'Vittata' ('Variegata') is reddish with yellowish green stripes. It tolerates very low humidity, high or low light intensities, and extended drought, making it a very tough plant that can survive the neglect of a variety of gardeners.

Moses in the boat can be used as a small potted specimen, ground cover under larger potted plants, or outdoors as summer edging. Propagate by carefully prying or cutting loose individual stems from the "mother clump" and repotting.

Night Blooming Cereus
Selenicereus grandiflorus and other species
Very bright to moderate light

Even though this cactus relative is one of the ugliest things ever put into a pot, the old "pass-along" plant has been shared for many generations, partly because it simply won't die. Many gardeners have memories of sitting up late at night to wait—hopefully—for it to come into flower. If you miss it, it's gone—the flowers are limp and wasted by early morning.

Several species have cylindrical or angular stems, but the most popular has a cascading mess of long, flat, leathery, serrated leaves, each producing more scraggly leaves in an almost random pattern. The plant is durable—surviving conditions ranging from broiling in a hot window to gathering dust in dim corners—and roots easily from leaf cuttings stuck directly into potting soil.

Its fat, pointed flower buds, produced on long, supple stems from serrated leaf tips after a period of drought (or neglect), open slowly at night into fist-sized trumpets of narrow petals, many protruding stamens, and an interesting spidery pistil. It is usually fragrant in a thin sort of way, not heavy or musky like other tropical night-bloomers. One of mine had nearly two dozen flowers open at one time (I have a faded photo to prove it), but most flower just one or two at a time.

Peace Lily
Spathiphyllum species
Moderate to deep shade

The large, dark leaves and pure white flowers of this extremely shade-tolerant calla lily relative cause it to be nearly overused as an indoor plant. It is everywhere, especially in airports, malls, and office buildings, and will even fill the void of a summer-dormant fireplace hearth. It will "talk" to you by wilting when it needs watering. One thing it will not tolerate is hot sun, so always make sure it is only near, not in, a south or west window.

A typical peace lily plant has several dozen leaves that arise directly from the soil, each a broad sword of extremely deep green on a stiff stalk. Each flower, produced on an individual stem at or above the top of the foliage canopy, is a white, leaf-like spathe partially cupped around a central flower spadix.

It is a favorite gift plant, but should in every case be repotted when received; because its commercial production involves lots of greenhouse watering, growers use a potting soil that drains too quickly for convenience to home gardeners. For continuous new growth of both foliage and flowers, fertilize lightly every few waterings.

Pencil Cactus
Euphorbia tirucalli
Full sun to bright light

This plant is sometimes called "milk bush" because of its thick shrubby growth and milky sap. So many gardeners have gotten their "start" of this tall, twiggy oddity from other gardeners that it may be the most passed-around potted plant in the country. Not a cactus at all (it's in the same milky sap family as the popular poinsettia), it is named for its thin, cylindrical stems, which look like lots of green pencils stacked end to end. The green stems are thornless and usually leafless; the leaves are tiny green things that last only a short while, hardly noticeable, and the stems have enough chlorophyll to keep the plants going with no foliage at all.

Like its close relative crown of thorns and other members of the *Euphorbia* genus, pencil cactus must be allowed to dry completely between soakings or its thick stems will rot. Also, like its milky-sap cousins, its sap can irritate the skin of some gardeners and even cause severe eye irritation, so be sure to wash your hands after cutting on the plant, especially when making lots of cuttings to root in a well-drained potting soil.

Philodendron
Philodendron species
Bright to medium light

Grown for their glossy leaves, this diverse but durable genus of tropical vines and sub-shrubs are among the most common houseplants in the country. Many are survivors from a "hospital basket" of mixed plants and are kept alive for decades on little more than an occasional watering. I have one rooted in a cola bottle of water, left over from my son's hospital birth back in 1986!

Very few gardeners ever see a philodendron flower, which is a creamy white, calla-like spathe hidden within the foliage canopy. The foliage is glossy, slick (almost rubbery), and durable even in low humidity. Most grow best in bright but indirect light.

Split-leaf philodendron (*Philodendron bipinnatifidum*) has huge, elephant-ear leaves, deeply divided almost to the midrib, produced from a stocky, shrub-like trunk with incredibly strong aerial roots used for support. It and a near relative (*Monstera deliciosa*, which often has holes in the leaves like Swiss cheese) can reach six or eight feet tall and nearly as wide, with leaves up to three feet long. 'Xanadu' is a super-tough "dwarf" form used in mass plantings or as a potted specimen for low-light, low-humidity, breezy spots.

Heart-leaf philodendron (*P. scandens*) and spade-leaf philodendron (*P. domesticum*) are fast-growing vines that attach to supports with smaller aerial roots. Their leaves are glossy and deep green, and the vines can wrap around an entire kitchen window from a small pot on the sink. 'Royal Queen' is a spade-leaf with deep red foliage. Many other cultivars are available.

Pothos or Devil's Ivy
Epipremnum aureum
Bright to medium light

As the strikingly bright, long-lasting foliage of the pothos vine climbs or cascades, it creates a tropical contrast that you'd expect to see in a real jungle. This plant often outlives its gardener, moving from one generation to another by stem cuttings.

The rarely flowering vine has a tough, stiff stem that wraps and attaches with stubby aerial roots. Depending on the amount of humidity and care, its thick, glossy green leaves, usually splashed or marbled with large yellow blotches, can easily surpass a foot or more long and more than half that wide, with mature leaves sometimes deeply cut. The yellow is more pronounced in bright light.

It is best used as a hanging basket plant, as a climber or cascading "trailer" planted with a taller plant, or even as a summer ground cover at the base of landscape trees, in sun or shade.

Relatives include heart-leaf philodendron (*Philodendron scandens*) and arrowhead vine (*Syngonium podophyllum*).

Rubber Tree

Ficus elastica

Full sun to moderate light

I have had a rubber tree, which I named "Big Jim," since the mid-1970s. It has survived many moves before, during, and after my college years and gets watered maybe ten or twelve times a year, fed once a year, and pruned back to bare trunks whenever it gets too big. And it just keeps on growing. Its sticky, milky sap, which can irritate eyes, is what rubber is made from.

Pruning these usually single-trunked trees forces new stems to come out right at the cut, which thickens the plants into indoor shrubs of broad, thick, foot-long leaves of green, sometimes variegated or tinged with red. New growth is usually sheathed in a red covering that quickly sheds.

Unlike its cousin the weeping fig (*Ficus benjamina*), which is fairly tough but drops its leaves at the slightest provocation (even turning it halfway around to get more light), rubber trees tolerate lower light and humidity than any other indoor potted tree. Interesting relatives include fiddle-leaf fig (*F. lyrata*), creeping fig (*F. pumila*), and the edible fig (*F. carica*).

Snake Plant or Mother-in-Law's Tongue

Sansevieria trifasciata

Very bright light to very low light

Talk about tough—this succulent from Africa can grow in an ashtray on top of the TV! And can go months without water—really! I have collected many different kinds of *Sansevieria* (sans-see-VAIR-ee-uh); some are still alive after minimal care for over thirty years, in the same pots. I even have one that my grandmother grew in a big paint bucket lined on the outside with aluminum cooking foil.

The plants thrive in moderate light, but tolerate full sun or dark corners, as long as they are not overwatered. Rhizome-like runner stems can be divided, and you can even cut leaves into small pieces, which root to form new plants.

Common cultivars include variegated ('Laurentii') and dwarf ('Hahnii'), but many more species and varieties are available from collectors and through Internet companies, including kinds with long, pointed, carrot-like cylindrical leaves, and some with wide leaf blades that look like beaver tails.

Spider Plant or Airplane Plant
Chlorophytum comosum
Nearly full sun to moderately low light

One of the most popular hanging basket plants, from Africa, spider plant grows as a sprawling clump of long, narrow, arching, grass-like leaves, either solid green or variegated. It sends out two- or three-foot flowering stems, also arching up and then back downward, covered with half-inch white flowers and ending in miniature plantlets, each of which can be cut off and quickly rooted into a new plant. 'Variegatum' and 'Vittatum' have broad white stripes on leaves and plantlets.

Spider plants can be used as fast-multiplying hanging baskets, ground covers in other potted plants or in shaded summer flower beds, and as easy "give-aways" to get kids started on gardening. They are often combined with other contrasting plants such as ornamental sweet potatoes and impatiens. The plants need repotting every couple of years or so, during which they can be divided into more plants. Slice off the starchy tuber-like root appendages, which simply take up potting soil space.

Other Good Potted Plants

African Violet (*Saintpaulia ionantha*) - Popular flowering plant with many thousands of cultivars and even its own plant society; easily grown in medium light with high humidity.

Aluminum Plant (*Peperomia obtusifolia*) - Many-branched foliage plant with crinkled variegated leaves; best used under other plants for shared humidity.

Arrowhead Vine (*Syngonium podophyllum*) - Philodendron-like vine with narrow, arrowhead-shaped leaves, usually variegated. Tolerates very low light.

Aucuba (*Aucuba japonica*) - Medium shrub with croton-like variegated leaves.

Bird of Paradise (*Strelitzia reginae*) - Clump of many upright canna-like leaves, with fantastic orange and purple flowers; needs bright light and root-bound conditions to flower.

Boston Fern (*Nephrolepis exaltata*) - One of many popular ferns, requires medium light and protection from heaters and air conditions that dry them out too quickly.

Burn Plant (*Aloe vera*) - Old standard potted plant with several "fans" of narrow, slightly toothed succulent leaves (sap is a good salve for cuts and burns). May flower in bright light.

Burro's Tail (*Sedum morganianum*) - Long, hanging stems covered with overlapping, thick, gray-green leaves.

Calamondin Orange (× *Citrofortunella microcarpa*) - One of several small potted citrus plants that do best in very bright light indoors. Fragrant flowers, edible fruit. Scale insects may be a problem.

Cast Iron Plant (*Aspidistra elatior*) - Normally used outdoors in the South, but also a very good indoor potted plant for low-light areas.

Crown of Thorns (*Euphorbia milii* var. *splendens*) - Multiple-stemmed upright shrub with thorny stems and milky sap, topped with bright red, pink, or white flowers.

Fatsia (*Fatsia japonica*) - Coarse-leaved evergreen shrub.

Fiddle-Leaf Fig (*Ficus lyrata*) - Large indoor tree with huge leaves, up to two feet long and half as wide, with prominent veins. Same family and genus as rubber tree.

Grape Ivy (*Cissus rhombifolia*) - Vining plant with grape-leaf-like leaves, usually grown as a hanging basket.

Holly Fern (*Cyrtomium falcatum*) - Large leaflets give a holly-leaf effect, very good for both outdoors in the shade, or low light indoors.

Ivy (*Hedera helix* cultivars) - Outdoor plant with many cultivars, including forms with small or large leaves, green or variegated; can be trained and pruned onto wire forms.

Jade Plant (*Crassula ovata*) - Thick, shrubby plant with fat succulent leaves on stubby stems. Very easy to root from leaves. Prefers dry conditions to avoid root or stem rot.

Kentia Palm (*Howea forsteriana*) - One of several popular indoor palms, which tolerate medium light. Low humidity and spider mites are often problems.

Norfolk Island Pine (*Araucaria heterophylla*) - Large tropical tree with needle-like leaves on whorls of stems every few inches up the very straight trunk. Needs bright light; often outgrows its space.

Rex Begonia (*Begonia rex*) - Begonia with many variations in leaf colors and patterns, usually densely hairy and showy. Easy to root leaves in water; requires humidity and medium light. Avoid getting water on the leaves.

Sago Palm (*Cycas revoluta*) - "Birds nest" growth habit, many dark green fronds arise at one time from around a thick, stubby "trunk." Does best in very bright light.

Ti Plant (*Cordyline terminalis*) - Dracaena relative with narrow stems and brilliantly colored, pink, magenta, or orange variegation. Easy to root.

Umbrella Tree (*Schefflera actinophylla*) - One to many trunks topped with large leaves of many oval leaflets. A large indoor tree that can remain in the same pot for years, with pruning for size control.

Wax Plant (*Hoya carnosa*) - Cascading or climbing vine with thick, oval leaves, often curled or variegated, with clusters of flowers that look like they are made of wax. Tolerates drought and low humidity.

Zebra Plant (*Aphelandra squarrosa*) - Upright small shrub with many stems of striking variegated leaves, topped with exotic yellow flowers. Requires high humidity.

Felder's Personal Potting Soil Recipe

I researched various potting soil mixes in college and came up with my all-purpose blend that holds up a long time, keeps plants upright in the pots, stays moist without staying wet, and holds nutrients so they don't wash out too quickly. It is easy to make and inexpensive; I mix it on the driveway and store it in a plastic garbage can.

Ingredients: One part cheap potting soil and one part finely ground pine bark mulch. That's it. The bark allows good water and air penetration; the potting soil holds moisture and nutrients. Sometimes I put a few rocks in the bottom of the pots to help keep top-heavy plants from tipping over.

Dumpster Divers Unite!

Someone said that a "rose is a rose, is a rose…"

The same holds true with flower pots. Whether your garden is formal like Versailles, where everything, including antique pottery, matches *just so*, or a funky cottage garden with "mismatch" being the only standard—*plants really don't care* what type of container they grow in, as long as it has drainage and they get watered now and then.

Don't believe me? Drive around town and see for yourself. In addition to fake classical and real Victorian urns, you'll find lots of plastic pots in natural and unnatural tones, clay pots that are cracked and flaked but still functional, and concrete monstrosities all around the courthouse downtown, all sporting the same kinds of plants.

Look carefully, and you'll also discover beautiful combinations of plants growing in wash pans, metal cans, trash bins, wooden boxes, bathtubs, even

Scott Kunst Victorian Urn, Ann Arbor, Michigan

toilets; don't smirk, they are in every town I have visited! My grandmother grew stuff in big plastic paint buckets, sometimes with used aluminum foil crinkled around the outside "for looks."

What really gets me, is the holier-than-thou attitude towards certain kinds of planters. It really bothers me that gardeners cheerfully admit admiring planters made from recycled whiskey barrels, which are expensive in the first place, then last maybe three or four years before falling apart. Then the same folks turn up their noses at those of us who recycle a more durable, common material: car tires.

An English landscape artist named Ian Finley once said "Better truth to intellect, than truth to materials." In other words, get off your high horse—if a recycled whiskey barrel is okay to plant in, then so is a tire. An artist would just call it an "alternate medium."

The simplest concept for "arranging" flowers in a container garden—or even in a cut-flower vase—uses the florist terms "line, mass, and filler." This translates into having something spiky, something roundy, and something frilly. For a large potted plant, adding something "floppy" to cascade down one side helps tone down the overall design. Use these guidelines, and people will think you know what you're doing.

While some plants do double-duty (hosta, canna, coleus, and ornamental grasses have a roundy leaf effect but with spiky flowers), good examples of *spikey* plants include iris, snapdragon, gladiola, lythrum, salvia, liriope, and larkspur; *roundy* plants include begonia, geranium, caladium, pansy, small roses, zinnia, boxwood, polka dot plant, and basil; *frilly* plants include parsley, gomphrena, yarrow (foliage), asters, asparagus fern, violas, marigold, and cosmos; *floppy* plants include moss rose, petunia, wintercreeper euonymus, ivy, golden moneywort, oregano, ajuga, and sweet potato.

Include one or more plants from each group, make seasonal changes as needed, and you'll be well on your way to a nice design that everyone will love!

Just for fun, I asked a knowledgeable group of folks, called the Herb Thymers of Mercer and Grove City, Pennsylvania, to take a challenge. I showed member Terry Conner (who wrote the foreword to this book) how to make a planter out of a tire, and he then made one for each of six very diverse members of the group, and they all planted them with only these guidelines: Paint the tire however you want, but remember my rule of thumb—plant something spikey, something roundy, something frilly, and something floppy.

ON THE FACING PAGE: *Top:* Herb Thymers; tire planters by *Left:* Cyndi Burk; *Center:* Deb Miller; *Right:* Elaine Timulak

ON THIS PAGE:
Upper Left: Michele English; *Upper Right:* Karen Fors; *Lower Left:* Maureen Conner; *Lower Right:* Terry Conner

The result—no two are alike, and all are filled with cool plants. Imagine each combination in an urn, or a whiskey barrel, and see if it really makes a difference what kind of container is used.

The Herb Thymers members were surprised to find themselves agreeing that it really does not matter, because in the end, to their flowers, a pot is a pot, is a pot—regardless of its pedigree.

Keep Your Tropics

I couldn't quite put my finger on what was uncomfortable about my latest trips to South America and Africa. It wasn't the spider I watched eating a bird, or the bat that fluttered onto my bed. Or the killer bees, the alligators in the canal next to my guest home, the piranhas in the creeks, or the ten-foot, volcano-looking termite hills, or how people normally eat lizards and rats. It wasn't even the lukewarm beer.

And it certainly wasn't the banana and papaya trees—loaded with ripe fruit—in one friend's backyard, mere feet from two coconut palms from which I drank fresh milk from the fallen coconuts. Heck, who can complain about a pineapple growing in the front yard?

Picture this: bougainvilleas the size of a garage, two-story hibiscus, and miles of canals lined with elephant's ear, sugar cane, snake plant, wild "candlestick" plants, and flowering lotus. Fragrant frangipanis, towering Norfolk Island pines, and rubber trees dripping with bromeliads and orchids, wrapped in climbing philodendrons. Poinsettias ten feet tall and wide, in full bloom.

I sincerely enjoyed hundreds of beautiful gardens planted with gusto, often lined with planters made of tires, practical in a flood-prone land where water from the Amazon Basin stands for months on end, and where clay pots are an expensive premium. The gardens made up for the rest.

But I was still bothered—a lot—by the lack of a weather change. There are no seasons on the equator, no planting dates. Spring, summer, fall, and winter roll one after another, with nary a hint of change in the air. You want to plant okra in December? No problem. Want to eat tomatoes fifty-two weeks out of the year? Ho hum.

Forget the lack of window screens, and having to sleep under mosquito nets, slathered with Deet. And don't worry if that bat is a vampire, which is common in those parts. What I wanted was a cool breeze to let me know it's time to slow down. I needed to see daffodils, which won't flower without winter's chill. Give me brilliant red and yellow fall colors, which signal a dormant rest ahead.

Tropical climes can keep their bananas. Give me seasons, so I can mark time, and to help me grow daffodils.

STEADFAST
Shrubs

Want to really have a low-maintenance landscape that looks good every month of the year? Your choice of hardy "woody" plants—and how they are planted that very first time—can make or break the landscape.

Shrubs, vines, and trees create the basic framework around which other flowers revolve. They are the "bones" of the garden, providing year-round focal points, lines, hedges, masses, and security. Plus, when compared with annuals and perennials, and especially the lawn, these long-lived plants are generally as close to low maintenance as anything.

The ones described here are beautiful, useful, and tough enough for our soils and climate, and give a special "sense of place" unique to any other place on earth. Many other good plant choices are out there, but these keep rising to the top of the heap for durability and beauty—and include even some of the "edgier" ones that many garden designers once turned away from as old-fashioned or common.

This chapter, like the rest of the book, is packed with an unusual selection. After many years of poking around small towns—including back alleys between streets—and driving around with area horticulturists and local Master Gardeners, I think I've spent almost as much time backing up to take second looks as going forward, leaping out of my jeep or truck to yak with surprised gardeners and take photographs, and occasionally even help move or plant something. I've dug around in old compost piles, taken cuttings to root, and turned leaves over to look at weird bugs. In short, I think I have come to

London, Ontario

TO SHEAR OR NOT TO SHEAR, which removes stem tips only, is a question facing many gardeners, whose evergreen shrubs get tall and "leggy" and grow up over the window ledges. Rule of thumb: The more you cut, the more compact and dense the new growth will get. Yew, boxwoods, hollies, privet, and other hedge or foundation plants should be sheared in the spring or early summer for new growth to have time to "harden off" before winter. Avoid shearing spring-flowering shrubs in late summer, fall, or winter—or lose the next year's flowers!

know tough shrubs for the North. Plus, I have run every one of these plants by old friends who are well-known garden experts and authors, from Iowa to Massachusetts, who have signed off on them all.

Planting Shrubs

The secrets to success with new shrubs, which I have used for many years, are iron clad:

- Choose good plants (that's what this book is about).
- Place them in appropriate conditions (sun or shade, and no standing water).
- Dig a wide, raggedy hole, keeping the dirt that came out of it (if the hole is smooth-sided it will hold water like a bucket—shrubs need drainage).
- Loosen the roots of container-grown shrubs and plant at the same depth they originally grew.
- Fill around the roots with mostly original soil. Note: Amending your soil with organic stuff (compost, bark, whatever) means *adding to*, not *replacing*, native soil.
- Cover the planted area with mulch, feed lightly, and provide only occasional deep soakings.
- If the plants suffer or die from weather, diseases, or pests, *plant something else* in that hole!

That's what I do, over and over, sometimes with individual plants, sometimes with entire beds. But these simple steps, without overdoing anything, get

plants established well so they can survive—even thrive—for decades with little or no attention. Really.

Want to do more in your garden? *Go for it*—but there is no need to go to extremes or "bite off more than you can chew." Think of your neighbor's grandmother or retired uncle, and how they would do it: nice and easy, with a long-term view. That's the ticket!

Winter Interest

Keeping in mind the ideal textural combination of "spiky, roundy, and frilly," you can create an interesting winter landscape by combining several kinds of shrubs and trees for contrasting forms and foliage. My favorites include the bright green, teardrop-shaped dwarf arborvitae contrasted perfectly with the burgundy foliage of barberry; throw in a soft-tip yucca, and an airy, tree-form rose of Sharon with its dried seed pods, underplant it all with a ground-cover spreading yew, and you've got an eye-catching combo! Go to a garden center and mix and match hardy shrubs, right on the lot, until you find your own combination of shapes, sizes, colors, and textures.

Corkscrew plants with gnarly, twisted trunks are often used as novelty accents, most effectively when placed against a backdrop of solid green evergreens, or against a building or fence. They can easily be highlighted with underplantings of dwarf spring-flowering bulbs such as grape hyacinth and 'Tête-à-Tête' daffodils. Very long-lived, small to medium-sized flower bed shrubs with contorted trunks and stems include corkscrew hazel (*Corylus avellana* 'Contorta', sometimes called Harry Lauder's walking stick after an old Vaudeville entertainer) and corkscrew flowering quince (*Chaenomeles* 'Contorta', with white or pink late winter flowers).

There are also shrubs that provide the surprising element of scent during the winter. Mid-winter delight: Driving slowly around an old part of town on a moderately warm day, window down, and snagging sweet wafts of fragrance from elaeagnus, winter honeysuckle, witch-hazel, and the hard-to-find old-garden clove currant—all of which bloom with fragrant bouquet in mid-winter to very early spring.

Adam's Needle Yucca

Yucca filamentosa
Full sun to light shade

Yuccas have a bad rep—just because someone lost a beach ball to one. Truth is, soft-tipped native kinds are neither dangerous nor invasive. Their bold forms and striking flowers are useful accents for architectural or tropical effects, plus they grow well in tight, dry, sloped spots or small areas in pavement with reflected heat where not much else will, while contrasting well with more traditional garden plants.

FLOWER: Tall tree-like panicles of two- to three-inch-wide white bells in the summer. Flower stalks arise from the center of each plant; there can be as many flower stalks as there are crowns in each clump. Very showy, slightly fragrant, and edible.

PLANT: Spreading rosettes of slender, sword-like leaves up to two and a half or more feet long with sharply pointed tips, often forming thick mounding clumps of many rosettes. Slow growing at first, they usually become quite solid and hard to get rid of—digging them completely out, or even burying them, often only slows them down. Tolerant of prolonged dry spells, they also tolerate normal rainfall, most hardy kinds being native to the eastern United States.

INTERESTING KINDS: Though the "plain green" Adam's needle can set off a collection of more colorful evergreens or contrast with perennials, stiff-leaved Adam's needle (*Y. filamentosa*) has several cultivars, including 'Bright Edge' with yellow edges, 'Variegata' with blue-green leaves and creamy white margins that turn pinkish in winter. *Yucca filifera* 'Golden Sword' has a yellow stripe down the middle of each green leaf.

SOIL: Any well-drained, dry soil with moderate to low fertility. Drainage is essential or they rot.

PROPAGATION: Divide clumps or root plant portions—remove suckers, or "pups," from the base of plants and root in moist potting soil, or bury root sections of stems in sandy soil.

TIP: XERISCAPE IS NOT A DRY WORD when it comes to low-maintenance gardening. Far from being all rocks and yucca with a scattered cactus or two, it simply means designing and planting with rainfall in mind. The result can be smaller lawn areas, more mulches and ground covers, and groups of hardy trees underplanted with tough shrubs and old-time perennials. It's common-sense gardening without the pop-up sprinklers; choosing and using plants that have proven themselves to be hardy on rainfall alone for many decades and still look good—that's xeriscaping.

Azalea

Rhododendron species

Shade to part sun

Azaleas and other rhododendrons are almost irresistibly beautiful when in flower, which is why so many gardeners throw out common sense and plant what for the rest of the year look like big green meatballs!

In 1939, Massachusetts nurseryman Peter J. Mezitt cross-pollinated some new rhododendrons from China, and accidentally developed the first really cold-hardy azaleas for the North, which became the now-common 'P.J.M' series whose flower buds are hardy to minus 30 degrees, with foliage that turns bronze in winter.

FLOWER: Showy clusters of single or double funnels of red, pink, white, orange, mauve, purple, and spotted or streaked combinations.

PLANT: Rounded mounds from four to ten feet tall, some evergreen, with pointed oval leaves from two to six or more inches long. Tip-pruning after flowering and into midsummer can help produce thicker plants.

INTERESTING KINDS: Hardiest azaleas include University of Minnesota's Northern Lights series in fragrant pink, orange, yellow, or white; and the very commonly planted 'P.J.M' hybrids, which are evergreen with purplish fall foliage and almost gaudy lavender-pink flowers in late winter. The large-leaf native Catawba rhododendrons (*R. catawbiense*) have yielded several great cultivars, including the white 'Alba', bright red 'America', and rosy pink 'English Roseum'. There are many new cold-hardy varieties; your best bet is to buy from a reputable local nursery owner who chooses varieties carefully for your climate.

SOIL: Rhododendrons must have well-drained soil, partially blended with peat moss and finely ground bark for acidity and better internal soil drainage. They will not tolerate heavy clay, wet, or alkaline soils. Sun tolerance is directly associated with a wide, mulched root system. Overfeeding increases susceptibility to disease and winter damage. "Rhodies" have a tough time with dessication, as stems and foliage dry in the winter sun and wind. Prepare them by watering deeply in the late fall and perhaps during an unusual warm spell in the winter.

PROPAGATION: Summer stem cuttings, or just buy new plants as needed.

TIP: WHAT'S THE DIFFERENCE between a rhododendron and azalea? Technically, an azalea is a member of the larger *Rhododendron* genus. But in general, rhododendrons are larger shrubs than azalea plants, with larger leaves. Also, most azalea flowers have five yellow pollen-bearing stamens, while the rhododendron flowers have ten stamens. Finally, unlike rhododendrons, many azaleas are deciduous.

Burning Bush

Euonymus alatus
'Compactus'

Full sun or light shade

Few shrubs polarize preening garden designers more quickly than euonymus, which is so easy to grow it is one of the most common roadside planting shrubs. You may hate its overuse, the occasional insects or diseases, or how it escapes by seed into our natural woodlands, or whatever other reason—it's still one tough plant!

FLOWER: Small cream-colored flowers in the spring are not showy at all, and birds eat the small fruits before people really even notice they are there.

PLANT: Bushy, twiggy member of the bittersweet family, a shrub to ten feet or more tall and wide with dull-green summer foliage that turns a brilliant crimson in the fall. Young twigs have corky "wing" growths.

INTERESTING KINDS: While the commonly grown 'Compactus' gets huge as a shrub, the "regular" winged euonymus is a small tree. A cultivar of the European euonymus, *E. europaeus* 'Red Cascade' has bright red fruits and is still hardy throughout the North into parts of Canada. *Euonymus fortunei*, the "wintercreeper" euonymus seen so often in cemeteries and landscapes as a ground cover or cascading vine, can easily be pruned into a small, durable shrub; shrubby cultivars include the vigorous 'Vegetus' and variegated 'Golden Prince'.

SOIL: Any soil, but has best fall colors when grown in a soil that does not stay wet and is not high in fertilizer.

PROPAGATION: Super easy to root from short stem cuttings in the summer or fall. Roots quickly.

TIP: NO NEED TO HATE THE PESTS of euonymus— they're easy to control. The popular shrubs are very susceptible to small, crusty scale insects, which attach to the undersides of leaves and stems and can sometimes completely defoliate the plant, and powdery mildew fungus. All are very easy to control with hard pruning and an application of dormant or summer oil.

Cool Compact Conifers

Very few plants give the "instant oomph" of dwarf conifers as accents, companions to perennials, or as tough container plants. Their unique shapes and shades of green, gold, or near-blue are dramatic. And talk about *tough*— these heat- and salt-tolerant plants can be found growing perfectly well in cemeteries, or in the "horticultural hell" of parking lot dividers.

Keep in mind that most are very slow-growing and may take years to get to the size you expect— then they keep growing until you either have to remove them or learn to live with them.

PLANTING AND CARE: As a group, with notable exceptions, conifers perform best in full sun and require well-drained, dry soils. They thrive on little or no fertilizer and occasional deep soakings. Many are susceptible to spider mites for which, really, there is no practical control even with regular spraying. Bagworms are caterpillar larvae of moths that cover themselves with portable bags of dead leaves and feed on conifer foliage; hand pick them or use a safe "biological worm spray" (commonly available) early in their July or August feeding cycle. Or add bird feeders to attract bagworm-eating feathered friends!

Hard pruning often kills conifers; if you prune a stem back to where no needles remain, it will usually die all the way back to its point of origin. It's best to just shear only new growth very lightly for thickness, or thin individual cluttered or wayward branches and limbs on aging conifers and let Nature take her course.

Mercer, Pennsylvania

Best Conifers for Beginners:

Arborvitae (*Thuja occidentalis*) has among the most interesting cultivars of all the conifers. Unlike the old huge kinds, new compact varieties include round, three-feet high and across 'Globosa' ('Little Gem' and 'Little Giant' are very similar); 'Rheingold' is cone-shaped, slow-growing, and bright golden, only four or five feet tall; 'Woodwardii' is an old-fashioned globular arborvitae that grows very slowly up to around eight feet. 'Degroot's Spire' and 'Brabant' are narrow and columnar. There are many, many others, including 'Golden Berkman' and the egg-shaped *T. orientalis* (*Platycladus orientalis*) 'Blue Cone'.

Dwarf Mugo Pine (*Pinus mugo*) is a sturdy compact little true pine with fine needles in irregular clumps at the ends of its branches; 'Mops' is dense and globe-shaped.

False Cypress (*Chamaecyparis obtusa*) or Hinoki cypress has soft needles. 'Nana Gracilis' with twisty flat foliage has appealing texture; 'Crippsii' is a dense pyramidal shrub, green tipped with rich yellow gold, and can get very large.

Junipers (*Juniperus* species), especially the ground covers that grow from six inches to two feet high and spread many feet in every direction, and pfitzer (*J. chinensis* 'Pfitzeriana') that can get to six feet and spreading, with many varieties such as 'Gold Coast' (three feet by five feet with lacy, yellow foliage).

Boston Common

Yews (*Taxus* species) are generic, ancient shrubs commonly used as foundations, backgrounds, hedges, and topiary; they tolerate dry shade. 'Densiformis' is a low spreader to four feet; 'Brownii' is rounded; 'Hicks' is narrow and upright.

There are many, many variations on all these, and quite a few other species as well. Any good garden center will have a great selection and someone to help you choose the right one for your garden. Remember that they are slow growing, yet often outgrow where you plant them!

WASPS LOVE NEEDLE-LEAF EVERGREENS and often nest in the inner coolness of the foliage. When getting ready to shear thick hedges or even to work near dense shrubs, carefully nudge them and be prepared to run if a few sentry wasps appear! Try to find the general area where the nest may be, and gently waft an aerosol insecticide their way from a safe distance or from the protection of a car with windows nearly rolled up; straight-shooting hornet and wasp jet sprays often burn foliage, so use those only as a last resort.

Cotoneaster

Cotoneaster apiculatus
Full sun to light shade

Let's get the pronunciation right: It isn't "cotton-easter," it's ko-TO-ne-AS-ter. Got it? Then grow it! Cotoneasters come in a wide range of shapes: low growing and spreading, tall and upright, weeping, evergreen or winter-bare, and everything in between, with just as many landscape uses. All are very hardy, and tend to need plenty of room to spread out with their crisscrossing branches, though they all prune very well.

FLOWER: Musky-smelling clusters of small white or pink flowers, similar to firethorn (*Pyracantha*) but not as showy. Fruits can be red or black, bird's-eye size or as large as crabapples.

PLANT: Cotoneasters are fine-textured evergreen or semi-evergreen shrubs or ground covers with layered branches but no thorns. The densely twiggy branches of some ground-hugging and low-growing spreading varieties make removing fallen leaves and trash somewhat difficult. Fall colors can be great or just so-so.

INTERESTING KINDS: Willowleaf cotoneaster (*C. salicifolius*) is tall, large, and open with flexible arching branches, narrow leathery leaves, and red berries. Cranberry cotoneaster (*C. apiculatus*) is a low-growing ground cover or trailing rock wall plant with bronzy-red or purplish fall colors that persist into November or later, with very showy red cranberry-like fruits. Hedge cotoneaster (*C. lucidus*) can be sheared into a medium hedge more than six feet tall, with pinkish white spring flowers, yellow or orange and red fall colors, and black fruit. Both spreading cotoneaster (*C. divaricatus*) and rock cotoneaster (*C. horizontalis*) are medium-sized spreading shrubs. *Cotoneaster multiflorus* looks like a weeping crabapple with many showy white flowers in May that are followed by crabapple-like fruits, which drop with the leaves in the fall. Creeping cotoneaster (*C. adpressus* 'Tom Thumb' and 'Little Gem') only grows to a foot or more tall.

SOIL: Any well-drained soil, including very dry summer soils. Cotoneasters tolerate roadside salt, making them great for along sidewalks or parking lots.

PROPAGATION: Stem cuttings taken in the summer root fairly readily under humid conditions.

TIP: IT'S DIFFICULT TO WEED or clean out around ground covers and low, spreading shrubs after falling leaves and wind-blown stuff gets matted in. Using landscape "weed barrier" fabrics is a good idea when planting, but can look ratty later as well as prevent some natural plant spread; mulches are difficult to replenish without working it in through foliage and tight-massed twigs. No way around the chore of weeding but to get down on your knees and start pulling.

164

Deutzia

Deutzia scabra

Sun or shade

As a kid trying to avoid chores, I used to hide behind and beneath my grandmother's "fuzzy deutzia" without really appreciating what a fragrant plant it is. Botanic gardens use deutzia effectively as a "disappearing bridge plant" to provide important color and flower texture when the main show of azaleas and wisteria is over and before roses and summer perennials come into their glory. After that, they disappear into the backdrop as other more substantial summer shrubs come into bloom. Deutzia is an excellent understory shrub to use between trees and showier foliage plants.

FLOWER: The ends of every branch of this shrub sprout partially upright sprays of small pinkish white clusters, mildly fragrant, after azaleas and other mid-spring shrubs have made their showiest splash. Flowers are formed on the previous year's stems, but appear on long twigs as leaves come out in the spring.

PLANT: Small to large deciduous shrub six to ten feet tall with arching branches of oval, sharply toothed leaves up to three inches long. Rough to the touch, leaves have curious little "uplifts" in each cut in the leaf margin. Shrubs are many-stemmed, with larger cane-like trunks sporting attractive shredded exfoliating bark, which gives a craggy old look to mature plants. Pruning is best done by simply culling out older or taller stems close to the ground, rather than shearing the entire shrub.

INTERESTING KINDS: Fuzzy deutzia (*Deutzia scabra*) is a large old-garden specimen, up to fifteen feet tall with arching branches; it has pink cultivars ('Pride of Rochester' has double, frilly, pink-tinged flowers). Showy deutzia (*D. × magnifica*) has very showy white flowers and gets six to eight feet tall and wide. Slender deutzia (*D. gracilis*) has slender stems three to six feet tall that are easily pruned into a small hedge or accent behind statuary, with small, bright green leaves and pure white flowers; its dwarf form 'Nikko' makes an outstanding ground cover to about three feet tall with burgundy fall colors when grown in the shade. New cultivars I have seen in European gardens have names such as 'Pink Charm' and 'Strawberry Fields'—very difficult to find commercially, but they hint at the variety that is becoming available thanks to plant explorers and observant nurserymen.

SOIL: Any well-drained soil, even heavy soil or dry sites under trees.

PROPAGATION: Roots incredibly easily nearly any time of the year and is very easy to divide in the fall or winter by digging up outer stems from clumps.

TIP: HOW MUCH IS TOO MUCH MULCH? The rule of thumb for organic (leaf- or bark-based) mulches is to use exactly enough to completely cover the ground, then add that much more to allow for settling and decomposition. Always spread evenly; never pile high on trunks or at the base of shrub stems, pulling it away from the trunks at least two inches.

Dwarf Flowering Almond

Prunus glandulosa

Sun or light shade

One of my earliest childhood garden memories was of running my thumb and forefinger up a long, willowy cane of my grandmother's flowering almond (not really an almond, by the way), to capture a "bouquet" to throw in someone's face. My grandmother used the freshly bare twig to switch my legs for ruining her shrub's only reason for being in the garden—its early spring show. But I don't hold my experience against the flower, or my grandmother.

FLOWER: Pink or white double flowers, looking very much like little double roses, are bunched up and down the entire length of the previous summer and fall twig growth. Cutting stems back severely after flowering causes long, upright new growth, which when in flower looks like pink shooting stars. Single-flowering kinds produce red fruits up to one-half inch in diameter.

PLANT: Small multistemmed, generic, deciduous shrub, up to about five feet tall and nearly that wide—it really doesn't look like much except when in flower in the late spring, before its two- to three-inch long leaves emerge. Because it is such an ordinary plant most of the year, and just takes up space and gets leggy, I usually cut mine way back after flowering, and let the new growth just "do its thing" the rest of the year behind summer perennials. Its long, arching new growth, up to two feet or more, loads up with flower buds for next winter without my really having to deal with it. Trunks may split apart under a heavy snow load.

INTERESTING KINDS: 'Alba Plena' has double white flowers; 'Sinensis' (also called 'Rosea Plena') has double pink flowers.

SOIL: Requires the same growing conditions as flowering cherry and apricot: slightly fertile, well-drained soil. Does very well in dry sites or in the back of flower beds

PROPAGATION: Roots like a rose in the fall or late winter, but is very easy to divide some of the many small plants ("suckers" that sprout off side roots up to a foot or more from the main plant).

TIP: USE A LITTLE KNOW-HOW about plant physiology to make plants grow in whatever direction you want them to; new growth on a clipped stem shoots out of the bud closest to the pruning cut; when pruning, cut just above an outward-facing bud, and the new growth will grow in that direction. This is called "directional pruning."

Dwarf Fothergilla

Fothergilla gardenii

Sun or light shade

New gardeners overlook some plants because of their weird names alone. But when in bloom, fothergilla, a surprisingly underused, sturdy Alleghany Mountains native shrub—a close relative of witch-hazel—causes passersby to stop, look, touch, and sniff. Even better than the flowers is the brilliant autumn show of foliage colors. Too bad it was labeled forever with the nearly unpronounceable British physician's name—but its common name, witch-alder, ain't much better!

FLOWER: Stubby spikes of many petal-less flowers that look like fuzzy bottlebrushes at the tips of every twig, in late winter, have a slight honey-like scent, making the plant a good choice near walkways.

PLANT: This small accent shrub is highly decorative toward the back of a flower bed, or mixed in with evergreens, with interesting leaves, and nearly zigzag twig growth for winter interest. Its foliage, which appears after flowering in the spring, is toothed, crinkly, and a dull dark green or blue-green, but turns super-showy, bright red, orange, and yellow in the fall—often with all three colors present at the same time. Fothergilla does not need routine pruning, but can be cut back fairly hard every few years to rejuvenate and renew the plants. However, the larger native fothergilla (*F. major*), really a small tree, can be planted along walkways, and should be "limbed up" to keep from knocking people's hats off; underplant with spring bulbs and summer shade perennials such as hostas or ferns.

INTERESTING KINDS: 'Blue Mist' has blue-green foliage and requires partial shade in the summer; its fall colors are somewhat disappointing. *Fothergilla major* flowers later and is generally a larger species; 'Mt. Airy' is more upright and rounded, though not as large as the species, and has the most spectacular fall foliage colors—a true landscape kaleidoscope.

SOIL: Any woodsy, well-drained soil, with plenty of mulch to keep roots cool and moist in the summer (and to help roots through harsh winters in northern areas). As with most natives, fertilize lightly and water deeply but not often.

PROPAGATION: Root stem pieces, or divide from the suckers that come up around the base of mature plants.

TIP: IF A PLANT SEEMS DRAB part of the year—no one really pays much attention to it for one reason or another—add another plant to complement it. Try to create contrasts with shape or leaf texture to avoid their "running together" visually, and make sure all plants in the area tolerate the same growing conditions. Or add a hard feature: birdbath, piece of driftwood, stone, bench, or the like.

Harvard University

167

Elderberry
Sambucus canadensis
Full sun or part shade

I'm not "into" elderberry wine—not my taste—but that doesn't stop me from growing the native plant as a magnificent flowering shrub! Occurring naturally from Nova Scotia to Minnesota, and south to Texas and Florida, it's a handsome plant and both its flowers and berries are edible. Very attractive to wildlife as well.

FLOWER: Each stem is topped in the late spring with a large, flat, plate-like cluster of small, creamy white florets with a pleasant scent. The flowers appear on new growth, so pruning in the winter does not affect the show. As berries begin to mature, they turn from reddish to blue to black, and the entire berry cluster will droop downward when it is ripe for harvest.

PLANT: Elderberry is a large, spreading, semi-woody herbaceous shrub with several stems, each of which can reach ten feet or more in a season. Leaves have up to eleven pointed leaflets, each about five inches long, with finely toothed margins. To keep plants vigorous and within bounds, remove older stems at ground level when they are three or four years old; new canes will quickly replace them.

INTERESTING KINDS: 'Adams' is used in wildlife plantings and for culinary use, with berries ripening in early September. 'Nova' has large, sweet, less astringent berries and 'Scotia' (I'm not making this up) has very high sugar content. 'Laciniata' has lacy, cut leaves, 'Aurea' is a rounded plant with yellow foliage and red fruits, and 'Goldfinch' has leaves both deeply cut and yellow. 'Maxima' is a vigorous cultivar with larger flowers and leaves than the species, and purple flower stalks. There are variegated forms as well. *S. nigra*, European elderberry, is equally tough and has some interesting cultivars.

SOIL: Elder grows in nearly any kind of soil but produces the best berries in a moist soil. Its shallow, fibrous root system can shut down berry ripening during a prolonged summer drought. Little or no fertilizer is needed.

PROPAGATION: Stem cuttings taken in the fall or early in the spring, before new growth is too succulent, root readily. Stick foot-long pieces of mature stem into good garden soil, with at least one or two leaf joints buried and one bud sticking out of the ground; the buried buds will root, and the exposed one will sprout.

TIP: ADD RIPE ELDERBERRIES to an apple pie recipe, in a forty-to-sixty elder-to-apple ratio. Or for a real summer treat, cut an elderberry flower head while in full bloom, wash and dry it, then dip into thin pancake batter. Fry in hot oil until light brown, drain and pat dry, then sprinkle with powdered sugar and cinnamon. Enjoy!

Flowering Quince
Chaenomeles speciosa
Sun or shade

This indestructible shrub often comes into flower before forsythia, sometimes as early as February in lower parts of our region. Growing in sun or shade, it tolerates extreme neglect and never fails to flower with nearly the zeal of an azalea. Cut stems can be used to bring much-needed winter cheer into the home. Excellent for hedges and perfect for underplanting with shade-loving perennials that lure the eye from the quince itself, which is not a very showy shrub in the summer and fall.

FLOWER: Large, flattened, apple blossom-like flowers up to two inches across in a common scarlet, but also pink, white, orange, and salmon. Produced in small clusters tightly held against bare stems in February, March, and early April. Very attractive to bees on warm winter days, excellent cut flowers, especially when cut in bud and "forced" in water indoors. Small, lumpy, green to yellow, apple-like fruits are practically inedible, but smell good and make good pectin for jellies.

PLANT: Long-lived hedge or specimen plant has many thin but strong branches, sparsely thorned, which shoot upward for six feet or more from a small basal clump; some forms have twisted, curly stems. Leaves, which often have smaller leaf-like "stipules" wrapped partway around their base, are up to three inches long, oval and serrated, and emerge somewhat bronzy in the spring and often shed early in the fall. Not a handsome shrub, except when in full bloom when nothing else is. Prune by thinning older stems close to the ground (easy enough to do when bringing in flowering stems for indoor use), or completely cut the shrub nearly to the ground every spring to force strong new flowering shoots to grow over the summer.

INTERESTING KINDS: 'Apple Blossom' (white and pink, lots of fruits), 'Contorta' (white or pink with twisted branches, makes a good bonsai plant), 'Coral Sea' (coral pink and tall), 'Minerva' (cherry red), 'Red Ruffles' (ruffled red, almost thornless), 'Snow' (white), and 'Toyo Nishiki' (tall, with pink, white, pink-and-white, and red flowers all on each stem, good fruits).

SOIL: Literally any kind, anywhere, except in wet areas. Needs no fertilizer or water for years.

PROPAGATION: Rooting cuttings or dividing small plants from the base of older clumps is easy.

TIP: BRING SPRING INDOORS by cutting branches of early spring blooming shrubs and trees and place them in water in a warmish room (although the hotter the room, the shorter they will last). Flowering quince, forsythia, cherry, pear, and flowering almond can all be forced to bloom a little ahead of schedule.

Forsythia

Forsythia × intermedia

Sun or shade

Perhaps the most common late-winter showstopper, "golden bells" is an apt descriptive common name for this old-fashioned flowering shrub. Commonly escaped from older gardens, it can survive where an old homestead may have once stood but has long disappeared. Planted as a single specimen or in masses, tightly pruned or allowed to grow wild, this nearly indestructible shrub never fails to perform in mid- to late winter. Its long stems also make great indoor arrangements when cut in bud or flower and placed in tall containers of water for "forcing" in mid-winter.

FLOWER: Inch-long trumpets in bright to golden yellow, produced in clusters at leaf joints from one end of the stem to the other. The entire shrub looks like yellow fireworks.

PLANT: Fountain-shaped deciduous shrub with long, stiff, arching branches arising from a fairly narrow basal clump, with pointed, slender oval leaves up to four inches long produced in pairs. Few gardeners expect the shrub to get as large as it will; luckily, forsythia can be pruned by thinning old canes close to the ground or cutting the entire shrub to a few inches tall to force strong, arching, new growth to shoot up over the summer and fall. To rejuvenate a forsythia that is unsightly and to achieve the fullest fountain effect, prune a third of the old stems to the ground every year for three years; your patience will be rewarded. The plant itself, with its arching form and medium-green leaves, fits in well with other shrubs and makes a good backdrop to a flower border. Branches that touch the ground will root, forming an impenetrable mass.

INTERESTING KINDS: 'Lynwood' or 'Lynwood Gold' (standard in garden centers), 'Fiesta' (grows to less than five feet with deep-yellow flowers, with green and yellow variegated leaves that last all summer), 'Spring Glory' (pale yellow flowers), 'Gold Tide' (spreads rapidly by suckers, grows to only two feet tall). 'Primulina' has pale yellow flowers and foliage that turns mahogany in the fall.

SOIL: Any kind, even cemetery soils and into a woodland edge. No water is ever needed after the first season in the ground.

PROPAGATION: Division of crowded clump in the fall or winter, or stem cuttings taken in the fall or winter.

TIP: ROOT DECIDUOUS SHRUBS the easy way, as country folks with less than a lick of horticultural training have done for centuries. Simply take mature stems (near, but not directly on, the ends of recent branches), and stick them most of the way into a sandy-soil flower bed. Do this in the fall or winter, and the plants will root well enough to move by the following fall.

Hydrangea
Hydrangea species
Moderate shade to sun

Tradition dictates that every garden have a "hy-geranium"—if only because it is a rare summer-flowering showstopper, and its dried flower heads stand erect and tall even in the middle of the winter, making the shrub more than just another undulating mound in the snow.

FLOWER: Large round or flat "lace-cap" heads of smaller flowers in white, pink, or blue produced in the spring or summer. Flower clusters up to a foot in diameter have showy, petal-like sepals, which remain after "real" flowers fall, gradually fading in color to tan. Severe winter pruning or hard freezes do not affect flowering, which is on new growth.

PLANT: Medium to large deciduous shrubs with big bold leaves usually serrated along margins. Some make small specimen trees and should be given plenty of room to grow, or pruning can disfigure the show.

INTERESTING KINDS: Peegee hydrangea (*H. paniculata* 'Grandiflora') is a tall shrub with showy white flower clusters in the summer; smooth hydrangea (*H. arborescens*) is a smaller, more compact shrub to five or six feet tall. Two very popular cultivars are 'Snow Hill' and the extraordinarily large-flowering 'Annabelle'. Other cultivars of both are available depending on local suppliers. Lace-cap varieties are not as cold hardy.

SOIL: Get hydrangeas started right by preparing soil with generous amounts of organic matter blended into native soil in a planting hole that is much wider than deep. Thick leaf mulch will keep roots cool and moist. Light fertilization and only occasional deep soakings are all that the shrubs will need later.

PROPAGATION: Root stem cuttings taken in the late winter, or in summer after flowering.

TIP: FLOWERS OFTEN FAIL TO OPEN on the popular pink or blue "French" or big-leaf hydrangeas (*H. macrophylla*). Since they are produced from buds on the previous year's twigs, they often fail to flower in the northern reaches of our region, after a hard winter kills the plants back a bit. The shrubs put out new growth, but not with flowers—they end up being just big, coarse-textured lumps of foliage. In warmer areas where they do flower, soil acidity or alkalinity affects flower color. Adding lime to the soil will turn the flowers pink; aluminum soil acidifiers can ensure deep blue blossoms.

Japanese Barberry
Berberis thunbergii
Full sun to part shade

Widely used as specimen shrubs, masses of color, or accents in flower gardens, barberries have become a mainstay of the garden design world. And their needle-like spines are just stiff enough to help keep people—including those interested in checking out your windows "after hours"—on the straight and narrow.

FLOWER: Yellow flowers in early spring are not showy, and are usually hidden by emerging new foliage; however, many varieties have red fruit that can put on a show from October through the winter.

PLANT: Dense, rounded shrub is covered with bright green leaves that turn a brilliant orange to red in the fall. Many small, very fine thorns make it an excellent barrier when planted where people may need to be kept in (or out of) bounds. Older growth makes the best fall colors, so the less pruning done, the better.

INTERESTING KINDS: Red-leaf Japanese barberry (*B. thunbergii* 'Atropurpurea') is a full-sized barberry with reddish-purple leaves from spring to fall. 'Crimson Pygmy' is a popular old compact form, but quite a few unusual variegated forms shimmer with a golden or even pink glow. 'Golden Ring' has reddish purple leaves with a narrow golden margin; 'Rose Glow' has rose-pink foliage mottled with pink, purple, and cream blotches; 'Aurea' has yellow foliage and red berries, and grows to only two feet or so.

SOIL: Any well-drained soil, even outside a fast-food restaurant, will do. Heavy or wet soils can lead to root rot.

PROPAGATION: Cuttings taken in summer or winter.

TIP: PRUNING IS A NEAT IDEA for showy plants such as barberry, forsythia, and spirea—literally. While some plants look better the thicker they get from tip pruning and shearing, others look too contrived with that treatment and need to have branches selectively removed (it's a matter of personal preference, like plucking eyebrows versus shaving them off). Barberry can be thinned out (don't worry about the thorns, which point up and won't snag you like those on roses); put on a good pair of gloves and just snip out a few wayward branches, leaving most untouched. It will end up with a more relaxed, energetic look than when clipped into a tight box or gumdrop.

172

Kerria

Kerria japonica

Full sun to moderate shade

The old "yellow rose of Texas" isn't a rose at all—but it sure looks like one when it flowers, and it is in the rose family. Introduced to America in the early 1800s, kerria is often found in older gardens and is still a graceful addition to a lightly shaded shrub border beneath tall trees. And it's easy to share.

FLOWER: Solitary buttery yellow apple blossom-like single or very double rose-like blossoms, one to two inches across, appear in leaf joints in late spring, often "spritzing" through the summer and early fall.

PLANT: Upright, many-stemmed arching shrub, six to ten or more feet tall, with many non-invasive suckers appearing around its narrow base. Leaves up to two inches long are yellow-green, sharply pointed and almost triangular, heavily serrated or toothed and with prominent veins. Stems have a slight zigzag habit, angling slightly at every leaf joint, and remain light green all year, creating winter interest and making the plant an excellent specimen planted against a fence or evergreen backdrop. Prune by thinning old canes close to the ground, from which they will shoot back up with flowering vigor.

INTERESTING KINDS: 'Pleniflora' is the most common form, with large, frilly, double flowers on large, rambling, arching plants; 'Shannon' has large single flowers on vigorous shrubs; 'Kin Kan' has interesting yellow-striped stems and single yellow blooms; 'Variegata' or 'Picta' is variegated with white-edged leaves; 'Alisa' and 'Albescens' or 'Albiflora' have white flowers.

SOIL: Any well-drained soil, including very dry under trees and in competition with nearby shrubs.

PROPAGATION: Division of suckers nearly any time of the year except during very dry periods, but can still be done if plants are cut back to foot-high stubs and allowed to sprout in new locations. Mulch will help get plants established.

TIP: SURVIVORS FROM GRANDMOTHER'S GARDEN don't seem old fashioned when they are used well in contemporary landscapes. Many heirloom shrubs are making a real comeback because of four trends: they are historic or full of memories of bygone people or places; they provide unusual but valuable flowering or foliage alternatives to the "same old, same old" mass-production meatballs and gumdrops that fast-food designers, contractors, and growers have lulled us into depending on; they are generally pest resistant or they would have disappeared decades ago; and they have proven themselves to survive in ordinary or even abandoned garden conditions, thriving on rainfall alone—making them ideal for the twenty-first century and beyond.

Ligustrum or Privet

Ligustrum species

Sun or shade

FLOWER: Small, showy, very fragrant white flowers on the ends of the previous season's growth in mid-spring; some people claim to be allergic to the cloyingly sweet flowers, but often are reacting to wind-blown tree pollen. Late summer fruits are small, fleshy, and nearly black, highly attractive to birds, and can be a nuisance when dropped on cars.

PLANT: Upright, many-stemmed evergreen shrub with small oval leaves. Because privet tolerates heavy pruning, it is commonly sheared into tight specimens or hedges; this usually removes flowering growth and requires several clippings a year. Whiteflies can be a nuisance in the summer and early fall, but no practical control exists other than expensive, troublesome insecticidal soap sprays.

INTERESTING KINDS: European privet (*L. vulgare*) is one of the most common, large and rank if not sheared regularly. 'Densiflorum' remains dense and attractive even when not pruned a lot; 'Lodense' is a compact four- or five-foot compact variety. Amur privet (*L. amurense*) is a common privet, sometimes deciduous in harsh winters, very invasive, and easy to prune. It is resistant to the few diseases that sometimes damage European types.

An editor for *Horticulture* magazine in Boston told me that the only thing that could stop a snowplow is a privet hedge. And she had the hedge to prove it. Want a fast evergreen screen, cheap? Don't mind pruning for the rest of your life? Ligustrum or privet is the way to go. Plant 'em well, then run for your clippers.

SOIL: Any soil, other than one that is soggy or wet. Very drought tolerant. Salt tolerant.

PROPAGATION: Very easy to root cuttings in the summer or dig and transplant seedlings. Widely available in garden centers.

TIP: EVER TRY TO KILL A SHRUB by cutting it down, just to have it spring right back as vigorous as ever? This is known horticulturally as "rejuvenation" and, with the exception of junipers, is an excellent way to reclaim old, gnarly, half-dead, or overgrown ligustrum, lilac, and other shrubs—even azaleas. Do it early in the summer, and tip prune new shoots before fall to help plants thicken up quickly.

Lilac
Syringa vulgaris
Full sun or part shade

Because I was raised in the South, I didn't understand the nostalgic sway that lilacs—even more than peonies and rhubarb—can have over gardeners who move down from the North, until one warm early spring day some twenty years ago when I got my first whiff somewhere in the Midwest. I was hooked

FLOWER: Many clusters of lavender, rose, or white flowers, extremely fragrant.

PLANT: The small, open tree is of no particular interest most of the year, except for deep-green, heart-shaped foliage.

INTERESTING KINDS: Cut-leaf lilac (S. × *laciniata*) is the one most enjoyed south of the Mason-Dixon, but of the hundreds of cultivars in the North, the most fragrant is the common lilac (*vulgaris* is Latin for "common"), a large evergreen shrub brought to New England by early colonists. Mildew resistance is as important as fragrance in many common lilacs. Other species that perform superbly and are fragrant and mildew resistant, include S. *reticulata* 'Miss Kim' with icy blue flowers; and S. *meyeri* 'Palibin', a compact purple dwarf lilac, which blooms before leaves appear. Too many others to mention, including some with little or no fragrance for those who just don't "get it."

SOIL: Lilacs grow well nearly anywhere but prefer a well-drained soil that is neutral or slightly alkaline. If your soil is acidic, work limestone into a wide planting hole and scatter more around the outer edges of the plant's root system every three or four years.

PROPAGATION: Lilacs generally root fairly easily from stem cuttings taken in the fall or winter, stuck directly into well-prepared garden soil as with rose cuttings.

TIP: GROW FIRST WHAT GROWS BEST! Northern gardeners keep trying to grow Southern magnolias (there is one in Boyertown, Pennsylvania), and Southerners keep attempting lilacs (the "crape myrtle of the North"). Local horticulturists wish, as gardeners move around this huge country, that they'd leave favored "comfort plants" back home, and try their green thumbs at growing what does best in their new location.

Mock Orange
Philadelphus coronarius
Shade to part or full sun

A scraggly old garden shrub that brings the shade garden to life every spring with dogwood-like flowers.

FLOWER: Four-petaled white flowers nearly two inches across, some single, some semi- or fully double, completely cover the arching branches in mid-spring, usually after azaleas. Most varieties of this old-garden shrub are dependable in all parts of the North, at worst losing a few flowers after a relentlessly cold winter. Many are fragrant like oranges (see tip below), though if you want to be sure of what you get, root a division from an existing plant.

PLANT: Upright, arching, large deciduous shrub to ten or more feet high with many stems from suckers at the base, forming a fountain of medium green; older canes have reddish brown or orange exfoliating (peeling) bark. Leaves are oval with pointed ends, three or four inches long and in pairs, some with variegation or golden tinges. Prune out older canes close to the ground to keep the big plants tidy and fresh, either in the winter when you can see what you are doing or right after flowering in late spring or early summer; new growth will quickly shoot back up and have time to set flower buds by fall. Note: Mock orange forms a lot of suckers!

INTERESTING KINDS: Tall, old-fashioned "English dogwood" (*Philadelphus coronarius*) is the most common, a bold species best suited for screens, 'Aureus' being a cultivar with bright golden yellow leaves turning to light green in the summer; *P. × lemoinei* is a smaller species to around six feet with the well-known single-flowering cultivar 'Avalanche' and double-flowering 'Enchantment' (which has somewhat confused parentage); *P. × virginalis* has several excellent cultivars, most double, including the dwarf double-flowering 'Glacier' (four to five feet tall) and 'Dwarf Minnesota Snowflake' (a mere three or four feet tall). 'Natchez', reportedly the showiest of them all, has flowers up to two inches across. 'Snowbelle' is another good cultivar.

SOIL: Any well-drained soil of moderate fertility.

PROPAGATION: Difficult to find in garden centers because they look so scraggly in pots in the spring, so either order from reputable mail-order or Internet plant centers or divide pieces of stems from around older plants in the winter. Mulch until established. Softwood cuttings can be taken in the summer.

TIP: ONE MAN'S FRAGRANCE IS ANOTHER MAN'S STINK, at least according to Gerard, the famous herbalist who wrote over three hundred years ago that the flowers of mock orange "have a pleasant and sweet smell, but in my judgement troubling . . . I once gathered the flowers and laid them on my chamber window, which smelled more strongly after they had lain a few hours, but with such an unacquainted savour that they awaked me from my sleep, so that I could not rest until I had cast them out."

Ninebark

Physocarpus opulifolius

Full sun or light shade

It is rare that I recommend a plant without having seen it grow for more than just a few years—it takes decades to convince me that a plant is tough enough to pass muster! But this "new" shrub just blows me away—partly because it is so showy, and partly because the plant parent of this European love child is a North American native whose range is from Quebec through the entire Northeast and Midwest. Ninebark, by the way, gets its name from a belief that it has nine layers of bark, which is peeling and cracked.

FLOWER: White flowers have a faint pinkish cast and occur in two-inch, round "snowballs" made up of tinier blooms. Regular ninebarks follow the blooms with half-inch green to reddish seeds in summer and autumn, which birds like to eat.

PLANT: Ninebark is a thicket-forming Northern native, a deciduous shrub that grows upright into a vague fountain shape up to six or ten feet and spreads into small colonies by underground runners. In the garden, it rarely becomes invasive, and usually grows only to six feet or so high; it can be easily pruned into a small, very compact shrub.

INTERESTING KINDS: Though the native ninebark is fascinating on its own, several cultivars exist, including golden-leafed and dwarf varieties. 'Monlo' (marketed under the trademark name 'Diablo') is the most striking. 'Diablo' ninebark blooms late, May through July, and its white flowers are followed by seeds of a bright vivid red in clusters two or three inches wide. The most striking feature of 'Diablo' is the deep, dark purplish red leaves that last through summer. In hot humid weather, however, they sometimes fade to green with only a blush of the spring purple remaining in summer. Toward autumn the leaf color fades back toward a deep burgundy red. Perhaps in light shade, or with plenty of rain, the color would remain in midsummer. Sometimes sold as 'Diabolo', for anyone squeamish about buying a plant named 'Diablo'!

SOIL: Ninebark is highly adaptable. It grows best in a moist, well-drained soil in the sun or half sun, but it will tolerate more shade, clay soil, and drought once established.

PROPAGATION: Root stem cuttings or dig and divide multiplying plants from thickets.

TIP: EVERY TRIP I MAKE TO EUROPE brings home the amazing fact that some of our most common native "weeds" are very popular landscape plants in other lands: ninebark, sumac, sweetgum, bald cypress, asters and goldenrods, and coneflowers. So many common North American natives are not only celebrated there, but also improved upon with aggressive breeding programs. Not using them more ourselves is really a missed opportunity.

Pieris
Pieris japonica
Shade to part sun

Late winter and early spring, just as the 'P.J.M.' azaleas come into magenta splendor, this "lily-of-the-valley" shrub kicks in and tones things down with an almost Gothic elegance.

FLOWER: In the late winter and early spring, the tip of every branch is draped heavily with a cluster of three- to six-inch stems studded with dozens of waxy, urn-shaped florets, hanging like miniature white bunches of grapes. Flowers of most varieties are fragrant and white, though some are pink or rose-red. The flowers persist for three weeks or longer, well after new growth begins to appear.

PLANT: Upright, many-stemmed evergreen shrubs from three to eight feet tall and half as wide, each stem topped with a rosette of narrow, finely toothed, lustrous green or dark green leaves that appear with the flowers; some varieties have pinkish or reddish new growth to create an even more dramatic contrast to the flowers.

INTERESTING KINDS: 'Mountain Fire' has red new growth and pure white flowers. Foliage of 'Variegata' is edged with creamy white. 'Dorothy Wycoff' has pink florets, 'Flamingo' has rose-red. 'White Cascade' has longer chains of flowers that also last longer than others. The hybrid cultivar 'Brouwer's Beauty' has flower clusters that are thick and heavy with larger, more tightly packed florets. For naturalizing in wooded settings, choose the scrappy, pest-resistant mountain pieris (*P. floribunda*).

SOIL: Though pieris is often planted as a foundation or specimen shrub in full sun, it is best suited for light shade and woodsy soil conditions—moist and high in organic matter as for an azalea or blueberry. Heavy or clay soils stunt roots or cause root rot during heavy rainy spells and early spring snow melt. Those planted in the light shade with plenty of soil preparation are generally more lustrous than the ones in tight planting holes and broiling sun.

PROPAGATION: Stem cuttings root somewhat readily, but small mature plants are fairly inexpensive and very common.

TIP: LACEBUGS ARE SMALL INSECTS that pierce and suck sap from the undersides of pieris and azalea leaves in midsummer, causing discoloration. While this doesn't seriously harm the plants, it is unsightly, and no really good controls exist (even powerful chemical sprays have their limits, so why use them?). Lacebugs and mites are attracted to and do much more damage on sun- and drought-stressed plants—you can dramatically reduce pest problems on pieris and azaleas by planting them in light shade and watering them every few weeks in the summer.

Pyracantha or Firethorn

Pyracantha coccinea

Sun or part shade

Problems with pyracantha include thorns, rambling growth habit, disfiguring "scab" disease, and lack of cold hardiness. And its flowers stink. But where it grows, it really shows off—making it worth a shot. Faint praise for what is actually a very showy shrub.

FLOWER: Delicate, small, single, white apple blossom-like flowers produced by the dozens in two- or three-inch clusters amongst the leathery foliage in late spring, giving the entire plant a soft cloud-like look. Flowers have a "dusty" kind of off-odor, not really unpleasant. Many loose clusters of showy berries persist into the fall until cedar waxwings or other berry-eating birds wipe them out. Each berry is really a slightly flattened, orange or scarlet "apple"—pyracantha is in the rose family with apples, pears, and crabapples, though pyracantha fruits are too small and tasteless to be worth fooling with.

PLANT: Upright or arching stems, each studded with many small branches ending in very sharp, stiff points that leave a burning welt when careless gardeners get too close. Leaves are two to three inches long and fairly thin, lustrous green when the lacebugs don't brown them out (no real good cure for this, but doesn't seriously hurt the plant). Very effective "burglar" plant because of its thorns. Long stems are fairly weak, so it will need tying if grown espaliered against a wall.

INTERESTING KINDS: Hybrids 'Fiery Cascade' and 'Mohave' have good cold tolerance; *P. angustifolia* 'Monon' (same as 'Yukon Belle') is perhaps the most cold hardy, and 'Gnome' is more compact.

SOIL: Any decent, well-drained soil of moderate fertility.

PROPAGATION: Cuttings taken in midsummer root fairly well under humid conditions such as those found in a greenhouse or shaded flower bed. Best to buy rooted plants at a garden center.

TIP: FIRE BLIGHT is burning the North, and there isn't a lot to be done about it. The bacterium, which damages twigs and fruit clusters of apples, pears, ornamental pear, pyracantha, and related members of the rose family, is spread by pollinating insects, usually just in the early spring when infected plants are in flower and being worked by bees. Twigs turn brown as if burned, and affected fruiting plants usually lose their fruit. Fire blight sprays are not cures, and have to be applied while bees are working freshly opened flowers (the bactericide does not harm bees or people). Pruning infected plants usually has a mere cosmetic effect and often spreads the fungus on the pruning shears. Either spray while in the plant is in bloom, or learn to live with the results.

Rose-of-Sharon or Althea

Hibiscus syriacus

Sun or shade

A drunk driver once ran over my great-grandmother's old althea (which most of us pronounce AL-thea), and it came right back with new flowering growth. That's one tough shrub if it can be pruned with a pickup truck! This old-garden plant graces many older neighborhoods out of sheer persistence. Interesting varieties are all over the place, but are difficult to find commercially because the plant doesn't look like much in a pot. Once set out, it quickly becomes a focal point from summer to fall for its prolific large flowers, and even in the winter when its long branches are tipped with light-brown seed capsules—which some people enjoy as winter interest.

FLOWER: Single or double, open, bell-like typical hibiscus flowers up to four inches across, in white, pink, red, lavender, pale blue, sometimes with a contrasting "eye" or flower streaks, all produced in late spring through fall on new growth, even in the shade. Flowers are great bee attractors. Some gardeners prune off the slightly showy dried seed capsules (which have many seeds, producing unwanted seedlings).

PLANT: Upright, vase-shaped shrub to ten feet or more with medium-sized, lobed leaves that sometimes turn golden in the fall. Sooty mold (black, sticky, fungus-like growth) is sometimes a problem on altheas grown under insect-drippy shade trees, but does not harm the plant or reduce flowering much. Pruning the shrub can thicken it up, but the best shape is open and upright. Only moderate thinning is needed, which will also increase the size of flowers on the unpruned parts of the shrub. Althea is easily trained into a single trunk by removing excess branches, or you can train it as an espalier against a wall or fence.

INTERESTING KINDS: There are many great old cultivars, but the National Arboretum has introduced sterile (seedless) kinds that have much heavier flowering, including 'Minerva' (ruffled lavender pink with reddish eye), 'Aphrodite' (rose pink with deep red eye), 'Diana' (pure white), and 'Hélène' (white flowers with deep red eye). One of my favorites is the pale 'Blue Bird', which appears a bit lavender in the summer heat.

SOIL: Any well-drained soil, especially dry, even under trees. Moderate fertility if any.

PROPAGATION: Seedlings may be transplanted, or foot-long cuttings rooted any time of year.

TIP: SOME SHRUBS AND TREES ARE WEEDY and show up all over the place. Althea, sweetgum, and others that come up readily from seed can be pains to pull from flower and ground cover beds. The best thing to do is to just put on a pair of gloves and pull them while they are small, which is most easily done a day or two after a good rain, when the ground is soft and yielding.

180

Roses

Rosa species and hybrids

Full sun to very light shade

'Nearly Wild' Rose

For too long, the "fancy rose" folks have been pushing us to become great rose growers when all we want is to grow a few roses without a lot of fuss. From Nebraska to Cape Cod, rose hybridizers have been coming up with really hardy roses for cold climates, and amateur "rose rustlers" have been discovering rose "survivors," then taking and sharing rooted cuttings. As more of these show up in gardens, maybe the word will spread that you don't have to be an expert or own a power sprayer to enjoy good roses.

FLOWER: Colorful pointed buds clasped in tight green calyxes and borne either singly on long stems or in loose masses. Buds open into many petals of red, white, pink, yellow, orange, burgundy, near blue, and nearly every combination; there are singles and doubles, some open flowers remaining tight while others flop open shamelessly, and many are heady with fragrant perfume. Though some old varieties bloom only once in the spring, many others continue to flower off and on through the summer and right up to fall freezes. Pruning stems back by a third after flowering will stimulate increased new flowering shoot and bud formation, but many shrubs continue to flower repeatedly with no summer pruning at all.

PLANT: Small compact bushes to tall leggy shrubs and a few multiple-stemmed "vines" that require tying to keep them on trellises or arbors. Most plants have thorny stems and beautiful leaves up to six inches long, with five to seven or more oval leaflets each an inch or more long. Foliage is a major concern for rose growers, because a large percentage of roses are highly susceptible to leaf diseases (black spot and powdery mildew) for which even regular fungicide sprays have poor success at best; roses are now being developed with disease resistance.

INTERESTING KINDS: There are way too many great roses—old and modern, shrub and bush and climbing—to go into detail; suffice it to say, old roses sold in your part of the region are good to start with, along with some Internet research. And just treat hybrid teas as one-shot annuals—buy 'em cheap, then let 'em go.

SOIL: Roses require well-drained soils of moderate fertility. Amend your native soil with about a third that much potting soil, finely chipped bark, compost, or the like (don't overdo it). Mulch with hay, shredded bark, or other organic mulches to keep roots cool and moist in the summer (pine straw and conifer needles look good but don't add much to the soil as they decompose—better to use leaves). Occasional deep watering and very light fertilizing at least once a year (no more than twice a year) will improve plant vigor and flowering, but hold back on both as you move toward fall, or risk even more winter damage.

PROPAGATION: Foot-long cuttings taken from mature stems in the fall or late winter, stuck most of the way into garden soil amended with sand or a half-and-half mixture of potting soil and sand. Rooting powders and covering cuttings with cut-off plastic bottles will increase the numbers that root. Layering is easy on roses with flexible canes.

TIP: HYBRID TEA ROSES DON'T NEED SPRAYING if you plan on yanking them out of the ground when they start looking bad. If you really like hybrid tea roses but don't want to spray, simply buy two or three new ones every year, then pull up two or three old ones that don't look so hot, rework the soil, and plant the new ones in the old holes. It takes discipline and tough decisions, but works without much fuss. Having companion plants mixed in with the roses helps, including daffodils, mint, daylilies, iris, salvia, and artemisia.

Felder's Picks: Roses Proven to Grow for Decades

Believe it or not, there are some tough roses for the North! Among old standbys (particularly the rugosas, with crinkled leaves and powerful fragrance, which never need spraying or covering) are "Buck's" roses, developed by Dr. Griffith Buck at Iowa State in the 1950s and left out in the cold and heat and neglect. Two new Canadian series have roses that can survive deep freezes with only snow protection, are disease resistant, and repeat flowering all summer: the Explorer series (named after Canadian explorers) and Parkland series (most notably those beginning with "Morden"). Also, many shrub roses that are on "own roots" (not grafted) can come back from heavy winter damage to flower on new growth. For more information on hardy roses, contact the Canadian Rose Society (www.mirror.org/groups/crs) or the American Rose Society (www.aars.org).

My "short list" of cold-hardy, disease-resistant shrub roses was graciously tweaked by Peggy-Anne Pineau of Heirloom Roses in Halifax, Nova Scotia, who also recommends any of the Pavement series of rugosa roses. She emphasized that "no rose will be garden-worthy without a *little* TLC (mostly watering in dry spells) and cannot be totally ignored. Believe me, in my twenty-odd years owning a rose growing nursery, people need to know this!!"

'Ballerina' (pink)
'Blanc Double de Coubert' (hybrid rugosa, fragrant white and ironclad hardy, six feet by six feet)
'Bonica' (shell-pink double)
'Carefree Wonder' (pink semi-double)
'Golden Unicorn' (the hardiest, most vigorous, and most disease resistant Buck rose)
'Henry Hudson' (pink buds open to white fragrant double flowers)
'Jens Munk' (semi-double medium pink with great fragrance)
'Knock Out' (ever-blooming raspberry pink flowers and bluish green foliage, disease resistant)
'Nearly Wild' (large single pink flowers on small twiggy shrub)
Rosa rugosa **'Alba'** (white)
Rosa rugosa **'Robusta'** (red)
'Roseraie de l'Hay' (fragrant, intense red double, six feet by six feet)
'The Fairy' (tight clusters of double pink on small shrub)
'William Baffin' (strawberry pink semi-double, climber)

TIP: DO HARDY ROSES NEED WINTER PROTECTION?

It has been said that there are four ways to get roses through a hard winter: (1) Stick with the old-timey once-bloomers; (2) grow hybrid teas as showy one-shot annuals; (3) carefully follow all the fussy advice about sprays and pruning and covering them up, then lose the roses anyway; or (4) move south where this is not a challenge.

Keep in mind that most winter damage comes from drying in the wind when roots are frozen solid so plants can't take up water, and from alternate freezing and thawing cycles that confuse canes, buds, and grafts. According to rose experts who have planted and replanted more roses than you and I will ever see, here are some tips to ease the loss, edited down to the chores most likely to actually get done by garden-variety (non-rosarian) rose lovers:

■ Plant cold-hardy rugosa, Buck, Explorer, or Parkland roses, preferably "own root" kinds rather than more tender grafted shrubs and vines; if they die back to the ground in a particularly severe winter, they will grow back from the roots fairly quickly.
■ In the fall, reduce the amount of nitrogen fertilizer used, to slow the production of new tender growth and allow plants to "harden off."
■ Stop pruning in late August, to allow the plant to form hips, which also slows growth and causes canes to start hardening for dormancy.
■ After the first freeze of the season, cover rose crowns with a foot of dirt, and after that freezes, cover it with a foot of mulch (then remove it in the spring).

Spirea
Spiraea species
Sun to moderate shade

With their small, narrow leaves, clusters of tiny blossoms, and arching mounds of wiry stems, spireas are a fine-textured element in the garden, to contrast with more bold-textured plants. Some forms have bright chartreuse or yellowish foliage that provides color even when the plant is out of bloom, is a foil for dark green or blue foliaged plants, and can be a shining backdrop for perennial and annual flowers.

FLOWER: Depends on the species. Classic "bridal wreath" types have many clusters of small single or double white flowers produced along arching stems from the previous season's growth; the more shrubby pink spireas have broad clusters of pink, white, or red held above the current season's foliage from late spring through summer. Most have a dusty fragrance and no fruit.

PLANT: Durable, long-lived deciduous or semi-evergreen shrubs from two to six feet tall, tolerant of extreme weather conditions with no fertilizer or supplemental irrigation for decades. Prune spring-flowering bridal wreath spireas after they flower in late spring, and summer-flowering pink spireas in the late winter before new growth gets too far along.

INTERESTING KINDS: Bridal wreaths, in order of blooming: baby's breath (*Spiraea thunbergii*), earliest bloomer with many thin canes of single white flowers, with narrow leaves that turn reddish gold in the fall; favorites include *S. thunbergii* 'Ogon' and 'Goldflame'. True bridal wreath (*S. prunifolia*) flowers soon after baby's breath with clusters of small, tight, button-like, double, white flowers and small oval leaves; Reeves spirea (*S. cantoniensis*), clusters of white flowers surround thin, arching leaves as serrated long leaves appear, the double form is 'Lanceolata' or 'Flore Pleno'; and Van Houtte spirea (*S. × vanhouttei*), the latest and perhaps most popular, with two-inch flat clusters of small white flowers held above new angular foliage (shaped like a ragged fingernail) at every leaf joint along the stems. Shrubby pink spireas, generally summer-blooming compact bushes, include hybrids and cultivars involving *S. japonica*, such as popular 'Anthony Waterer', 'Gold Mound' (chartreuse foliage), 'Limemound' (lime-green turning gold in the fall), 'Golden Princess', and 'Bumalda'. Quite a few others that are somewhat hard to locate are generally all as tough as the old favorites, if you can find them.

SOIL: Any well-drained soil, even tolerates close competition from mature tree roots. A light feeding in the spring helps foliage color. Adding organic matter to the soil at planting time, loosening potting soils, spreading roots, and mulching will get these long-lived shrubs off to a great start.

PROPAGATION: Division of mature plants, or short cuttings made in the fall or winter.

TIP: AZALEAS AREN'T THE ONLY SHOW IN TOWN when you consider how the even-tougher spirea, forsythia, quince, mock orange, snowball, and pieris are all flowering around the same time—not to mention vines such as wisteria and trumpet honeysuckle, and redbud and dogwood trees. Why put all your eggs in one azalea basket?

Staghorn Sumac
Rhus typhina
Full sun, at least half a day

My garden would not be complete without its tall central mound of sumac, planted on the pile of clay that came out of my water garden hole. I dug mine from a rural fence row, the same kind of sumac cherished in European gardens and increasingly planted as outstanding specimens in modern American landscapes, from naturalistic hillsides of goldenrods and asters, to formal containers. And it isn't poisonous.

FLOWER: Large, almost football-sized, pointed clusters of pale yellow or greenish small flowers held above foliage in late spring, an outstanding pollen or nectar source for bees, butterflies, and hummingbirds. Plants are either male or female; only the female flowers form the fuzzy burgundy-red berries held in tight, triangular clusters above branches like fat fuzzy red candles, which are very showy well into winter.

PLANT: Fast growing, sparsely branched small trees that grow in colonies from many suckers, creating a large flat or rounded-top mound sometimes fifteen feet high and several yards across in unrestricted areas. Because shoots come up nearly everywhere around, it can be a real chore pulling small plants—attached to roots headed back to the main clump—in the summer. Unbelievably gorgeous fall colors on leaves that are up to two feet long with many narrow, pointed leaflets. Some stems may break under heavy snow loads.

INTERESTING KINDS: 'Laciniata' and 'Dissecta' are naturally occurring staghorn varieties with finely divided, almost ferny leaflets and distinct orange fall color; less vigorous than the species, these make superb container specimens for hot dry spots. Fragrant sumac (*R. aromatica*) is a spreading, upright ground cover type with three leaflets—very similar to poison ivy, to which sumac is related. Illinois Nursery Selection "Gro-Low" sumac (*R. aromatica* 'Gro-Low') is a two-foot, dense, pachysandra-like ground cover with red, showy fruit in the late summer and good orange-red fall colors. It makes an excellent bank cover, or can be planted to cascade over a wall.

SOIL: The poorest, driest to be found. Sumac in moist, fertile soil will have poor fall color and get leggy and weak. Plant on top of a pile of hard-packed clay, and walk away from it.

PROPAGATION: Find a colony with good fruit clusters along a roadside near you, and (with permission) dig small trees from the edges, cutting them back to knee high.

TIP: POISON SUMAC has stubby foliage and clusters of white berries; it is nearly always found in low, wet, boggy soils, not on dry hillsides like "good" sumacs. If you aren't sure, clip a branch (carefully, into a trash bag) and take it to a county Extension Service office to send to the university for identification. Or buy the "sure thing" from a nursery!

Summersweet

Clethra alnifolia 'Hummingbird'

Shade to moderate sun

Sweet pepperbush is one of the most fragrant summer flowering shrubs to come out of our native woodlands. Its love of shady, damp areas makes it perfect for low garden areas that stay wet most of the year.

FLOWER: Masses of scented white or pink-tinged flowers on fuzzy little six-inch spikes are so sweet-smelling they can fill an entire garden with fragrance in July and August from just one or two plants—sometimes in bloom for a month or longer, at a time when warm summer nights seem to carry fragrance throughout the landscape. Plant near a doorway, deck, or patio, or along a shaded walkway. Keep in mind that bees also love the flowers for their rich nectar, so place plants far enough back in the bed so busy bees don't unnerve your garden guests.

PLANT: The shrubby, upright stems form a dense oval, and over time spread into small colonies with underground roots, making the shrub a good soil-holder on hillsides or shady berms. Dense, shiny foliage has a nice yellow-orange glow in the fall, especially when plants are grown in woodsy conditions.

INTERESTING KINDS: The native *Clethra* can reach ten feet or more tall, which is fine for naturalistic woodland landscapes; *C. barbinervis* can reach up to eighteen feet, with mottled bark and tiny white flowers on drooping stems. But the real showstopper is 'Hummingbird', a charming dwarf (to four feet), compact shrub with dark green leaves and large spikes of white flowers. Other cultivars include pale 'Pink Spire', 'Rosea' with dark pink buds and pink flowers, and 'Ruby Spice' with deep-pink flowers.

SOIL: *Clethra* grows naturally in moist, woodsy, lightly shaded areas where the soil is slightly acidic and holds moisture all summer. Toward the bottom of a woodland hillside, in light shade, is perfect, but also near the water's edge. Thick natural mulches help keep roots cool and moist, and "feed" the soil and roots as they compost.

PROPAGATION: Division of suckers formed by spreading colonies is the easiest, though stem cuttings root readily.

TIP: FLOWERING SHRUBS FOR THE LIGHT SHADE include mock orange, weigela, summersweet, rhododendron, doublefile viburnum, burkwood daphne, dwarf fothergilla, dwarf flowering almond, kerria, hydrangea.

Viburnum

Viburnum species
Full sun to moderate shade

Viburnums are a diverse lot ranging from hedge or screen shrubs, foundation plantings or borders, low masses, containers in public spaces, and accents or specimens. Native Americans used the stems of one type (called arrowwood) for making arrow shafts.

FLOWER: White, sometimes pink-tinged, flowers in spring or summer, on huge round heads at the ends of stiff upright branches, or flat disks along nearly horizontal stems. Some are fragrant. Berries can be rich blue, red, or black.

PLANT: Highly variable forms, depending on species. Leaves can be glossy green, crinkled, or slightly hairy. Some have spectacular fall colors.

INTERESTING KINDS: Arrowwood (*V. dentatum*) is one of the showiest American native shrubs with creamy white flowers in flat disks along outstretched, stiff, long, arrow-like stems, lustrous dark green leaves that turn burgundy in the fall, and blue-black berries that are very attractive to birds (which also love to nest in arrowwood); cultivars include 'Chicago Lustre' ('Synnesvedt') and 'Northern Burgundy' (also known as 'Morton'). Doublefile viburnum (*V. plicatum tomentosum*) also has long, stiff stems with double rows of white "lace cap" flowers and dark berries after fall foliage turns red. Koreanspice viburnum (*V. carlesii*) and burkwood viburnum (*V. × burkwoodii* 'Mohawk') both have rounded heads of pink buds which open to cream-pink with an intoxicating fragrance, and red or red-plum fall colors.

SOIL: Any well-drained soil, including alkaline or dry; root rot occurs in heavy clay soils. Low fertility is nearly a requirement with viburnums, or rank leggy growth will occur.

PROPAGATION: Stem cuttings taken in late summer or early spring before new growth begins.

TIP: HOW DO YOU FIND hard-to-get tough plants? Ask your local garden center owner (nicely) to try to order a few for you and some friends. If this doesn't work, check out the Internet. Your local library is connected.

Weigela
Weigela florida
Sun or light shade

Some old-fashioned shrubs just won't fade away. These include weigela, of which new cultivars are currently being developed in both North America and Europe for their better flowers and more compact growth, and for how they "color bridge" after lilacs finish blooming and before perennials kick in. Easy to root and easy to prune once a year and then forget—until late spring flowers knock your socks off. And you can't kill it with a pickup truck.

FLOWER: Narrow trumpet flowers an inch and a half or more long in loose clusters of deep-red, rose, lavender, pink, or white in mid- to late spring, with a few flower clusters appearing through the summer. The clusters appear at leaf joints all along the branches about the same time as the foliage, often weighing branches to the ground as if to show off the flowers. Outstanding hummingbird shrub.

PLANT: Arching branches arising from a central clump give this deciduous shrub a fountain-like effect up to six or so feet tall and wide; dwarf varieties exist. Narrow, oval leaves up to four inches long appear in pairs, dark green or variegated with pale yellow or creamy white. Preserve its natural shape by pruning after flowering, cutting the entire shrub back to a foot or two from the ground so new shoots can arch back out undisturbed until the next spring's floral display, or selectively thin older canes and leave others to fill in.

INTERESTING KINDS: 'Red Prince' is one of the hardiest, even into Minnesota and Maine. 'Polka' is a Canadian introduction considered the "best pink" weigela that blooms from June to September. Others include 'Bristol Ruby' (ruby red), 'Bristol Snowflake' (white), 'Java Red', 'Variegata' (variegated leaves, rosy red flowers), 'Candida' (white tinged with green), 'Minuet' (dwarf variety to around three feet high with purplish foliage and flowers of red, purple, and yellow), and my current new favorite, 'Wine and Roses' ('Alexandra') with burgundy leaves and hot rose-pink flowers.

SOIL: Any well-drained soil, but prefers a good loamy soil for best foliage and flower color, and moderate fertility.

PROPAGATION: Roots very easily from dormant twigs taken in the late fall or winter or from softwood cuttings in the summer stuck in well-drained flower bed soil or a half-and-half mix of potting soil and sand. Layer by bending and looping a section of a long cane into the soil with the tip coming back out, held in place over the summer with a rock.

TIP: UNDERPLANT DECIDUOUS SHRUBS with bulbs, such as grape hyacinth, early flowering daffodils, snowflake, and painted arum, which get the sunlight they need in the winter and are dormant in the summer when shrubs are leafed out.

Easter Egg Shrub
Plastic tackysanthemum
Full sun or shade

Let's have some fun! This seasonal plant pops up around the middle of March in even the most upscale neighborhoods, much to the chagrin of curmudgeonly neighbors who can say nothing without being tacky themselves.

FLOWER: Oblong (egg-shaped) plastic balls in pastel pink, yellow, blue, or green hung from wire or string.

PLANT: Medium sized evergreen shrub, preferably a conifer, or small deciduous tree with low-hanging branches.

INTERESTING KINDS: Egg carton bush (*Ovi cartonii*), the bottom halves of styrofoam egg cartons cut into a dozen tulip-looking flowers and stuck onto the tips of small trees or bare shrubs, or on small sticks in flower beds.

TIP: KEEP THEM ALL THE SAME COLOR (blue, yellow, pink, or white) or neighbors will *know* you are tacky.

EVER NOTICE ALL THE "FENCE SECTION HARD FEATURES" in the corners of yards? It's easy to make one for your own garden. Just put up a single fence post, and lean one or two rails down toward the ground, and you've got an instant garden accessory. It isn't high-end sculpture, but does create a focal point and allows you to plant roses, bulbs, or other stuff out in the middle of nowhere—and get away with it, because your neighbors think you've got a plan!

Buddleja and Other Nearly Tough Shrubs

I wish I could highlight more tough shrubs, because some are all-time favorites of mine, and of literally millions of other gardeners. But the following woody plants all have at least one of the following challenges: They are not universally tough, they need to be babied part of the year, or they are not easy to find commercially. But if you can find them, give them a try, and some may outlive your great-grandchildren.

Bayberry (*Myrica pensylvanica*) is an overlooked, rugged native evergreen up to ten feet tall with waxy blue berries used for candle wax. Super drought- and salt-tolerant, it can be used around public walkways.

Beautyberry (*Callicarpa* species) includes native and imported deciduous shrubs with arching stems studded with golf ball-sized clusters of shocking magenta berries in the summer and fall. Very showy for lightly shaded areas.

Blueberry (*Vaccinium* species) is a medium sized deciduous shrub with many suckers, delicate pinkish white spring flowers, showy summer fruit, and outstanding red fall colors. Sun or light shade; needs azalea-like soil preparation and occasional deep summer soakings. 'Patriot', 'Blue Ray', and 'Jersey' are early-, mid-, and late-season berry producers.

Bottlebrush Buckeye (*Aesculus parviflora*) is a spreading, colony-forming native woodland plant with large buckeye leaves that turn yellow in the fall, after very showy, tall spikes of white flowers light up the woodland edge in the middle of the summer. Seriously overlooked tough shade shrub for summer blooms.

Boxwood (*Buxus* species) is a generic roundish shrub used almost interchangeably with smaller yew hedges. Best bets for the North are 'Northern Find', 'Winter Gem', and dwarf English box (*B. sempervirens* 'Suffruticosa').

Birds Love Shrubs

Not only do shrubs provide texture, flowers, and fragrance for our gardens, they also make terrific perching, feeding, and nesting sites for native birds. Anything evergreen or with berries is a plus, but the real key to providing good wildlife habitat is diversity—special attention needs to  be given to planting something for all seasons, because our native wildlife is out there all year, not just in the seasons convenient to humans.

Butterfly Bush (*Buddleja davidii*) is one of the showiest summer shrubs, loaded all summer with long, thick, drooping spikes of purple, burgundy, white, or pink flowers that fairly drip with butterfly- and bee-attracting nectar. Great as a container plant or annual where winters are too long or severe for outdoor culture (though it does dry out too quickly to be considered a "tough" plant). Also, requires regular pruning of faded flower clusters for continuous bloom.

Camellia (*Camellia* hybrids) is a surprising fall- and winter-flowering shrub; the Ackerman hybrids are camellias bred for cold climates; 'Polar Ice', 'Snow Flurry', and 'Winter's Dream' are evergreen cultivars which can take temperatures of a -15 with protection from drying winds. Best to grow only as an experiment.

Clove Currant (*Ribes odoratum*) is a hard-to-find old-garden shrub, native to the Midwest, with stiff upright stems to eight feet tall and extremely fragrant yellow flowers clustered the entire length of the long stems in late winter, followed by small acidic fruits.

Best for Beginners:

- Flowering Quince
- Forsythia
- Hollies
- Lilac
- Rose of Sharon
- Spirea

Kinda Tricky:

- Butterfly Bush
- Hybrid Tea Roses
- Magnolias
- Rhododendron

Coralberry (*Symphoricarpus orbiculatus*) is a rambling woodland ground cover shrub whose arching stems are studded with pairs of stiff oval leaves, which drop to show tight clusters of showy purplish berries nearly six months of the year.

Daphne (*Daphne × burkwoodii*) a small, intensely fragrant shrub with a reputation for being hard to establish; 'Carol Mackie' is perhaps the best form. Its fragrance near a walk in a protected area can be worth the hand wringing.

Holly (*Ilex × meserveae*) 'Blue Boy' and 'Blue Girl' are evergreens for coarse-textured screens.

Oregon Grape Holly (*Mahonia aquifolium*) spreads freely as a ground cover or mass planting with bronze fall foliage. Low-growing 'Compactum' is fairly cold hardy.

Potentilla (*Potentilla fruticosa*) is a native Midwestern shrub with showy, five-petaled yellow flowers. Very durable, but will not tolerate wet, poorly drained soils.

Prickly Pear Cactus (*Opuntia compressa*) is a cold-hardy native cactus with flat "pads" (actually stems), looking like bristly pancakes stuck together on end. Interesting texture plant for drier parts of the garden, particularly nice in rock gardens or with yucca and native grasses for a "xeriscape" or dry garden style.

Red Twig Dogwood (*Cornus stolonifera*) is a welcome sight poking out of the snow in mid-winter. The small, clump-forming, spreading shrub has bright red new stems and tolerates wet soils.

Spicebush (*Lindera benzoin*), host plant for a large purple swallowtail butterfly, is a native shrub with small, fragrant, yellow early spring flowers and bright red berries against clear yellow fall foliage. Thrives in any soil, anywhere, full sun or deep shade.

Strawberry Bush (*Euonymus americanus*) is a woodland native with sparse solid green branches and showy winter fruits of orange and red. Outstanding for shade.

Virginia Sweetspire (*Itea virginica*) is a spreading ground cover shrub with arching branches to four feet or more, slender drooping flower stalks in the summer, and red early fall colors. 'Henry's Garnet', discovered on the Swarthmore campus in Pennsylvania, is particularly deep red.

Winter Honeysuckle (*Lonicera fragrantissima*) is a large, rambling deciduous shrub with intensely fragrant yellowish white flowers in midwinter. Very fragrant and good for pollinators active in mid-winter, but can escape into surrounding natural habitats.

Green Thumb Is Official

At last, the "green thumb" has been officially declared a type of intelligence!

As a horticulturist, I was taught that the so-called "green thumb" we've always heard about is merely an indication of certain positive human qualities such as the ability to be observant, pay attention to detail, plan ahead, follow through on projects, and be flexible while working with the vagaries of nature.

But, while studying educational psychology in college, I learned of Harvard professor Howard Gardner's "Theory of Multiple Intelligences" in which he noted and found regions of the brain which "light up" when certain abilities are activated. In addition to the most widely accepted, pattern-smart "logical-mathematical" and language-oriented linguistics aptitudes, he also found evidence of body-kinesthetic (athleticism and control in handling objects, such as surgeons possess), spatial (accurate mental visualizations), musical, interpersonal (awareness of others' feelings and motivations) and intrapersonal (awareness of one's own feelings and goals).

Sounds complicated, those seven kinds of intelligence I learned about. But I always felt that gardeners should be in there somewhere. Look around, and you'll see people who have an obvious nurturing tendency, and that some folks with no formal training in horticulture seem to be gifted with the ability to quickly recognize subtle distinctions in the natural world, and easily relate everyday things to their environment.

And sure enough, now Gardner has found physical evidence of an eighth intelligence, called "naturalist" intelligence, with even its own special brain region that supports it. Simply put, people with naturalist intelligence have the ability to identify and classify patterns in nature, and make predictions based on seemingly random events.

My great-grandmother Pearl, whose garden sported huge collections of daffodils and wildflowers, had a "Bird Sanctuary" sign in her side yard, which embarrassed us as kids because we thought people would think our family weird. But it was she who showed me the difference between black-eyed Susan and purple coneflower, and how caterpillars eat flowers but turn into butterflies without really harming the flowers in the long run. She explained how a bird's wing works, and showed me how to tell if pecans were moldy before bending down to pick them up by stepping on them to see if they were firm or soft.

Naturalists like Pearl are very comfortable outdoors; when on vacation, they watch people, or go to a botanical garden rather than a ball game or opera. They are constantly aware of their surroundings, looking around as they drive, watching weeds and hawks, and braking for butterflies. They observe, touch, and compare even "yucky" things, and often collect stuff—shells, rocks, and flowers (often in mixed cottage gardens, or extensive collections of roses or daylilies or African violets).

They also manipulate things to see what happens; ever-curious plant hybridizers fall into the category of naturalist, as do "giant tomato" or "perfect lawn" gardeners. So do wildflower enthusiasts, bonsai artists, bird watchers, and garden teachers, whose naturalist leanings are coupled with strong interpersonal and linguistic abilities.

Any of this apply to you? Mix in doses of other intelligences, and no wonder gardeners have such different approaches, and levels of success and satisfaction. We may not all be smart—but we sure are intelligent!

STOUTHEARTED
Trees

Walk away from your garden and, within a few short years, the entire place will become a shaded woodland. Because of our soils and climate, trees are the "climax species" in the natural landscape of the Midwest and Northeast, started from seeds spread by wind, birds, and other animals, and quickly growing large enough to shade out the "meadow" plants we call flowers.

This chapter deals with only a few of the very toughest trees suitable for flower-garden-type landscapes. Most make fine specimen or standout trees because of their flowers or foliage. Some are easy to work into existing beds; others make good shade for more tender plants, and several are excellent "understory" or "in between" plants—taller than flowers, shorter than other trees.

Because they are so dramatic in size and effect, trees provide the most important landscape framework for your garden, apart from your home and

other structures; they are the "walls" and "ceiling" where shrubs are the furniture and flowers the knick-knacks. Trees enclose and cool, and they provide nesting places and food for wildlife. They capture the sound and motion of the wind and deliver color, texture, line, mass, and lots of other design goodies.

Even if you plant small specimens, keep in mind that trees need elbowroom to grow. Small ones can fill a void beneath other larger trees with their spreading branches and roots. It is best to include only very small tree species in new flower beds, and to wait until

Wellesley College

larger kinds are established before planting shade perennials and ground covers underneath. Meanwhile, nothing beats a clean layer of natural mulch to make trees "look right" while protecting the new roots from hot summer sun, cold winter nights, and attacks from lawn mowers and string trimmers. Plus, as leaves and bark decompose, they feed the soil around tree roots in a most natural way (it's how things have worked in the forest for a long, long time).

The selection of ones that are super easy to grow and enjoy is astounding. Whether you choose tall or short, evergreen or bare in the winter, flowers or foliage, spring blooms or fall colors, there are kinds—and varieties within each kind—to suit every need and season.

Smaller Is Better

It's an oddball fact, but a small tree will nearly always outgrow a larger tree of the same species planted at the same time. I've watched this happen for many, many years now. This is because a smaller tree has a higher proportion of roots to top, so it doesn't waste time trying to play catch-up, as does the larger tree, which spends months just sitting there trying to stay alive as it builds its root system to accommodate its branches and foliage. Choosing a tree that is smaller can be important both for your wallet and your back, and it will help determine how quickly the tree will get established and begin growing.

Getting Trees in the Ground

C'mon—throwing a tree into the ground isn't nearly as complicated as some horticulturists make it seem. To encourage roots to roam far and wide to access water and food, trees need to get adjusted to their new home quickly; in fact, when planting new trees around Habitat for Humanity homes, I rarely add anything at all to the native soil—no matter how hard the clay. Here are a few quick tried-and-true planting tips for trees:

- Dig a wide hole, not a deep one, and rough up the sides by chopping grooves into the sides and bottom.
- For balled-and-burlapped trees, remove any wire and as much burlap as possible.
- For container-grown trees, loosen the pot-shaped root ball a bit and mix the potting soil with your garden's native soil.

- Set the tree so its original soil line is even with or barely higher than the soil around it—*an inch too deep can stunt it for life!*
- Fill in around roots with mostly original soil, with a small amount of compost or potting soil blended in.
- Cover the planting area with leaves, bark, or other natural mulch.
- Water thoroughly—but don't keep it wet, or root rot can quickly set in.

After-planting care for trees is about as easy as it gets. Only five or six *really* good soakings will be needed the first summer, one or two the next year, and after that the trees should make it on their own for decades. In general, little or no fertilizer is needed the first year a tree is planted, because it needs to get its roots established before putting on a lot of top growth. A little "root stimulator" can help, but don't push a new tree too much—let it get rooted, and it will really "jump" the next year. Any fertilizer given to nearby flowers or lawn will generally take care of the tree's needs from then on.

Protect Your Trees

A tree's worst fear is being hit by a lawn mower or string trimmer. Even one good cut on tender bark can interfere with food movement from leaves to

WHEN IN DOUBT, plant in groups. Woodland trees love company, to the point that if you don't give them neighbors, they will ignore your best efforts at "making" them grow. Just as you never see a solitary dogwood growing along a sunny fence row—they grow best on shaded slopes—you won't find redbuds surviving for long standing alone in hot, sunny landscapes. Best to put them under existing trees for protection from hot afternoon sun. Leaves used as mulch also help a great deal by shading the soil and roots, and "feeding" woodland trees as they decompose, creating a nice woodsy soil.

roots, which starves the roots and causes the tree to suffer for years to come. Meanwhile, it also introduces dirt and contaminants that can cause long-term heart rot. You get the picture.

Prevent this number-one cause of tree death by mulching around the base (in a ring around the area, not a mound on the trunk) and edging the planting hole with bricks, rocks, or other ornate barrier. Or plant a ground cover such as pachysandra or wintercreeper. Keep in mind that two or more nearby trees can be "connected" at their bases by a large mulched area, in which small shade-loving shrubs or perennials such as ferns, hosta, or astilbe can be planted. The whole area will instantly take on a more "finished" look.

AN INSTANT "TREE" is easier than you'd think—if you think about how easy a large deck umbrella can be. One large-diameter post, at least ten feet high, set into the ground and planted with a vine can create the same effect as a tree. Setting up a two-post arbor—again, at least ten feet high, using six-by-six posts instead of cheap-looking four-by-fours—is only a little more expensive, with nearly twice the appeal. Or you can build a more extensive arbor, with four or more posts and supports across the top, for gourds or grapes to hang from.

To Prune, or Not to Prune?

When should a tree be cut? Forget what you've been told, and think like a tree. By all means remove dead or broken limbs or branches, or ones that are getting in your way or shading a plant too much. Remove them any time of the year, leaving no stubs. Cut nearly flush right where the limb or branch is attached, just to the outside of the growth "collar" at the base of the branch. If you leave a stub, rot may get into the stub before the cut heals; if you cut off the collar, the tree will have a much harder time healing over the cut.

Best for Beginners:

- Crabapple
- Japanese Maple
- Maple
- Saucer Magnolia
- Star Magnolia
- Winterberry

Kinda Tricky:

- American Holly
- Apple
- Ornamental Pear
- Witch-Hazel

If you want to "limb up" a tree to allow more sunlight or a better view, do a few a year, leaving some here and there for a natural shape instead of zipping straight up the trunk leaving a "top knot" effect.

If you just want to "thin out" some cluttered or competing branches, it makes little difference to the plant which ones go and which stay.

If you want to "bob it back" like a shrub, most experts (and I) recommend that you get a poodle dog instead and leave the tree alone.

And by the way, "pruning paints" are purely cosmetic and have no effect on how fast a cut heals or whether or not insects and fungi get into the cut area. Use them only for approval from a spouse or neighbor.

American Fringe Tree

Chionanthus virginicus

Full sun or shade

The native "old man's beard" is a stunningly pure white spotlight in the spring landscape.

FLOWER: Spectacular masses of slightly fragrant, white, fringe-like flowers held in lacy clusters of four inches or more. Female trees produce small, dark fruits that are very attractive to birds.

PLANT: Upright, shrubby-looking tree with glossy green, pointed oval leaves that have deep or bright yellow fall colors.

INTERESTING KINDS: Chinese fringe tree (*Chionanthus retusus*) is more shrub-like with smaller flower clusters and blooms earlier, looking like a white lilac. Furrowed gray-brown bark is golden on new stems, providing winter interest.

American Holly

Ilex opaca

Part sun or shade

Holiday decorations wouldn't be the same without holly (for "Holy") berries—and our native holly tree is one of the largest and hardiest!

FLOWER: Clusters of yellowish white in the spring on previous season's twigs, followed by red, orange, or yellow berries in the fall and winter. Plants are separate male and female; for fruiting, both male and female plants (and bees) are needed.

PLANT: Upright evergreen tree with a strong central stem; dull, sometimes yellow-green leaves may have many "stickers" along edges. Needs protection from cold wind.

INTERESTING KINDS: 'Jersey Princess' is a heavy-bearing female; 'Jersey Knight' is a good pollinator. Several other cultivars are available, varying widely due to local suppliers and demand, including 'Howard' and 'Miss Helen'.

Apple
Malus sylvestris var. *domestica*
Full sun to very light shade

John Chapman, "Johnny Appleseed," was from the same small Massachusetts town as Don Featherstone, the inventor of the pink plastic flamingo. Both men have had a long-lasting influence on American gardening!

FLOWER: White with a pinkish blush usually on spurs of last season's growth. Fruit ripens in August and September.

PLANT: Multiple-trunk trees that produce much better when thinned and pruned annually (and the picking is easier).

INTERESTING KINDS: Of the more than eight thousand varieties of apples, about ten are used for 90 percent of commercial production. There are many more out there. Best old Northern varieties include 'Red Delicious' and 'Golden Delicious', 'Northern Spy', 'McIntosh', 'Jonathan', 'Ida Red', 'Rome', and 'Winesap'. Contact an Agriculture Extension office for more apple details.

Crabapple
Malus species
Full sun or very light shade

Many new crabapple varieties are less messy, and more disease resistant, than the kinds I was raised with. Among the showiest of spring flowering trees, it's worth the time to seek out a good one for your garden.

FLOWER: Many dense clusters of frilly apple-like blossoms in red, white, pink, and everything in between; edible fruits vary in size, color, and sweetness according to variety.

PLANT: Open, rounded, many-branched tree can be upright or mounded, even weeping, with very hard wood.

INTERESTING KINDS: Good cultivars include 'Snowdrift', 'Red Jade' (glossy fruit), the dwarf M. *sargentii*, and the very disease-resistant 'Narragansett' from the U.S. National Arboretum. Many more are available.

Dogwood
Cornus florida, Cornus kousa
Shade to full sun

Native flowering dogwood is tricky to get established, and suffers from diseases—but where it survives, it's the perfect flowering tree! Kousa dogwood blooms later, after it has leafed out, and is much tougher.

FLOWER: Very showy, flat, four-petaled flowers two or more inches across borne in late winter (*C. florida*) to early summer (*C. kousa*), followed by bright red berries.

PLANT: Small tree with many curvy trunks and branches, excellent red fall color when grown in full sun. Kousa is very disease resistant.

INTERESTING KINDS: Many cultivars of flowering dogwood, including pink and red forms, and the disease resistant Stellar series; several cultivars of kousa dogwood have exceptionally showy summer flowers and fall fruit.

Flowering Cherry
Prunus species and hybrids
Full sun or very light shade

Among the first flowering trees to make a big splash in the spring, flowering cherries—closely related to flowering plums, apricots, peaches, almonds, and nectarines—compete with one another for the spotlight.

FLOWER: Single or double flowers in white, pink, or rose in early to mid-spring; small black fruit better for birds than people.

PLANT: Upright rounded small trees, sometimes with curved limbs and cascading ("weeping") branches.

INTERESTING KINDS: Higan cherry (*P. subhirtella* 'Pendula') is the classic weeping cherry, pink flowers on drooping branches; 'Snow Fountain' is white. The little Amur cherry (*P. maackii*) has glossy red-brown bark striped with black and gray like a birch. Sargent cherry (*P. sargentii*) has deep pink flowers, bronze leaves that redden in the fall, and glossy mahogany bark in the winter. Other popular favorites are 'Okame', 'Kwanzan', and *P.* × *yedoensis* (Yoshino cherry). *P.* × *cistena* is easy, and one of the hardiest purple-leafed plants.

Ginkgo
Ginkgo biloba
Sun

The maidenhair tree is a bona-fide antique—perfectly formed leaf fossils date it to North American dinosaur days. Stately old trees have dark brown bark that contrasts starkly with the breathtakingly brilliant yellow-gold fall leaves.

FLOWER: Small flowers are not showy, but female trees drop a fetid (nearly awful) smelling fruit-like seed.

PLANT: Tall, single-trunked tree with deep, chocolate-brown bark. Fan-shaped leaves with one deep slit turn solid yellow all at once, hang on a week or more, then fall suddenly into a yellow carpet beneath the tree.

INTERESTING KINDS: 'Autumn Gold' is a tall, upright "tree" shape; 'Saratoga' is rounded, with deeply slit leaves that droop; 'Princeton Sentry' has a taller, more narrow shape; there are many others.

Hawthorn
Crataegus species
Sun or light shade

Hawthorns are nice small trees with good foliage, flowers, and fruit—perfect as specimens in small gardens or grouped in larger settings.

FLOWER: Small white apple-like flowers for two weeks or longer in the spring, with a husky odor. Orange-red fruit is very showy in the fall and winter.

PLANT: Strong horizontal branches are very architectural, but may break during heavy ice or snow loads. Some species are quite thorny as well.

INTERESTING KINDS: Washington hawthorn (*Crataegus phaenopyrum*) and *C. viridis* 'Winter King' are heavy-berried in winter. Cockspur hawthorn (*C. crus-galli*) has glossy leaves, one-inch red fruit, and long, sharp thorns (the variety 'Inermis' is thornless).

Japanese Red Maple

Acer palmatum and cultivars

Full sun to part shade

Spring to fall, and even in the winter, Japanese maples are stunningly beautiful—graceful and colorful, and in a huge array of forms and hues of red or green. Japanese maples are perfect eye-catchers in flower beds, as accents, or even as container plants—like natural but oversized bonsai plants.

FLOWER: Not showy, purplish-red clusters followed by classic winged maple seedpods (called "samaras").

PLANT: Medium to small trees, even shrub-like dwarfs, with gnarly, dark trunks and branches and deeply divided leaves from light yellow or green to red-tinged, blood red, or deep burgundy. Plants seem to hold their color and suffer less leaf-tip burn when planted in light afternoon shade. Some have a weeping habit.

INTERESTING KINDS: 'Bloodgood' and 'Garnet' are upright and deep red, 'Dissectum Atropurpureum' has very finely divided burgundy leaves and a weeping form. 'Aureum' has soft yellow-green spring foliage with crimson-purple fall colors. 'Viridis' is all green, while 'Sango Kaku' has an electric combination of green leaves on red stems, the latter providing winter interest.

WE TAKE FOR GRANTED the common names of plants, and say them often without giving them a second thought. But once you pause and think about the words, your curiosity might be piqued. Discovering the origin or meaning of these common names can become a bit of a game. "Buckeye" comes from the resemblance of the large shiny seeds to the brown eyes of a deer, for example. "Haw" refers to the fruit of the hawthorn, and the meaning became expanded to include similar trees, thus "possum haw" (although a holly and not related to hawthorns) means "fruit for possums."

Japanese Tree Lilac
Syringa reticulata
Sun or light shade

Upright and flowering a good month after common lilac (S. *vulgaris*), the tree lilac is somewhat less troubled by the diseases that affect lilac shrubs.

FLOWER: Large, foot-long, pointed panicles of lightly fragrant, creamy-white flowers stand upright in late spring and early summer. Most gardeners prune the flower heads as they "brown out" to prevent seeds from forming, which just create seedlings to weed.

PLANT: Single- or multiple-stemmed small tree with typical heart-shaped leaves and smooth, reddish stems, which are striking in the winter.

INTERESTING KINDS: Compact, heavy-flowering 'Ivory Silk' is widely available. Another cultivar is 'Summer Charm'.

Maple
Acer species
Sun or shade

Nothing says "North Woods" like maples in autumn splendor! Every child has made a crayon rubbing of a maple leaf, and it's what brings out tourists and natives alike on drives through town and the countryside.

FLOWER: Not noticeable, but has showy, typical twin-winged maple seedpods that twirl like helicopters.

PLANT: Upright, teardrop-shaped with usually one central trunk. Brilliant fall colors of red, yellow, or orange are determined by species and growing conditions. Shallow roots make growing grass underneath difficult.

INTERESTING KINDS: Sugar maple (A. *saccharum*) is what maple syrup is made from, and has many good cultivars including 'Bonfire'; Norway maple (A. *platanoides*), which often drops limbs in wind storms; and red maple (A. *rubrum*), including cultivars such as 'Red Sunset', are also very popular trees. The bark of paperbark maple (A. *griseum*) has good winter interest.

Mountain Laurel
Kalmia latifolia
Moderate shade to part sun

Henry Hudson may have seen mountain laurel when he wrote of "rose trees" on Cape Cod. This small native tree is dramatic when set against a dark woodland backdrop.

FLOWER: Showy clusters of light pink cups, often with contrasting throats, each flower up to an inch across, from May to July. State flower of Pennsylvania and Connecticut.

PLANT: Small, shrubby tree native to steep slopes and lightly shaded, well-drained sites, grows slowly up to fifteen feet tall. It's fine-grained wood is used for making eating utensils.

INTERESTING KINDS: Many colorful cultivars are available, some less hardy than others, including dwarf shrubs. Flowers range from pure white to blood red and bicolors.

Ohio Buckeye
Aesculus glabra
Shade to part sun

A buckeye seed carried in your pocket is supposed to bring good luck. I'd rather plant mine!

FLOWER: Seven-inch long spikes of yellow-green flowers bloom among the foliage in the spring. Big, shiny, mahogany-brown seeds are considered poisonous.

PLANT: Rounded, many-branched tree with almost tropical-looking leaves of fanned-out, finger-like, multiple leaflets with yellow to reddish orange fall colors. Branches reach nearly to the ground then curve back up.

INTERESTING KINDS: The very showy red buckeye (*A. pavia*) is not hardy in all parts of the North.

Ornamental Pear
Pyrus calleryana
Sun

Sometimes overdone in plantings around malls and businesses because of the uniform shape and predictable habits, ornamental pears are still showy with spring flowers and fall colors, and their soldier-like predictability

FLOWER: "Dusty" smelling clusters of white flowers make the plants appear solid white when in bloom, before or sometimes right at spring leaf-break. Small brown summer fruits are usually insignificant.

PLANT: "Lollipop" tree with many upright limbs forming a neatly pointed teardrop shape that spreads and opens up with age. Dense limbs with narrow angles are susceptible to ice load damage. Brilliant red fall colors.

INTERESTING KINDS: 'Aristocrat' and 'Chanticleer' (may be the same as 'Cleveland Select') are less likely to split under ice loads than the common 'Bradford'; 'White House' is narrow and upright and 'Redspire' is broad and pyramidal. 'Autumn Blaze' is more cold hardy.

Redbud
Cercis canadensis
Light shade or sun

A naturalistic group of three or four redbuds is breathtakingly beautiful in a woodland edge setting. Redbuds are edible and perfectly delicious, tasting exactly like raw peanuts (after all, they're both in the pea family). Try one or two when no one is looking.

FLOWER: Showy clusters of small, pea-like, reddish pink or white flowers, rarely with any fragrance at all, form along trunks, branches, and twigs, sometimes in nearly solid masses. Flat, bean-like seedpods follow.

PLANT: Vase-shaped trees with rounded crowns, often with multiple trunks; because their wood is not very strong, older trees often form sturdy, fresh sprouts from the base to replace dead or damaged older trunks. Foliage is generally heart-shaped, the size of a man's hand, and glossy green, turning yellow in the fall.

INTERESTING KINDS: 'Flame' has double red flowers. 'Minnesota Strain' is selected from winter-hardy stock. 'Forest Pansy' has glossy wine-colored leaves.

Saucer Magnolia
Magnolia × soulangiana
Sun or light shade

It seems like the blooming of "saucer" or "star" magnolias—a real aristocrat— actually causes a freeze; mid-winter warm spells trigger them to erupt into massive splashes of huge pink, purple, or white blossoms, then a freeze browns them out. Happens nearly every year. Still, their Mardi Gras spectacle makes them worth the risk.

FLOWER: Each stem tip has several large, fuzzy buds that open into bowl-sized saucers of pink or purple petals, some of which are fragrant on warm days.

PLANT: Single- or multiple-trunk trees with upright branching get up to thirty feet tall and half that wide with oval leaves that look ratty after a hot, windy summer.

INTERESTING KINDS: 'Alexandria' blooms later with deep red-purple flowers that often miss the late freeze.

Serviceberry
Amelanchier canadensis
Sun or light shade

This overlooked native, also called shadblow, is a true four-season tree, great for small spaces such as townhouse or patio gardens, especially when underplanted with dark spreading yews.

FLOWER: Delicate white flowers show off on naked gray branches before spring kicks in, followed by tasty, purplish black fruits in June, good for lucky gardeners who beat the birds to them (the tree is also called juneberry).

PLANT: Multiple-stemmed understory tree with yellow to orange-red fall colors and smooth gray winter bark.

INTERESTING KINDS: Several species are native to the North, including A. *laevis* and A. *arborea*, and garden centers often offer named cultivars.

Star Magnolia
Magnolia stellata
Sun or shade

One of the best, although slow-growing, small flowering trees for the mid-winter garden, up to fifteen feet across, becomes a cloud of white, water-lily blooms.

FLOWER: Each floppy flower, three or four inches across, has many narrow, strap-shaped, white petals.

PLANT: Rounded small tree or large shrub that seems to flower just fine in the shade.

INTERESTING KINDS: 'Merrill' (M. × *loebneri*) is the cold-hardiest cultivar, followed closely by M. *stellata* 'Waterlily' with pink buds. Lilac-pink M. × *loebneri* 'Leonard Messel' is deservedly popular.

Witch-Hazel
Hamamelis species
Shade to part sun

Few plants flower during freezing winter weather, when we are least likely to be out in the garden—but witch-hazel is up to the task. Be sure to plant where you will see and smell it, lest you miss it entirely.

FLOWER: Many very thin petals of yellow or orange in hairy-looking, golf-ball-sized clusters along gray stems appear for several weeks in mid-winter, closing during freezing weather. Fragrance is good on warm days.

PLANT: Woodland natives with multiple stems up to fifteen feet or so tall. Wood is used for divining rods.

INTERESTING KINDS: Common witch-hazel (H. *virginiana*) has yellow flowers from October to December; vernal witch-hazel (H. *vernalis*) blooms in January and February. Chinese witch-hazel (H. *mollis*) has orange or reddish flowers and orange-red fall colors. H. × *intermedia* 'Diane' and 'Jalena' are popular cultivars.

Bottle Tree

Silica transparencii

Full sun to dense shade

Originating in ancient Arabia, this rare but sturdy specimen migrated from rural Southern gardens to create a dazzling year-round focal point that is close to zero-maintenance perfection, while being whimsical, daring, and artistic. Similar to "Easter Egg" shrubs (see entry in Shrubs chapter) and ornaments hanging from holes punched in ears.

FLOWER: Small to medium, hollow glass cylinders of clear, amber, green, blue, and occasionally a rare red, found on the ends of stems, remain every day of the year (particularly colorful when backlit by sunshine). Though occasionally damaged by hailstorms, bottle trees can be quickly and easily repaired.

PLANT: Upright to eight or ten feet, with many short branches. Sometimes a strictly upright specimen similar to a large fence post with stout nails, often more like an old Christmas tree with limbs bobbed back to finger-sized branches, and occasionally a rambling collection of several lesser trees wired together; rarely one is seen that looks like heavy welded rebar. Collectors save glass "flowers" to line kitchen or bathroom windows, with a stained glass effect. Some bottles have been seen as neck-down edging around nice flower beds (in Europe, gardeners have used them this way for centuries).

INTERESTING KINDS: 'Kaleidoscope Stroke' (formerly 'Gaudy') is a popular old multicolor display, usually with no particular color pattern, being edged out by unique cultivars including 'Beer Bottle Delight' (delicate blend of clear, green, and brown bottles) and the rare 'Milk of Magnesia' (pure cobalt blue). 'Mardi Gras' is festooned with old necklaces and strings of beads.

SOIL: Any firm soil will support a heavy bottle tree, though ready-mix concrete can be used for strength. Occasional watering cleans the foliage and flowers; selecting vines such as cypress vine or moonflower can enhance the bottle tree.

PROPAGATION: The tree itself is easily made any time of the year, sometimes taking just a few minutes. Most bottles are very easy to locate, either at home or behind local pubs. Upscale restaurants often share choice longneck amber or even blue bottles at no charge. Annual bottle collector meetings can yield some very fine colors at a reasonable cost, as can Internet auction sites and garage sales.

TIP: GARDEN ACCESSORIES CAN BE SERIOUS, classical, contemporary, whimsical, or downright humorous, but they always add a special accent or personal touch. Birdbaths, urns, statuary, driftwood, boulders, bottle trees, whatever—in your own personal space, "anything goes." No matter what you do, your neighbors will talk about you anyway!

Other Good Trees

Amur Cherry (*Prunus maackii*) has pinkish-white spring flowers, violet berries attractive to wild birds, and shiny cinnamon bark that peels in the winter.

Bald Cypress (*Taxodium distichum*) is a tall, narrow, many-twigged deciduous conifer for many soil types (including dry), with ferny green foliage and rusty red fall colors. Very little leaf litter.

Black Cherry (*Prunus serotina*) is one of the showiest red fall color trees.

Catalpa (*Catalpa speciosa*) is a large tree with huge heart-shaped leaves and big clusters of purple-spotted white orchid-like flowers and long beans that hang on well into the winter. Very showy, too large for most flower gardens.

Chinese or **Lacebark Elm** (*Ulmus parvifolia*) is a small, blight-resistant elm with long, spreading, drooping branches of leathery green leaves, and outstanding mottled bark for winter interest.

Cornelian Cherry (*Cornus mas*) is actually a dogwood with small tufts of early-blooming yellow flowers, bright red cherry-like fruits in the late summer, and gorgeous red fall colors. Excellent specimen tree for sun or light shade.

Golden Rain Tree (*Koelreuteria paniculata*) is a rounded tree with ferny foliage and large loose spikes of yellow flowers in early summer, followed by showy papery seedpods.

Japanese Flowering Apricot (*Prunus mume*) is one of the toughest winter-flowering trees around, blooming way before anything else. Tolerates a wide range of soils, but may freeze in northern areas.

Mountain Ash (*Sorbus* species), though somewhat short-lived, has long been a favorite native garden tree for its white spring flowers and the wild birds attracted to the showy reddish-orange fall fruit.

Pawpaw (*Asimina triloba*), an upright, rounded native of moist bottomlands in the Midwest, has maroon winter flowers and egg-sized or larger "custard apple" fruits in summer. Great orange fall colors. Prefers deep, moist soil.

Red Horse Chestnut (*Aesculus* × *carnea*) is a horse chestnut-buckeye hybrid with big upright panicles of scarlet flowers.

River Birch (*Betula nigra* 'Heritage') is a multiple-trunk tree with peeling, papery outer bark and near-white or salmon-white inner bark; *B. platyphylla* 'Whitespire', developed at the University of Wisconsin, resists birch borers.

WHY WON'T MY DOGWOOD BLOOM? Seed-grown trees have huge variations in genetics and performance, so always buy named or grafted cultivars. Also, excess water or fertilizer from the lawn encourages foliage growth over flowers. Root prune by cutting a few outer roots in the late summer, which stresses plants into forming flower buds.

When planting dogwoods, mix in a little fresh soil from beneath an established tree to "inoculate" the soil with mycorrhiza, a beneficial root-extending soil organism.

ERICACEOUS PLANTS—mountain laurel, rhododendron, azalea, blueberry, pieris, and other members of the family Ericaceae—love well-drained, acidic soils; if soil is not acidic, they can't absorb iron, causing yellow leaves with green veins. Sulfur or aluminum sulfate increases soil acidity.

Russian Olive (*Elaeagnus angustifolia*), a silvery old-garden evergreen widely considered invasive (but not as pesky as autumn olive, *E. umbellata*); makes a fine windbreak, screen, erosion control, and wildlife habitat. Has sharp spines—so don't plant anywhere you might pass on a riding mower!

Sassafras (*Sassafras albidum*), a colony-forming tree, has orange fall colors and root bark from which root beer was once made. Great host for larvae of large butterflies and moths.

Smoke Tree (*Cotinus coggygria*), a small shrubby tree, has many cultivars with burgundy foliage; hairy seed plumes clothe the entire tree in a smoke-like effect. Grows in tough conditions. 'Velvet Cloak' is an outstanding purple. Native species (*C. obovatus*) has outstanding fall color, but is more difficult to locate in the nursery trade.

Snowbell (*Styrax* species), including native and Japanese species of small trees, is good for light shade, with spring clusters of fragrant white flowers that droop like bells from twigs. Easy to plant beneath.

Sourwood (*Oxydendrum arboreum*), with sprays of finger-like summer flowers and brilliant fall colors, is a popular native tree for slopes and banks, especially in the mid- and lower North.

Southern Magnolia (*Magnolia grandiflora*) has the showiest flower of any North American tree but is not cold hardy in the upper North; best bets for the Mid-Atlantic and lower Midwest are 'Edith Bogue', 'Bracken's Brown Beauty', and 'D.D. Blanchard'. Dwarf 'Little Gem' is long flowering and suitable for protected large containers.

Thornless Honeylocust (*Gleditsia triacanthos inermis*) is a native with sweet-scented white flowers and light, airy foliage, each leaf made of up to twenty leaflets. Yellow fall colors give way to brown, strap-like bean pods up to eight inches long that persist well into the winter.

Winterberry (*Ilex verticillata*) is a small-leaf deciduous holly tree with bright red winter berries and leaves that turn dark brown at the first heavy freeze, giving it the name "black alder."

DEUS EX MACHINA—No Last-Minute Bailout

Anyone remember the old "How to Serve Man" *Twilight Zone* program in which aliens came to Earth with all sorts of human-helping powers, before their manual was "outed" as a *cookbook*? What seem like miraculous bailouts often become horror stories.

Same with gardening. Whenever a new, seemingly spontaneous "cure" comes along for weeds, animals, bugs, or blights, a subtle but high price seems to come with it.

My wife got me on this line of thinking as we reminisced about high school days, and brought up a phrase I somehow missed in class (go figure—she was a member of the National Honor Society; I was a classic "underachiever"). The phrase is *deus ex machina*, or "god from the machine."

In this stage device, often used in Greek and Roman dramas, an apparently unsolvable crisis is solved at the last minute by the intervention of a "god" actor descending onstage by a wire suspended from the ceiling, or some other elaborate piece of equipment. It's the oldest version of being "saved by the cavalry."

I've been thinking about this "pie in the sky" approach to gardening. It took us a couple of generations to catch on that almost every new-fangled pest-eradicating chemical causes terrible, unforeseen hits on "non-target" species of plants, birds, or other wildlife, and sometimes ruins drinking water supplies. And the pests outmaneuver to come back with a vengeance (especially since some of their controls were eliminated in the process). There are no universal controls for deer, mice, voles, squirrels, slugs, groundhogs, or other furry or noxious pests. Few plants are totally resistant to them; fences, netting, wire mulches, and other barriers are cumbersome and ugly; poisons, baits, and repellants usually fail in the long run and kill "non-target" species as well. Sorry!

Truth is, gardening is a constant bailing of a very leaky boat. Wishful thinking won't make nature stop trying to fix itself: First come the weeds (nature's shock troops, called "pioneer species" by eco-gardeners), then birds that bring seed of larger plants to push the inexorable succession toward the old forest we cut down to make room for turf, potato patches, and daylilies (whose only contribution to wildlife is aphids).

Heaven didn't put lawns or hybrid tea roses here—we did, by enslaving and breeding plants from afar. And we wonder why they chafe and suffer and rebel from our domination!

When last-minute scientific breakthroughs fail to arrive, we should garden smarter by doing less counter-intuitive stuff like planting high-maintenance or pest-predictable plants, and by choosing tried-and-true plants that at worst can survive the onslaughts and at best will thrive in the face of adversity.

Vines
WITH VIGOR

Nearly every landscaper agrees that vines are the most overlooked group of plants available to gardeners. Yet they are everywhere, clambering up trees in the native woods, sprawling along roadsides, cascading down hillsides and creek banks, and softening the edges of fences and arbors in every small town and country garden. There are dozens of great vines that obviously need little or no care at all, other than occasional pruning to keep them out of our faces and off other plants.

Technically, vines are just flexible stems that don't stop growing in length; they constantly get longer, reach higher, and spread into new areas. Some are multiple-branched and make good screens or ground covers. There are annuals to be replanted every year, and tender tropical plants that must be brought in every winter. Others are herbaceous perennials that leap from the ground every spring, or long-lived woody landscape features that provide a year-round framework of texture for many years. Some grow so fast they can take over a porch in a few weeks or months; others seem to take forever to get established, and depend on their supports to give the desired vertical effect until they catch on.

Aggressive Vines

Bittersweet and poison ivy are normally not the first—or even last—choices for use in landscapes, but they have their places. Many gardeners and naturalists get upset over the use of "invasive exotic" plants in landscapes, such as Japanese honeysuckle and wintercreeper, because they have escaped from gardens and begun to take over natural areas, sometimes displacing native plants. Oddly enough, few complain about the similarly invasive native vines!

Anyway, a few vines that are real thugs should be planted with extreme care and contingency plans made for keeping them from escaping to neighbors' gardens, or into woodlands where they can do real harm to the environment. They include:

Ohio

- Bittersweet (both the native *Celastrus scandens* and Oriental *C. orbiculatus*)
- Fiveleaf Akebia (*Akebia quinata*)
- Hall's Honeysuckle (*Lonicera japonica* 'Halliana')
- Leatherleaf Clematis (*Clematis ternifolia*)
- Mile-a-Minute-Vine (*Polygonum perfoliatum*)
- Multiflora Rose (*Rosa multiflora*)
- Porcelainberry (*Ampelopsis brevipedunculata*)
- Trumpet Vine (*Campsis radicans*)
- Wisteria (*Wisteria floribunda* and *W. sinensis*)

Some of these "botanical pythons" can be strategically placed and carefully tended, controlled, and converted into mannerly garden favorites. Still, it is important to consider the impact of "weedy" vines on neighbors and nearby natural areas. Think twice before planting them, make sure they are in a good spot for control, and take care to keep them in bounds. If you choose to grow "weedy" vines, whether native or imported, expect criticism, but hold up your head and go on. After all, every plant has the potential to be a weed somewhere.

"FIRST YEAR WE SLEEP, second year we creep, third year we leap!" is an adage referring to hardy perennial vines. Have patience with them the first year or two.

Supporting Your Vines

Vines climb in weird ways, such as twining their stems around supports (cypress vine, honeysuckle, wisteria); using special extensions called tendrils that reach out to wrap around supports (grapes, gourds, cross vine, sweet pea, passion flower); clinging with tendrils that have hooks or claws, or with small stem roots with adhesive disks (trumpet creeper, Virginia creeper, wintercreeper euonymus); or being tied up with soft twine (climbing roses, tomatoes, coral honeysuckle). Clematis actually climbs by twisting the stalks of its leaves around supports. Choose an appropriate structure for the type of vine you're growing.

Vines that use slender stems, tendrils, or petioles to pull themselves up need something thin enough to wrap around; a honeysuckle or sweet pea, for example, won't stick to a flat board fence and needs something to get it started. Fishing line is so smooth it's hard for a twining vine to grip—use something with a little "tooth" to it, such as twine, tacked or nailed from the top of the fence to ground level near the vine. Once a vine has reached the top of the fence it will use the mass of its own stems to continue twisting and climbing.

Don't be weak when it comes to making an arbor, pergola, or other vine support. Vines often outgrow "store-bought" arbors, and it isn't unusual for climbing roses and trumpet vine to tear up wooden lattice. Use sturdy four-by-six- or six-by-six-foot posts at least ten feet high to allow vines to grow over and hang down a bit. One of the best "fabrics" for use between stout posts is heavy-gauge concrete reinforcing mesh, with large openings, to allow vines to grow through readily.

Vine Design

Vines and their supports lend crucial "vertical appeal" to landscapes. They provide framing, create focal points, and lift our view from the lawn and flower beds up to eye level and above. They mask bare walls and provide fast shade on the hot side of a house, or hide ugly scenery. Several provide erosion control or grow in areas that are too difficult to mow or too shady for grass. They provide colorful flowers in the spring, summer, and fall; gorgeous autumn colors; and evergreen texture or accents through our sometimes-dreary winter. On the following pages you'll find great vines—both annuals and hardy perennials—for the North.

American Bittersweet
Celastrus scandens
Sun

Normally thought of as an invasive weed, this native vine has its uses, including its fast screening ability, fall color, and winter fruit, which serves as both wild bird food and filler in dried flower arrangements.

FLOWER: Not showy, but the fruit is a dried capsule that splits and opens to expose an orange-red seed, which is harvested in the fall and hung upside down to dry. Note: Bittersweet vines are either male or female, meaning you will need at least one of both to have fruit.

PLANT: Rampant, sprawling stems with oblong leaves. Can be aggressive, so be careful.

INTERESTING KINDS: Oriental bittersweet (*C. orbiculatus*) can be sheared into a hedge, but is considered an invasive exotic by the environmental watchdogs.

Boston Ivy
Parthenocissus tricuspidata
Sun

The famous "Ivy League" ivy clambers all over buildings, providing both beauty and shade from the hot summer sun, before dropping its leaves to allow warming sun to reduce winter heating bills.

FLOWER: Insignificant.

PLANT: Dense, overlapping, glossy leaves are three-lobed (young seedlings are often mistaken for poison ivy), and turn deeply red in the fall. Autumn berries, which are poisonous, are blue. Warning: Boston ivy vines climb with "stick-tight" aerial rootlets, which can damage wooden house siding and door frames.

INTERESTING KINDS: 'Beverley Brook' has large leaves; 'Fenway' has yellow-green to gold foliage; 'Purpurea' has reddish purple leaves all season. 'Veitchii' and Lowii' have smaller leaves.

AERIAL ROOTS are clingy on stems of climbing hydrangea, Boston and English ivy, Virginia creeper, trumpet vine, and wintercreeper and will damage wooden walls and window frames. Grow them on masonry or brick.

Clematis
Clematis × *jackmanii* and others
Sun or light shade

A "best bet" for planting on mailboxes and small trellises, and on the canes of climbing roses.

FLOWER: Large, flat showstoppers, from two to nearly ten inches across, in white, purple, blue, red, pink, yellow, and bicolors; most also have very decorative seedpods.

PLANT: Somewhat delicate, brittle stems. Dark green leaflets have long petioles, which wrap around (slender) supports.

INTERESTING KINDS: Jackmanii group (large purple or white flowers), blooms on new growth; *C. henryii* has huge creamy white blossoms with dark stamens; sweet autumn clematis (*C. paniculata*) has billowy masses of small white flowers in the fall.

TIP: PRUNING CLEMATIS can be vexing; some bloom on new growth, and are pruned in the winter. Others flower on old wood, and are cut after flowering in the spring. If you aren't sure, simply do only minor snipping as needed.

Climbing Hydrangea
Hydrangea anomala petiolaris
Sun or shade

This stately, very slow-growing vine, is really an elongated "vertical shrub" that takes several years to reach its mature potential, but becomes a treasured landscape feature.

FLOWER: Layers of faintly scented, flat lace-caps of white "florets" and long-lasting white bracts cover the vine in the spring.

PLANT: Rich green, textured leaves. In the winter, the vine traces its growth with thick stems covered with rough, cinnamon-colored "peely" bark. Warning: It attaches to walls with aerial rootlets, which can damage wood.

INTERESTING KINDS: Japanese hydrangea vine, *Schizophragma hydrangeoides*, is smaller, less shrub-like, and has flower heads eight to ten inches across; one form is pink and another has silvery variegation to the leaves.

Climbing Roses
Rosa species and hybrids
Full sun

Nothing in the horticultural world says romance better than an arch covered with fragrant roses! To force roses the entire length of the stems, bend them over nearly to the point of breaking, and tie them down for a week or more. This "pegging" stimulates flower bud formation and forces more flowers, as does tying as horizontally as possible to a support.

FLOWER: Arching canes sport loose clusters of often-fragrant pink, white, red, or yellow flowers.

PLANT: Vining shrubs that need to be tied to supports, with usually thorny canes reaching several yards long.

INTERESTING KINDS: 'New Dawn', a prolific bloomer with huge pinkish-white fragrant flowers all season, was named the "Most Popular Rose in the World" in 1997 by the World Convention of Rose Societies; 'John Davis', developed in Canada, has three-inch old-fashioned double flowers of red to rich pink opening to show golden centers; 'John Cabot' is a fully double medium pink flower with orange fruits ("hips"); 'Henry Kelsey', another Canadian rose, has large clusters of vivid red, spicy-scented flowers; 'William Baffin' has strawberry pink, semi-double flowers.

Cypress Vine
Ipomoea quamoclit
Full sun or very light shade

Amazingly fast-growing, delicate-looking annual vine is loaded with flowers, butterflies, and hummingbirds all summer and fall, then reseeds itself for many years.

FLOWER: Bright red, flaring tubes scattered profusely between delicate, deeply divided, ferny leaves. One of the best butterfly and hummingbird flowers around.

PLANT: Super-fast-growing vine, twining up to fifteen or more feet, which can overpower nearby small shrubs. Makes an outstanding addition to arbors and good companion for other vines. Foliage is airy and ferny.

INTERESTING KINDS: A white-flowering form can be found and shared by gardeners. Cardinal climber (*Ipomoea multifida*) has identical flowers, but the two-inch wide leaves, instead of being fernlike, are roundish and hand-shaped with points.

219

English Ivy
Hedera helix
Shade or part sun

Evergreen vine forms a rugged ground cover in even dense shade but will climb up to forty feet in trees.

FLOWER: Insignificant.

PLANT: Tough vine that roots as it grows, either in the ground or on supports. Dull, dark-green leathery leaves, usually with pointed lobes, are not produced so thickly that they shade other perennials, but masses of the vine can create solid ground covers that can prevent erosion on steep shady slopes. Variegated forms are available, as are kinds with ruffled leaves.

INTERESTING KINDS: There are dozens of ivy cultivars, many of which are best suited for growing in pots (some are not as winter hardy). 'Thorndale' is perhaps the cold-hardiest.

"DOES IVY KILL TREES?" This is a common question, and everybody's mother says it will. But at the risk of starting an argument with Mama, it won't, unless it is so thick it completely shades the leaves of shrubs or small trees, or breaks them under the combined weight. If insects hiding in the thick vines are a concern, simply cut it all down every few years and let it start over again.

Goldflame Honeysuckle
Lonicera × heckrottii
Sun or light shade

Unlike the invasive Japanese honeysuckle, the informal native honeysuckles, often used on a trellis or mailbox, are never a nuisance.

FLOWER: Clusters of tubular flowers, bright coral outside and rich golden inside, appear in the center of two fused leaves at the ends of branches. Berries are bright orange and showy in the summer.

PLANT: Blue-green leaves on light tan stems, which develop peely bark as the vine ages.

INTERESTING KINDS: *Lonicera sempervirens* 'Sulphurea' has yellowish flowers, 'Superba' is bright scarlet; 'Magnifica' has large bright red flowers, yellow on the inside. 'Dropmore Scarlet' (*Lonicera × brownii*) has blue-green leaves and scarlet flowers.

Gourds

Lagenaria, Luffa, or Cucurbita species
Full sun

A friend once called gourds "vegetal white-out" for their ability to quickly cover up everything within reach. Some kinds are rampant enough to top a small tree in a single season, festooning it with large fruits that dry into huge pods. From the giant bird-house and dipper gourds, to the tiny ornamental kinds with warty skins and interesting colors and shapes, to the back-scrubbing loofah variety, gourds are among the toughest annual vines around.

FLOWER: Loofah and small kinds of gourds have small, yellow flowers; large true gourds have big, flat, white flowers. Separate male and female flowers are produced on the same plants, and both have to be open and pollinated by bees or moths to produce gourds.

PLANT: Large gourd vines require a lot of space, so plant them along chain link or another large fence. Some gardeners build special "gourd houses"—tall arbors over which gourds can clamber, with fruits hanging like ornaments.

INTERESTING KINDS: Loofah (can be skinned and the insides used to wash dishes or scrub body or hands), dipper (long handled), basket (huge and roundish), ornamental (many shapes and sizes and colors), and many others. Contact the American Gourd Society (www.americangourdsociety.org) for tips on growing, preserving, and ordering seeds of unusual varieties.

Grape

Vitis labrusca, Vitis vinifera
Sun

Grapes for backyard arbors can be rewarding, if tricky. Not all varieties are created equal some are very susceptible to late frosts or diseases of leaves and fruit clusters.

FLOWER: Rounded clusters of small whitish blooms.

PLANT: Best grown on sturdy wires stretched between stout posts set a few feet apart, and pruned hard every winter to keep vines short and productive.

INTERESTING KINDS: Improved native grapes (*V. labruscana* crossed with *V. vinifera*) include 'Concord', 'Niagara', 'Catawba', 'Fredonia', and Delaware'; European wine varieties for the North include 'Chardonney' and forms of 'Cabernet'; new hybrids with promise include 'LaCross', 'St.Croix', 'Mars', and 'Jupiter'. Get more information on varieties and training from your Agriculture Extension Service office. Good luck!

Hyacinth Bean
Lablab purpureus (or *Dolichos lablab*)
Full sun

This vine is a real traffic stopper! Among the largest specimens I have seen were those on a long, rustic arbor made of tree limbs at Monticello, Thomas Jefferson's mountaintop home in Virginia. This fast-growing vine requires an arbor or trellis for support. Start seed indoors and wait until the weather warms to move young plants out to the garden.

FLOWER: Spikes with loose clusters of lavender-purple, sometimes white, sweet-pea-like flowers, followed by showy burgundy-purple beans up to three inches long.

PLANT: Rambling, succulent stems with three-lobed leaflets often tinged purple.

INTERESTING KINDS: There is a white-flowered form.

TIP: WAIT UNTIL PAST FROST to plant seed of beans, gourds, and other hot-weather vines, or risk their rotting in the cold wet soil.

Japanese Honeysuckle
Lonicera japonica
Sun or light shade

I have seen this seriously invasive vine being sold in New York City for an astounding $75—for courtyard containers. Its delightful nectar and outstanding fragrance are loved by hummingbirds and kids of all ages.

FLOWER: Tubular white to cream flowers with flaring lips in clusters from spring to fall, which fade to a dull yellow upon maturity. Each extremely fragrant tube has a partial drop of pure nectar. It can be dragged out by pinching off the tip end and pulling the long, slender pistil through the narrow tube; then putting that drop on the tip of the tongue, where "sweet" taste buds are concentrated.

PLANT: Vigorous vine with deep green leaves and exfoliating bark, which can reach twenty feet or more.

INTERESTING KINDS: 'Halliana' has white flowers changing to yellow; 'Purpurea' has purple-tinged leaves and flowers that are maroon outside and white inside; 'Aureoreticulata' has leaves veined in gold.

Moonflower or Moonvine

Ipomoea alba

Full sun or very light shade

Watching moonflowers open at dusk is a magical event—the large white flowers spring suddenly from relatively small "twists" of buds, releasing a nearly overwhelming fragrance. Start seed indoors and move young vines outside once weather has warmed up.

FLOWER: Flat white trumpets up to six inches across, sometimes tinged with purple, often streaked with green, open from pointed buds shaped like swirls of soft ice cream. They remain open, almost glowing, all night, sometimes into the morning if the day is overcast.

PLANT: Large heart-shaped leaves are dark green.

INTERESTING KINDS: Morning glory, sweet potato vine, and cypress vine are all relatives.

Poison Ivy

Toxicodendron radicans (or Rhus radicans)

Sun or shade

Captain John Smith first called the plant "poison ivy" in 1609 after being warned about it (Native Americans believed it was put in the woods to make people more careful). Its fall colors, best viewed from afar, are spectacular, like flames licking up tree trunks. Best used as a screen along the back property.

FLOWER: Insignificant small clusters of flowers.

PLANT: Its signature three leaflets were the inspiration for the familiar saying, "leaves of three, leave it be." Vines are hairy with multiple aerial roots.

INTERESTING KINDS: The nonpoisonous staghorn, smooth, cut-leaf, and fragrant sumacs; and the poisonous poison sumac and poison oak. Also pistachio.

TIP: KILLING POISON IVY is not difficult; cut it back in the fall or late winter, and spray new growth with glyphosate (Roundup®), which does not harm tree trunks (it only affects plant parts that are green). It can damage nearby plants if the spray drifts, so pick a calm day with no breezes. Warning: The plant's sap oil (urushiol) can remain active for years, even on dead plants, tools, and gloves, and can cause a rash long after you have left the clean-up scene. Wash clothes thoroughly after working around poison ivy!

Sweet Pea
Lathyrus odoratus
Sun

This "grandma's garden" favorite has long been one of the swooning fragrances of the garden fence. Unfortunately, the sweet peas bred in the last century were for cutting flower size, not for fragrance; for the best fragrance, look for old-timey varieties—before 1900—and save their seed from year to year.

FLOWER: Intensely fragrant "pea" flowers in an amazing array of colors, on vines from four to six feet high. Soak hard-coated seed for a few hours to hasten germination.

PLANT: Pale green leaves and stems. Climbs by tendrils.

INTERESTING KINDS: Original sweet pea 'Cupani' first grown in 1699; 'America', beautiful ivory blossoms striped with crimson, introduced in 1896; deep burgundy 'Black Knight'; 'Grandiflora Mix'; many others. A perennial sweet pea with pink flowers, hardy to Zone 5, is *L. latifolius*.

Trumpet Vine
Campsis radicans
Sun or light shade

"Hummingbird vine" grows along every fence row and over every abandoned house or railroad telegraph pole in the country! It's a magnet for hummingbirds, and shades summer decks.

FLOWER: Clusters of thumb-sized buds on the ends of arching stems open into bright orange or reddish tubular flowers large enough for bumblebees to crawl into for nectar. Large, canoe-like seedpods five or six inches long split open to release flat seeds that float away on downy parachutes (and sprout up everywhere).

PLANT: Vine is robust to say the least, and can sprout from underground stems several feet from the main plant. Dark green leaves have nine or more coarsely toothed leaflets.

INTERESTING KINDS: 'Crimson Trumpet' is deep red; 'Flava' is yellow or pale orange; *Campsis* × *tagliabuana* 'Madame Galen', a hybrid between *C. radicans* and *C. grandiflora*, is bright orange to red.

Wintercreeper
Euonymus fortunei
Sun or shade

Whether grown as a slow-climbing vine or ground cover, wintercreeper is so common it's almost boring—except when used as a contrast to evergreen shrubs, to tone down the seriousness of a grave marker, or as a cascade from a rock wall.

FLOWER: Not showy at all, very inconspicuous florets hidden in the foliage; orange fall fruit can be showy.

PLANT: Evergreen vine or shrub that trails or climbs by rootlets produced along the flexible stem. Paired dark green leaves are usually edged with yellow, pale green, white, or silver. Extremely easy to root from stem cuttings taken in spring, summer, or fall. Powdery mildew is a common problem easily pruned out.

INTERESTING KINDS: 'Coloratus' has purple winter foliage. Many golden and otherwise variegated cultivars are available, including 'Canadale Gold' and 'Emerald 'n' Gold'.

Wisteria
Wisteria sinensis
Sun or light shade

A popular, vigorous, spring-flowering vine, often fails to flower in the North because of too much shade; too much fertilizer; too rich a soil; or just plain too much cold in the late winter, which kills flower buds.

FLOWER: Large, hanging clusters of bluish purple or white, fragrant, pea-like flowers in the spring or early summer. Seeds that may form are poisonous.

PLANT: Sturdy vine that with age can form a stout, twisted "trunk." Long stems sport graceful leaves of numerous, pinnate leaflets. Keep away from shrubs, which the heavy vines can overwhelm.

INTERESTING KINDS: Chinese wisteria (*W. sinensis*) often loses its flowers to freezes; Japanese wisteria (*W. floribunda*) blooms with eighteen-inch clusters after leaves appear ('Longissima' flower clusters can get three feet long!); native American wisterias (*W. frutescens* and *W. macrostachys*), which bloom after leaves appear, are not very invasive, and are very flower-hardy even in Minnesota—but are more difficult to find commercially.

Other Great Northern Vines

There are many good garden vines, but some require watering, spraying, or some other kind of maintenance, or aren't as tough in all parts of the North, or are nearly impossible to find at garden centers. You may have to shop around to find the ones listed here, or keep them in pots, but they are worth a little extra effort.

Akebia (*Akebia quinata*) is often called five-leaf akebia for its interesting foliage. Great tracery effect as it twines up supports to fifteen feet. Interesting fruit looks like a small sausage. Very invasive.

Black-Eyed Susan Vine (*Thunbergia alata*) is an old-fashioned summer annual, grown quickly every year from seed as a small climber or hanging basket plant. Lots of orange, yellow, or white flowers with dark throats. Related to twenty-foot sky vine (*T. grandiflora*), an annual with blue flowers.

👍 Best for Beginners:

- *Climbing Roses (some)*
- *Cypress Vine*
- *Goldflame Honeysuckle*
- *Hyacinth Bean*
- *Moonflower*
- *Wintercreeper*

Kinda Tricky: 👎

- *Bittersweet*
- *Clematis*
- *Climbinig Roses (some)*
- *Grape*
- *Poison Ivy*
- *Wisteria*

Climbing Tomato (*Lycopersicon esculentum*), a tender annual with delicious red fruit. Best fast climber: 'Sweet 100'.

Hardy Kiwi (*Actinidia arguta* and *A. kolomitka*), introduced from Russia, is grown less for its small, sweet berries (female vines only) than its showy foliage—green blotched with pink and white like a paint accident. Needs a trellis.

Scarlet Runner Bean (*Phaseolus coccineus*), an antique summer bean, is edible and beautiful. Vigorous vines run to fifteen feet with attractive foliage and many orange-red flowers all summer. Very attractive on wooden teepees in a garden setting.

Virginia Creeper (*Parthenocissus quinquefolia*) is a very common and fast-growing native vine for sun or shade, with five leaflets. Often confused with three-leaflet poison ivy, to which it is not related (Virginia creeper is in the grape family). Perfect for growing on tree trunks, fences, and walls; can take wooden shingles off a roof or wall and may need pruning to keep it out of rain gutters along rooflines, and from covering up windows. When grown in sun, it has attractive purplish berries on red stems and strong fall colors.

PLACES WHERE ANNUAL VINES GROW all summer are bare in the winter, and slow to fill in during the spring. During the "bare months" you can provide visual interest with a wind chime or other hanging accessory.

The American Cottage Garden: Out of the Parlor, into the Den

Cottage gardening is a style with the freedom of growing what you like, where you like, and how you like. Anyone can have a "slice" of one, a place to plant stuff "every which way" and enjoy using all the senses.

No two cottage gardeners are alike (nor are their gardens), though most share certain characteristics, including a love of being outdoors, keen observational skills, attention to detail, appreciation of variety, and a sharing spirit. Their gardens, filled with plants with proven hardiness and often shared between a diverse lot of gardeners, typically provide a strong sense of place.

- To outsiders, there is no apparent design, but a definite "personal" layout exists, usually best viewed from inside the house, not from the street.
- A fence, hedge, gates, and divided "rooms" connected with meandering paths create a sense of enclosure, as if you are in a special place (which you are).
- The lawn is minimal or nonexistent; grass is used in a "throw-rug" effect well defined by edged beds.
- Outdoor living is evident, from lots of seating, and signs of gardening activities (tools, gloves, pots, watering cans, and so on) in full view, where they can be reached easily.
- A strong vertical effect is created with flowering trees, arbors, and posts supporting vines.
- Plant diversity is incredible, almost to the point of being overdone: shrubs (evergreens often pruned creatively), roses, vines, bulbs, perennials, annuals, vegetables, and herbs provide a year-round display of texture, color, and fragrance.
- Potted plants and hanging baskets are everywhere, in a wide variety of containers.
- Few, if any, pesticides are used, both because they are troublesome and because cottage gardeners rarely tolerate plants that have serious pests or diseases.
- Abundant wildlife is present, often deliberately attracted, fed, and housed, especially birds and butterflies, but rabbits, lizards, and big yellow-and-black garden spiders are all tolerated, as is the occasional nonpoisonous snake left hiding under the rock pile to eat rodents.
- Expect to find many "hard features" such as birdbaths, urns, small statuary, signs, whimsical "yard art," and found objects (rocks, driftwood, and so on).

Not all of these are requirements. The main thing is to have fun growing plants for the love of it and to indulge in a few creative fantasies. Don't worry—it doesn't have to be an all-consuming obsession!

Bibliography

Instead of the usual bibliography, let me just tell you that I cross-referenced TONS of great books on gardening in the North, Midwest, New England, and even Canada. In them I found snippets of information and clarification of fine details, but mostly I used them to make sure I didn't overlook some really cool plants.

If a plant showed up in at least five or six books, I'd check to see what the Minnesota and New England experts thought of it, thinking that if it can survive in those places, it can grow ANYwhere! I pored over every Northern state's Cool Springs Press *Gardener's Guide*—which in my horticultural opinion have the most specific, up-to-date information available. Then I'd get on the Internet on sites like www.northerngardening.com to see what Master Gardeners, university horticulturists, and nursery professionals had to say about it. I also depended heavily on the best recommendations found in regional gardening magazines.

I made fifteen driving trips into the small towns of the North, crisscrossing Iowa and Illinois to Massachusetts, and every state in between, including a jaunt through parts of Ontario, always visiting solid-reputation nurseries (Old House Gardens in Michigan, for example), and photographing plants with old friends who live in the Midwest, Mid-Atlantic, and New England. So, while a lot of my information was gleaned from books, a good deal of it came from actual gardeners, toiling and sweating, and enjoying gardening in the North.

Garden Lingo

Love that *lingua franca!* Comfortable gardeners often speak plain, and plainly, to one another, slipping into a relaxed dance with country sayings and clichés that cause outsiders— and high school English teachers—to shudder.

It's not that we don't know better; though cognizant of the often confusing rules of our language, sometimes we prefer down-home lingo over more polished, high falutin' discourse. I've been criticized by more technical-minded fellow scientists for using vernacular, homespun phrases, as if my way of talking is just plain lazy. But some of our quirky descriptors are more meaningful to me than being precise.

For example, I recognize intellectually that it's not possible to put something both "up" and "under" at the same time, but how else can you get something "out from up under" the porch? And you need to "ask me something quick" 'cause I "just happen" to be busy.

I've picked up a few fun aphorisms from my English gardening buddy Rita Hall, who "bloody falls on her bum" every time she hears someone say they're "fixin' to do" something—

which we always seem to be doing: Fixin' to set out some 'maters. Fixin' to blow the leaves. Fixin' to pinch that boy's head off. Fixin' to git on a plane, or on a train.

Rita, who "bungs" (crams) plants into the ground, got her "nappies in a twist" (shorts in a knot) when she heard me tell someone that their green tomatoes would "red up" after being picked. "Red up? What's that mean?" she laughed.

Yet she says anyone who doesn't speak in a local jargon is just putting on airs—and real people can tell; after just a few minutes of hearing someone from England talk, Rita can spot their dialect, and pinpoint what part of England they are from. And on two trips to England, I've heard her revert to a normal English accent within an hour of getting through customs.

Jargon rules! A fellow called my radio program the other day to share how his rose bush—which he had pulled out of a pasture using a tractor so he could get the main root—had "growed up so good" that when it flowered "it was just a bo-kay." We all could tell how proud he was.

If you don't understand our patter—from the French *patois*—you ain't from around here, are you?

Still, there are some terms you outta know from this book, so here is my glossary (those that are not listed here, can be found in ANY garden book, anywhere, any time):

Glossary: A place in a book to look up words you might not know.

Agriculture Extension Service: Local county or branch of an agricultural university, with publications and advice on various aspects of gardening.
Annual: Seed- or cutting-grown plant that dies within a few months of when it is planted, usually from either hot or cold weather; some perennials in other parts of the world are annuals here.

New Jersey

Biennial: Green leaves one year, flowers the next. Then it's gone.
Bones: Evergreen plants and hard features which give a year-round structure to a garden or landscape, especially in winter.
Comes Back: Opposite of "goes down."
Cultivar: Variety that usually can't be grown true from seed, but has to be "cloned" (divided or rooted).
Cut Back: To prune stems moderately, leaving some of previous season's growth, to clean it up or to encourage new growth.
Deadhead: To remove spent flowers and seedheads, in order to frustrate plants into reblooming.
Dilettante: A gardener who dabbles in a little of everything, and knows more about some things that most folks don't really care about.
Divide: Pull or cut apart soil-level sections of a multiple-branched perennial or woody plant to make more plants, best done in the season opposite of when a plant flowers.
Dormancy: Often mistaken for death. The resting period for a plant, usually during either cold weather or really hot, dry weather, depending on the species.
Double Dig: British and Californian masochistic practice in which holes are dug twice too deep, causing root rot when they fill up with water in our wet winter and spring.
Force: To make a plant grow unnaturally, as in a vase on the TV; often done with bulbs, and cut stems of spring flowering shrubs.

Garden Club Lady: A member of an organized social club whose garden-related meetings often include plant swaps and flower shows; often performs valuable community beautification and educational services.

Goes Down: When either summer or winter perennials go dormant and their aboveground foliage disappears.

Herbaceous: Perennial that goes down part of the year, or is not woody.

Layer: To bury a part of a vine or shrub stem and let it root while still attached to the "mother" plant.

Master Gardener: Trained gardening volunteer with the Extension Service.

Melt: To collapse from heat and drought and overwatering and frustration with our climate; can happen to plants or gardeners.

Northern: Capitalized word representing a culture of people, plants, and environmental conditions peculiar to the northern portions of the United States.

Peg: To bend a vine or shrub, such as a rose, severely, attaching it to the ground with stakes, which forces flower buds to form all along the stem instead of just at the tip.

Perennial: A plant that lives for several to many years. Can be woody or herbaceous.

Pinching: To deadhead with your fingers, or to nip the tip off a plant so that it will branch down below.

Reseeding: Drops seeds everywhere that sprout the next season (think wildflowers and weeds).

Rogue Out: To remove a few unwanted plants somewhat brutally, by hand or with implements of destruction.

Root: Used as a verb—cut branches from plants, stick in soil or water, and grow new plants. Used as a noun—the part of the plant that goes in the ground when planting.

Run: To spread rapidly by way of vigorous underground stems; sometimes a good thing for ground covers, sometimes a weedy way of something "getting away from you" in flower beds.

Variety: Distinct kind of a certain type of plant that can be grown from seed.

Woody Plant: Perennial vine, shrub, or tree that has permanent stems and branches that get bigger every year.

Photo Credits

Felder Rushing: 4 (courtesy of the author), 7, 9, 10, 11, 12, 13, 14, 15, 17, 18, 20, 21, 22, 23, 26, 27, 28, 29, 33B, 38AB, 39A, 43B, 44A, 48AB, 62B, 74, 79, 80, 83B, 96, 99, 100, 102, 103, 108B, 109B, 111, 112, 115A, 118A, 119B, 123A, 128B, 129, 133, 137, 138, 139AB, 141A, 142A, 143, 144B, 145B, 146AB, 150, 151AB, 152ABCD, 153ABCD, 156, 158, 160, 162AB, 163, 166, 167, 168, 169, 175, 177, 181, 182, 183, 185, 189AB, 190A, 194, 196, 197, 198, 209, 211, 214, 215, 219A, 221A, 229, 230, 240 (courtesy of the author)

Thomas Eltzroth: 30B, 31AB, 32A, 33A, 34B, 35B, 36AB, 37A, 39B, 40A, 42A, 43A, 45A, 46AB, 51, 54, 58, 60, 61, 63, 65, 67, 68, 72, 77, 81ACD, 82BD, 84B, 85, 87, 89, 91, 93, 95, 104A, 105B, 106A, 107A, 108A, 109A, 114AB, 116AB, 117B, 118B, 119A, 121, 122A, 123B, 125B, 126B, 128A, 135, 140A, 141B, 144A, 145A, 147, 148A, 149, 159, 161, 164, 173, 174, 176, 178, 179, 200B, 201B, 208A, 217B, 219B, 221B, 224B, 225A, 226, 227AB

Jerry Pavia: 32B, 34A, 35A, 37B, 41B, 42B, 44B, 66, 70, 73C, 75, 81B, 82AE, 83C, 84AD, 104B, 113, 115B, 117A, 124A, 125A, 130, 155, 172, 190B, 201A, 203, 206B, 213, 220AB, 222A

Liz Ball and Rick Ray: 25, 30A, 40B, 41A, 45B, 53, 56, 59, 64, 73B, 106B, 107B, 110A, 120, 122B, 124B, 126A, 127AB, 165, 171, 180, 184, 186, 188, 193, 199B, 202AB, 204B, 205A, 206A, 207A, 208B, 218AB, 223B, 224A, 225B

Charles Mann: 57, 69, 84C, 157, 222B

Pamela Harper: 83A, 105A, 207B, 223A

Lorenzo Gunn: 142B, 148B, 200A

Mark Turner: 71, 110B, 187

André Viette: 62A, 73A, 199A

William Adams: 82C, 140B

David Winger: 205B, 217A

Cathy Barash: 204A

Ralph Snodsmith: 170

Key: A=first photo from top of page, B=second, C=third, D=fourth, E=fifth

Meet the Author

Felder Rushing is a tenth-generation American gardener whose quirky, overstuffed, low-maintenance cottage garden and its "yard art" have been featured in the *New York Times* and many magazines, including *Better Homes and Gardens, Garden Design, Landscape Architecture, House and Garden,* and others. He has driven more than a million road miles and acquired more than a million frequent flier miles, lecturing and studying gardens across the United States as well as in Canada, Africa, South America, and Europe, once taking a television crew to England and France.

Rushing's twice-weekly garden columns and live call-in radio program are syndicated. He has had hundreds of articles and photographs published in more than twenty-five magazines, including *National Geographic, Fine Gardening, Organic Gardening, Brooklyn Botanic Garden Record,* and *Garden Design.* He has written or co-written ten garden books and appears regularly on HGTV and the Discovery Channel. He serves as contributing editor for *Horticulture* magazine and *Garden Design.*

He is on the board of directors of the American Horticulture Society, is a national director of the Garden Writers Association, and recently retired from nearly twenty-five years as an "outside the box" university Extension Consumer Horticulturist and Master Gardener trainer and coordinator. One of his proudest moments was in 1990 when he was made an honorary member of the Garden Clubs of Mississippi—of which his horticulturist great-grandmother was a charter member in 1936.

Rushing, who believes that too many of his horticultural expert friends complicate things unnecessarily, says "We are daunted, not dumb." His lifework has been trying to make gardening as easy and fun as it is rewarding.

Index